Procedural Autonomy of EU Member States: Paradise Lost?

Diana-Urania Galetta

Procedural Autonomy of EU Member States: Paradise Lost?

A Study on the "Functionalized Procedural Competence" of EU Member States

Springer

Diana-Urania Galetta
Università degli Studi di Milano
Dipartimento giuridico-politico
Via Conservatorio 7
20122 Milano
Italy
diana.galetta@unimi.it

First publication D.U. Galetta, L'autonomia procedurale degli Stati membri dell'Unione europea: Paradise Lost? G. Giappichelli Editore s.r.l.(2009)

ISBN 978-3-642-12546-1 e-ISBN 978-3-642-12547-8
DOI 10.1007/978-3-642-12547-8
Springer Heidelberg Dordrecht London New York

Library of Congress Control Number: 2010932034

Cover design: WMXDesign GmbH, Heidelberg, Germany

Printed on acid-free paper

Springer is part of Springer Science+Business Media (www.springer.com)

Á Jacques Philippe Emmanuel,
mon mari,
avec tout mon amour

… … …
Amants, heureux amants, voulez-vous voyager ?
Que ce soit aux rives prochaines;
Soyez-vous l'un à l'autre un monde toujours beau,
Toujours divers, toujours nouveau;
Tenez-vous lieu de tout, comptez pour rien le reste.
J'ai quelquefois aimé; je n'aurais pas alors
Contre le Louvre et ses trésors,
Contre le firmament et sa voûte céleste,
Changé le bois, changé les lieux
… … …

(« Les deux pigeons », Jean de la Fontaine, Fables, Livre IX)

Foreword

This volume deals with a fundamental dichotomy which governs the existing system of European Union Law. On the one hand, it is a precondition of a functioning Union that its substantive law should be guaranteed in a uniform manner throughout the Union and it should prevail over the law of the Member States. On the other hand, European Union law is not only executed and interpreted by EU institutions. On the contrary, it is in principle left to national authorities and jurisdictions to handle it in accordance with the procedural rules of the respective Member States.

The latter phenomenon is referred to as the principle of procedural autonomy of the Member States of the European Union. Naturally, this principle may come into conflict with the demands of uniformity of European Union law not only in theory. The numerous case law of the European Court of Justice demonstrates that it has been up to the European Courts to reconcile the two conflicting principles in practice. This has been done by the judges more or less in a pragmatic way without any deep and thorough theoretic reflection.

Therefore, the topic of procedural autonomy of the Member States still presents a blank spot on the map of legal theory and dogmatic argumentation.

This excellent book devoted to the title of John Miltons' famous book "Paradise Lost" is shedding clear light upon this unclear matter. Diana-Urania Galetta, distinguished law professor of the University of Milan, well-known in particular for her fundamental books and articles in the field of administrative law and comparative public law (among others Diana-Urania Galetta, Principio di proporzionalità e sindacato giurisdizionale nel diritto amministrativo, Giuffrè, Milano, 1998, pp. XVII–273; idem, Violazione di norme sul procedimento amministrativo e annullabilità del provvedimento, Giuffrè, Milano, 2003, pp. XVIII–301) now offers a thorough and convincing legal study of a major issue of European Union law in its relation with the national legal orders of the Member States. Prof. Galetta comes to an European Union minded solution regarding the national judges also as a sort of "agents" in a functional sense of the European Union's interest. I find her argumentation which cannot be summarized here in detail well-founded and convincing. The book is full of inspiring ideas.

In the end, national procedural autonomy might be nowadays an "unsafe haven" as the author remarks in her last chapter. These two words cannot be used, however, to adequately characterise her study as a whole. On the contrary, the book provides us with a deep analysis of the term "procedural autonomy" and the legal problems connected with it. Thus, to rephrase the comparison, which the author draws, it is a safe harbour of dogmatic reasoning and a brilliant masterpiece of European Union Law.

University of Freiburg Professor Dr. Jürgen Schwarze

Preface to the English Edition

This volume is the translation of the book I published with Giappichelli Editore, in Italy, in 2009. In terms of content it differs from the original version only in as far as it was necessary to make reference to important ECJ judgements issued in the mean time (as for the Olimpiclub case I refer to in para. 3.4.) and I had to take into account the entry into force on 1st December 2009 of the Lisbon Treaty. In order to do this, each time I have added the reference to the articles of the consolidated version of the Treaty on European Union (TEU) and of the Treaty on the Functioning of the European Union (TFEU) and to the new wording when changes in the text have occurred.

In as far as terminology is concerned, I have used the terminology adopted in the Lisbon Treaty, even when it differed from the one used by the English speaking doctrine so far (it is the case, for example, for the word "supremacy", to which I have preferred the word "primacy" used in "Declaration n° 17 concerning primacy" annexed to the Lisbon Treaty. Or for the expression "sincere cooperation" which is now used in Art. 4, third paragraph, TEU instead of that of "loyal cooperation").

The idea of having my book translated into English was, first of all, a natural consequence of the considerable positive feedback I had received from Italian and foreign colleagues (and on this occasion I would like to thank them all!), most of them stressing the need to let the book circulate in a much wider circle than that of the scholars who are able to read Italian.

The second reason is related to the growing centrality of the topic of "procedural autonomy" and to the existing literature on this topic. As a matter of fact I wished to open a debate with English language scholars and especially with the UK doctrine which seems somewhat auto-referential, as only contributions in the English language are quoted by authors of papers dealing with the subject of procedural autonomy – as happens with so many topics of EU law.

Even if the translation work has cost a considerable amount of time and energy, we are still dealing here with a translation from Italian. So if, on the one hand, I have tried to always use the English language EU terminology, but I'm not sure whether I have always found the right one, on the other hand, the style is not always the one English native speaker academics would use. The sentences are sometimes a bit long and the style itself is somewhat different. Anyway I took the decision (and I'm therefore the only one responsible for that) that the "poor style" had to be corrected only if it hindered comprehension of my reasoning.

That's why I would like to thank, first of all, Anke Seyfried, Associate Editor at Springer, who shared this point of view and decided to publish the book without asking for too much (superfluous) editing work. I thank her also for the enthusiastic reaction to my publishing proposal and for the continuous support.

Many thanks also to Ana Aliverti (for the help in the first draft translation) and to my colleague at the "Università degli Studi di Milano" Mary Rubick, who helped me in revising and refining the text.

Università degli Studi di Milano Professor Diana-Urania Galetta

Acknowledgements

I am grateful for the very helpful comments from those who had the patience and kindness to read the provisional version of this book.

I would like to thank in particular Prof. Bruno Nascimbene for his support during these years and, in this case, more than ever...

I also want to thank Prof. Guido Greco and Prof. Vittorio Italia.

Finally, I want to express my gratitude to Prof. Jürgen Schwarze to whom I am indebted in many ways, not least for his foreword to this volume.

A honourable mention goes, though, once again, to my daughter Daphne Yael who, after asking me the title of my new book, at her seven and a half years old had exclaimed: Oh, that sounds interesting!

Contents

Chapter 1
Introductory Notes, Terminological Issues and Demarcation of the Scope of the Study

1.1 The Distinction Between Procedural and Substantive Law in EU Law

A large body of literature has focused on the question of the procedural autonomy of the Member States, especially from the first half of the 1990s onwards. That was in fact a season of important decisions by the European Court of Justice which – as a consequence of their impact, in practice very incisive – brought to the forefront the question of the possible limitations that this jurisprudence may have, or could have, on national procedural legal orders.[1]

Moreover, in the analysis of the EU jurisprudence on this matter it is necessary to take into account that, in order to distinguish between 'procedural law' – which concerns the object of our analysis – from 'substantive law,' it is not possible to use the categories of national law, that could in any case differ from one country to another. Instead, it is necessary to appeal to the relevant EU concepts.[2]

To this end, it is worth specifying at this point that the definition of procedural law indirectly adopted by *Mertens de Wilmars*[3] seems better suited to delineate the European Union distinction between procedural and substantive law.[4]

In fact, in a famous essay in 1981, he makes a distinction between EU norms of substantive law (the so-called material EU law) and national systems of norms aimed to 'sanction' the respect of the EU substantive law. In this context, the term

---

[1] I refer here in particular to the well-known judgements of the ECJ of 19 June 1990, Case 213/89, *Factortame* and 14 December 1995, Case 312/93, *Peterbroeck*.

[2] As has been recently noted by an influential author, the '*national approach towards the community law, even in the terminological realm*' should be abandoned and replaced by a more accurate '*community approach to law.*' See G. Tesauro, *Diritto comunitario*, p. XIV. Author's translation.

[3] Influential President of the first Chamber of the ECJ at the time of the decision on the *Rewe* case.

[4] In this vein, see also the reflections by W. van Gerven, *Of Rights, Remedies and Procedures*, p. 524, note n. 114, on the use by the ECJ of the expression '*procedural rules*' understood in a very broad and indeterminate sense.

D.-U. Galetta, *Procedural Autonomy of EU Member States: Paradise Lost?*,
DOI 10.1007/978-3-642-12547-8_1, © Springer-Verlag Berlin Heidelberg 2011

'sanction' should be obviously understood in a broad sense: since – as he himself specifies – it '... *designates the array of instruments of legal coercion that, in every Member State, guarantees the respect for the law in the case of conflicts arising in the course of its application.*'[5]

Understood in this perspective, it is clear that the EU notion of procedural law is much broader than the one we are used to considering as such. This is because it includes provisions that, in our mental scheme 'of national law,' we would identify as substantive law: but instead, from a EU perspective, they form part of the broad concept of 'procedural law' to the extent that they refer to *suitable legal instruments to sanction the observance of the EU law*.

As we will see, the problem of procedural autonomy and its limits emerges in this much broader context and – as has clearly appeared at least from the jurisprudence in *Kühne & Heitz*[6] – it is relevant also in terms of use of the institution which in the Italian administrative law is defined as '*ex officio* annulment.'[7] The *ex officio* annulment assigns the power to the national public administrations to annul administrative acts that are incompatible with norms in force.

This institution and its 'EU implications' will be specifically addressed in the course of Chapter 3. Additionally, other themes will be considered there, for example the authority of *res judicata* or State liability which from our national point of view are both matters of 'substantive law,' but which in the EU jurisprudence turn out to be instead elements pertaining to the procedural autonomy of the Member States and its limits.

1.2 The Concept of 'Procedural Autonomy': Cross-Reference

The scholarly works on the object of the present enquiry are almost all concentrated on the analytical examination of the EU jurisprudence on this matter. They are aimed at identifying the possible restrictive outcomes of this jurisprudence regarding the pre-supposed procedural autonomy of the Member States. This concept, however, is taken for granted without making an effort to examine and understand its nature and origins – even less its rationale.

---

[5]The '*sanction*' as '... *l'ensemble des moyens de contrainte légale qui, dans chaque Etat membre assure le respect du droit en cas de conflit à propos de son application*'. See J. Mertens de Wilmars, *L'efficacité des différentes techniques nationales de protection juridique contre les violations du droit communautaire par les autorités nationales et les particuliers*, p. 379 ff. (390). Author's translation.

[6]Judgement of the ECJ of 13 January 2004, Case 453/00, *Kühne & Heitz*.

[7]The Italian administrative law doctrine categorizes the "*ex officio* annulment" among the so-called "administrative acts of second degree": that is, among those acts through which the administration intervenes over its preceding acts modifying them. In particular, it is directed to eliminate, from the outset, the effects of an illegitimate administrative act.

The first objective of the present enquiry is therefore to provide (in Chapter 2) a definition of procedural autonomy that is also able to account for its inherent limits. These limits derive from, in the first place, the necessary coexistence of procedural autonomy with requirements and principles that are related, more generally, to the regulation of the relationships between internal law and EU law. This is because – as will be thoroughly examined – analyzing the concept of procedural autonomy outside the general context in which it is located is equal to distorting its role and importance.

To this end, before speaking of 'procedural autonomy' it is necessary to define the concept of 'procedural competence' of the Member States and delineate its scope of action. This is so since – as it will be argued – the procedural autonomy subsists only and to the extent that the procedural competence of the Member States exists and disappears the moment when – as in the case, for example, of the directives on public procurement procedures that we will briefly examine in Chapter 4 – the procedural competence is taken over by the Union. In the latter case, if the instrument used is the directive, the idea of procedural autonomy is substituted by that of the "choice" of the national authorities regarding "form and methods" given that, in terms of Art. 288 third paragraph, TFEU (*ex* Art. 249, 3, TEC) '*A directive shall be binding, as to the result to be achieved, upon each Member State to which it is addressed, but shall leave to the national authorities the choice of form and methods.*' And if, as we will see,[8] there is a substantial similarity between the idea of procedural autonomy and the mechanism underlying the use of the instrument of the directive, these are in actuality two entirely different scenarios.

1.3 The Analysis of the Jurisprudence: Delimitation to Preliminary Rulings and the Fundamental Decisions, in the Light of our "Well-Thought Path"

The third chapter will be devoted to the analysis of the EU jurisprudence considered more relevant to this topic. Moreover, the selection will be made only within the jurisprudence of the European Court of Justice (ECJ) enacted in the context of the preliminary ruling of Art. 267, TFEU (*ex* Art. 234, TEC), since it is in this specific area that the contours of the particular relationship between national judge and EU judge – which in doctrine is defined in terms of 'co-jurisdiction' –[9] are outlined. As we will see especially in Chapter 4, this is an essential aspect in the line of reasoning that I want to develop.

---

[8]In Chap. 2, para. 2.5.

[9]See E. Picozza, *Diritto amministrativo e diritto comunitario*, p. 308. This phenomenon corresponds to the '*intertwined nature of the EU's judicial function*' referred to by J. Ziller, *Separation of Powers in the European Union's Intertwined System of Government*, p. 31.

The objective of the enquiry that follows is not to describe in a systematic and exhaustive way the jurisprudence of the ECJ regarding the judicial process in general, and the judicial administrative law process, in particular, as this would repeat what has already been well done.[10]

The objective is, rather, to identify the rationale that underlies the interventions of the ECJ on issues of procedural autonomy and the common logic that, eventually, emerges from it.

Neither would it make sense – given the EU definition of 'procedural law' that has been mentioned in para. 1.1. – to restrict the enquiry only to the ambit of the judicial (administrative law) process. The scope of the enquiry turns out to be in fact – as stated above – necessarily much wider, since it is aimed at encompassing all those actions that are more generically ascribable to the power, that belongs to the authority of the Member States, to 'sanction' the observance of the EU law.

1.4 A "EU-Friendly" Approach: In Search of an Underlying Logic and Rejecting the Pessimistic 'Paradise Lost' Approach

Assuming that, in the current evolution stage, the EU law is and remains a legal order based on a system of treaties, and that the task of the ECJ is primarily to guarantee that the norms included in the treaties and the secondary legislation are applied and respected within the legal systems of the Member States, I consider it appropriate to emphasize how the present work draws from a "EU-friendly" approach.[11]

I set myself the target to try to demonstrate that – despite the apparent incoherence frequently regretted by certain commentators –[12] there is a coherent logic in the approach of the ECJ on the issue of the procedural autonomy of the Member States. It is a logic that has to be sought, however, not in the particularities of individual cases (as some tend to emphasize), but in the context of the interests at stake. Further, this expression of 'interests at stake' has to be understood in a broad

[10]Among others, see particularly, the monographic studies by F. Astone, *Integrazione giuridica europea e giustizia amministrativa: contributo allo studio dell'influenza manifestata dal diritto europeo sul sistema di giustizia amministrativa italiano e sui poteri del giudice amministrativo*; M. Burgi, *Verwaltungsprozess und Europarecht*; R. Caranta, *Giustizia amministrativa e diritto comunitario*; C.D. Classen, *Die Europäisierung der Verwaltungsgerichtsbarkeit*; O. Dubos, *Les juridictions nationales, juge communautaire*; Th. Dünchheim, *Verwaltungsprozessrecht unter europäischem Einfluss*. Lastly, see the monographic studies of 2008 by A. Barone, *Giustizia comunitaria e funzioni interne* and M. Eliantonio, *Europeanisation of Administrative Justice? The influence of ECJ's Case Law in Italy, Germany and England.*

[11]On this aspect see the conclusions, p. 123 ff.

[12]See, for all, G. Greco, *Superprimato del diritto europeo: le direttive sui mezzi di ricorso vincolano tutti, ma non la Commissione e la Corte di Giustizia.*

sense as it covers all the interests identified by the principles and criteria individualized in Chapter 2 and which concerns, precisely, the relations between national law and EU law.

Finally, a last consideration.

As a methodological choice, when analyzing the topic of procedural autonomy of the Member States, I decided to leave aside the consideration of the reasons of that debate – to be honest, of a too meta-theoretical character – that is built around the question of whether the procedural autonomy of the Member States has a value in itself, to be protected and safeguarded at any cost. In fact, I found it more interesting – and certainly more relevant to the role of a positive jurist, as I understand it – to consider the issues arising from the application of Art. 4, third paragraph, TEU (*ex* Art. 10, TEC), which concerns the duty of the Member States – of a 'constitutional' status – to ensure sincere cooperation (*coopération loyale*) to the EU institutions. This provision – as we will see – has a great importance in relation to the subject matter: in particular, regarding the relations between national courts and EU courts in the context of the preliminary ruling. This is so in the perspective, not least, of the fundamental principle of international law of *pacta sunct servanda* whose implications the critics of the jurisprudence of the ECJ too often seem to forget.

To conclude on a critical note, half serious, half jesting, it seems to me that the critique of the ECJ is often formulated in what – as the title of this book suggests – could be defined as a '*Paradise Lost*'[13] perspective: namely, that the ECJ imposes, as a divine punishment over the Member States, the definitive detachment from national procedural rules and, with it, the final expulsion from the Paradise of national legal culture.[14] The problem is however – as will be explained in Chapter 4 – that when the national doctrine heavily criticizes the responses provided by the ECJ, it often forgets to emphasize that they were necessary answers given in response to an 'unfortunate' preliminary reference in relation to the questions submitted to the ECJ and to their formulation. Therefore, they are responses to questions regarding which the national judge seems to have forgotten – as the appropriate title of a well-known essay suggests, with a metaphor that refers precisely to the preliminary reference to the ECJ – that the door of Paradise is the one to which he was knocking:[15] and then perhaps it would have been wise not to knock without a reason...

[13]The quotation refers obviously to the work by the immortal John Milton of 1667, which I read once again while I was writing these pages, drawing interesting starting points for reflection.

[14]To this end it is very useful to read the paper by C. Harlow, *Voices of Difference in a Plural Community*. See also – to quote only a few- G. Cocco, *L'insostenibile leggerezza del diritto italiano*, p. 629 ff., 636 ff.; S. Tarullo, *Il giusto processo amministrativo. Studio sull'effettività della tutela giurisdizionale nella prospettiva europea*, p. 77 ff.

[15]T. Tridimas, *Knocking on Heaven's door: Fragmentation, Efficiency and Defiance in the Preliminary Reference Procedure*.

Chapter 2
The Procedural Autonomy of the Member States from the Viewpoint of the Principles and Criteria Regulating the Relations Between National Law and EU Law

Freely they stood who stood, and fell who fell.
Not free, what proof could they have given sincere
Of true allegiance, constant faith, or love,
Where only what they needs must do appeared,
Not what they would? What praise could they receive?
What pleasure I from such obedience paid,
When Will and Reason (Reason also is choice)
Useless and vain, of freedom both despoiled,
Made passive both, had served Necessity,
Not me? They, therefore, as to right belonged,
So were created, nor can justly accuse
Their Maker, or their making, or their fate,
As if predestination overruled
Their will, disposed by absolute decree
Or high foreknowledge

(John Milton, Paradise Lost, Book III)

2.1 The Procedural Autonomy of the Member States from the Viewpoint of the Principles and Criteria Regulating the Relations Between National Law and EU Law: Brief Introductory Remarks

The problem of what procedural autonomy is and the limits of the so-called procedural autonomy of the Member States is a matter that the doctrine has examined at least since the judgement of the ECJ in the *Rewe* case.

With the *Rewe* jurisprudence the ECJ explicitly stated that: '... *in the absence of community rules on this subject, it is for the domestic legal system of each Member State to designate the courts having jurisdiction and to determine the procedural*

D.-U. Galetta, *Procedural Autonomy of EU Member States: Paradise Lost?*,
DOI 10.1007/978-3-642-12547-8_2, © Springer-Verlag Berlin Heidelberg 2011

conditions governing actions at law intended to ensure the protection of the rights which citizens have from the direct effect of community law.'[1]

The reading of the passage of the *Rewe* ruling quoted above enables us to focus immediately on an essential aspect of the matter: that of the necessary coexistence of the procedural autonomy with the requirements and principles related, more specifically, to the rules governing the relations between national law and EU law.

The question of the necessary coexistence – and, hence, of the necessary balance – between the so-called procedural autonomy of the Member States and the principles and criteria[2] that govern the relations between national law and EU law, is one that I would define as absolutely crucial. I think that the fact that it has not been adequately appreciated in the numerous academic works on this subject can be the reason for many of the misunderstandings among the authors in this regard.

This issue must necessarily be framed in the context of the complex system of relationships governing the juridical and institutional relations between national law and EU law. We should start from the fundamental – and too often overlooked – principle of conferral (*principe d'attribution*), with all the consequences deriving from it in relation to the question of what the EU law can do (through the adoption of binding acts) and what, by contrast, it cannot do simply because it has no competence on the matter.

The direct effect and the primacy[3] of EU law over national law are issues extensively examined by the doctrine, but they need to be re-examined here from the specific perspective of procedural autonomy. The aim is, in fact, to define and delimit their scope of action in this specific context.

Therefore, through the theory of the *effet utile* of the direct effect, a much needed understanding of the contour – which will prove crucial in our specific context – of the effectiveness of the EU law will be achieved. Also, we will re-assess the aspects relating specifically to the effectiveness of the judicial protection that is here a simple corollary of the main requirement of the effectiveness of EU law.

Finally, regarding the obligation for consistent interpretation of the EU law (which is, as we shall see in Chapter 3, the keystone to a correct interpretation of the jurisprudence of the ECJ on the topic of procedural autonomy), it will be necessary to allude also to the important role played, in this specific context, by the preliminary ruling. In fact, it constitutes the essential glue, that allows – or not, if used wrongly, as we shall see more clearly in Chapter 4[4] – the operation of the

---

[1]Judgement of the ECJ of 16 December 1976. Case 33/76. Rewe. *European Court reports* 1976 Page 01989. This ruling has been often reiterated by the Court in its subsequent jurisprudence. For an indication of the main decisions in this regard, see F. Grévisse, J.C. Bonichot, *Les incidences du droit communautaire sur l'organisation et l'exercice de la fonction juridictionnelle dans les Etat membres*, p. 298, note n. 2.

[2]Here, I prefer to refer to the expression of 'principles and criteria' in order to avoid inadequately using the concept of principle. On this topic see the observations by H. Lecheler, *Der Beitrag der allgemeinen Rechtsgrundsätze zur Europäischen Integration*, p. 338 ff.

[3]S. note n. 31.

[4]On this point, see Chapter 4, para. 4.3.

entire, complex and variegated system of relationships between national law and EU law. It is precisely within this system that the procedural autonomy of the Member States necessarily falls.

2.2 The Procedural Competence of the Member States as a Consequence of the Principle of Conferral: The Absence of a Legal Basis, the Implicit Competences and the Notion of *Effet Utile*

According to Art. 5, TEC – introduced as is well known by the Maastricht Treaty – '*The Community shall act within the limits of the powers conferred upon it by this Treaty*.' This is indeed the so-called principle of conferral of competences,[5] which we find now in Art. 5.1. TEU, according to which "*The limits of Union competences are governed by the principle of conferral*".

According to the interpretation of this principle by the ECJ, it involves an action of the EU based on either the competences derived specifically from the provisions of the Treaty, or on the competences that could be implicitly inferred from these provisions. This principle – as the uniform doctrine reminds us – conforms to a basic requirement for all international organizations and, even more, for an organization such as the European Union, which exercises "*responsabilités de puissance publique*" and has the task of pursuing specific goals.[6]

The allotment of objectives and the responsibility that this entails are likely, therefore, to attenuate the rigour of the principle of conferral,[7] which is obviously interpreted by taking into account the implicit competences. Anyway, in our specific context – as we will see below – the implicit competences play a role only in their attenuated form identified by the so-called *effet utile*.

Let me proceed step by step.

Without the need to consider here the definition of legal basis,[8] that can be deemed to be known, it is important to note that, even after the entry into force of

[5]See, among others, R. Adam, in R. Adam, A. Tizzano, *Lineamenti di diritto dell'Unione europea*, p. 16 ff.; R. Alonso García, *Sistema Jurídico de la Unión Europea*, p. 76 ff.; C. Blumann, L. Dubouis, *Droit institutionnel de l'Unione européenne*, p. 314 ff.; G. Tesauro, *Diritto comunitario*, p. 101 ff.

[6]In this sense, J.V. Louis, Th. Ronse, *L'ordre juridique de l'Union européenne*, p. 17.

[7]V. Michel, *2004: Le défi de la répartition des compétence*, p. 31.

[8]On the intrinsic implications of the concept of legal basis, see J.V. Louis, Th. Ronse, *L'ordre juridique de l'Union européenne*, p. 17 ff.; R. Alonso García, *Sistema Jurídico de la Unión Europea*, p. 87 ff. and the jurisprudence mentioned there. Here it is only reminded, incidentally, that the matter related to the identification of the legal bases of the action is a fundamental question for EU law. Also because -as in the case of Arts. 114 and 115, TFEU (95 and 94, TEC) – to the different legal bases correspond different procedures for the adoption of norms that, in turn, have

the Lisbon Treaty,[9] it is not possible to specify within the Treaty a legal basis for the potential competence of the Union on procedural matters.[10] In fact, there is no specific legal basis to this regard in the EU Treaties.[11] Neither is it possible to refer to those generic legal bases that concern the rapprochement between national legislations aimed at the establishment or the functioning of the common market: in general terms, in fact, neither Art. 115, TFEU (*ex* Art. 94 TEC), nor, even less, Art. 114, TFEU (*ex* Art. 95, TEC) proves to be proper legal bases to that end.[12] Even if it was possible to appeal to them (and particularly to Art. 95 TEC) in the adoption of the well-known directives on public procurement procedures[13] a generalized application of these legal bases in order to reconcile national norms has been explicitly ruled out by the ECJ jurisprudence.[14]

---

important practical consequences. On this aspect, see the recent work by J. Ziller, *Bases juridiques et compétences en droit de l'Union européenne*.

[9]The new provision of Art. 298 TFEU states that "*1. In carrying out their missions, the institutions, bodies, offices and agencies of the Union shall have the support of an open, efficient and independent European administration.*

2. In compliance with the Staff Regulations and the Conditions of Employment adopted on the basis of Article 336, the European Parliament and the Council, acting by means of regulations in accordance with the ordinary legislative procedure, shall establish provisions to that end". It can therefore be used as a legal basis only for the adoption of procedural rules referring to the EU administration.

[10]For this reason, I do not share the thesis of C.N. Kakouris, *Do the Member States possess Judicial Procedural "Autonomy"?*, in particular p. 1395 ff., who, from a literal understanding of the passage of the *Rewe* judgement already mentioned in para. 2.1. (*in the absence of community rules*), deduces the existence of a EU competence over this matter, without specifying however the legal basis referred to. In this sense, G. Tesauro, *Diritto comunitario*, p. 101, note n. 28, notes that the legal basis has in this sense a 'constitutional' nature.

[11]In this sense, J. Kokott, *Europäisierung des Verwaltungsprozessrechts*, p. 338 ff. On this point, see also the recent comments by G. Greco, *Illegittimità comunitaria e pari dignità degli ordinamenti*, p. 507 f.

[12]On a specific comment on these provisions see, among others, F. Caruso, *Art. 94 TCE*; Id., *Art. 95 TCE*.

[13]I refer here to the Directives 89/665/EEC and 92/13/EEC, recently modified by Directive 2007/66/EC of 11 December 2007, aimed at improving the effectiveness of review procedures concerning the award of public contracts (in *Official Journal of the European Union* L 335/31, 20.12.2007), which will be considered in Chap. 4, para. 4.4.

[14]See in particular Judgement of the ECJ of 5 October 2000. Case C-376/98. Federal Republic of Germany v European Parliament and Council of the European Union. *European Court reports* 2000 Page I-08419, para. 83 of the grounds, where it is stated that '*... the measures referred to in Article 100a(1) of the Treaty are intended to improve the conditions for the establishment and functioning of the internal market. To interpret that article as meaning that it vests in the Community legislature a general power to regulate the internal market would not only be contrary to the express wording of the provisions cited above but would also be incompatible with the principle embodied in Article 3b of the EC Treaty (now Article 5 EC) that the powers of the Community are limited to those specifically conferred on it.*' From this point of view the shifting of Art. 94 TEC in Art. 115 TFEU and of Art. 95 in Art. 114 TFEU has been made with the clear purpose of recalling the fact, that the provision of Art. 94 was the exception and that of Art. 95 the rule (and not viceversa!).

Neither is it possible to argue that there is an actual implicit EU competence[15] in procedural matters[16] that would derive from the competences granted by the Treaty to the EU in the different areas of substantive law. Such a line of reasoning is explicitly at odds with what the ECJ has repeatedly stated since the 1960s. In fact the ECJ has already pointed to what can be correctly identified as a *procedural competence* of the Member States in the jurisprudence of *Lück* of 1968,[17] a competence whose limits were to be defined later by the ECJ itself – as we will see – in the jurisprudence of *Rewe*[18] and *Comet.*[19] It did so without undermining the base principle, still valid while an immediate binding prohibition subsists, according to which: '*The direct effect of the prohibition in question requires national courts to apply it without any possibility of its being excluded by rules of national law of any kind whatsoever; it is for the internal legal system of every Member State to determine the legal procedure leading to this result.*'[20]

Therefore, while there is neither a suitable legal basis (and, thus, a EU competence in the strict sense), nor a genuine implicit competence of the EU law in procedural matters, there is however – as already anticipated – an implicit competence of the EU in procedural matters in an attenuated form identified by the so-called '*effet utile.*' As we will see later,[21] this particularly concerns the question of the so-called *effet utile* of the direct effect.

2.3 *Continued.* From Procedural Competence of the Member States to Procedural Autonomy: Specifications, Not Only Ones Related to Terminology, on the Concept and Scope of the Notion of Procedural Autonomy

Before continuing with our line of reasoning it is necessary to stop for a moment to consider a number of issues, related not only to terminology. I am referring,

---

15 On this subject, see among others, R. Alonso García, *Sistema Jurídico de la Unión Europea*, p. 80 ff.

16 Instead, regarding the 'executive' competences recognized to the Commission by the EU jurisprudence, as well as on the implicit competences regarding international agreements, see N. Bassi, *Principio di legalità e poteri amministrativi impliciti*, p. 49 ff.

17 Judgement of the ECJ of 4 April 1968. Case 34/67. Lück. *European Court reports* 1968, Page 00245, which I will consider in para. 2.3.

18 See para. 2.1, above.

19 Judgement of the ECJ of 16 December 1976. Case 45/76. Comet. *European Court reports* 1976 Page 02043.

20 Judgement of the ECJ of 11 December 1973. Case 120/73. Lorenz. *European Court reports* 1973 Page 01471. In the same direction, see the decisions of the same date in Case 121/73, *Markmann* and 141/73, *Loyrey*, both of them in *European Court reports* 1973, respectively Page 01495 and Page 01527.

21 See para. 2.5.

obviously, to the questions posed by the concept of procedural autonomy, including those regarding its scope of applicability.

If – as already shown – there exists a competence of the Member States in procedural matters, this still does not explain the origin of the notion of 'procedural autonomy'. This notion is taken for granted by many scholars, who do not thoroughly examine its origins, and barely considers its rationale and its effective scope of applicability.

In this regard, the analysis of the jurisprudence provides an explanation, in particular, in the first decision in which the ECJ asserted that an implicit EU competence on procedural matters does not exist.

In the well-known jurisprudence in *Lück*, being asked about the implications derived from the primacy[22] of the then Art. 95, EEC (now Art. 110, TFEU), the ECJ responded that '*Although Article 95 of the treaty has the effect of excluding the application of any national measure incompatible with it, the Article does not restrict the powers of the competent national courts to apply, from among the various procedures available under national law, those which are appropriate for the purpose of protecting the individual rights conferred by community law.*'[23] Thus the ECJ recognized the existence of a procedural competence of the Member States understood as an 'autonomous' choice of the means aimed at guaranteeing the effectiveness of EU law. Whereas the adjective 'autonomous' refers to the requirement of flexibility that is common to a legal order (like the EU one) that is implemented by a diversity of national orders that do not always have the same instruments available.

Therefore, the appeal to the expression of 'procedural autonomy' – widely referred to in the doctrine, but much less frequent in the language of the ECJ –[24] is probably derived from this expression of '*autonomous* choice of the means,' to identify the competence of the Member States to 'sanction' the respect of the EU law. In this sense, an evidently broad meaning of the term 'sanction' should be used here – according to what some scholars convincingly explain – which (as was

[22]S. note n. 31.

[23]See Judgement of the ECJ of 4 April 1968, Case 34/67. In the same vein see also Judgement of the ECJ of 19 December 1968. Case 13/68. Salgoil. *European Court reports* 1968, Page 00453. On this decision see the comments by R. Kovar, *Droit communautaire et droit procédural national*, p. 233 f.

[24]When a word search was made on the Eur-Lex site (that is better done in the German language, as in this case it is necessary to introduce only one word "Verfahrensautonomie" in the terms of the search) I found -on 4 February 2009 – only 26 decisions in which the ECJ has used this terminology. Moreover within these, in six cases, this expression has been used only by the parties or the Commission. Regarding the Conclusions of the Advocates-General, the use of this expression was also limited to only 57 cases. To this regard see the observations of Th. Von Danwitz, *Europäisches Veraltungsrecht*, p. 311.

already explained in para. 1.1.) '... *designates the array of instruments of legal coercion that, in every Member State, guarantees the respect for the law in the case of conflicts arising in the course of its application.*'[25]

Therefore, as pointed out in Chapter 1, this broad meaning will be used when referring to the concept of procedural autonomy.

Put as such – and to conclude with this point – it seems evident to me that the concept of 'procedural autonomy' is the result of the union of two different elements.

The first element is the absence, as already shown, of a EU competence on procedural matters in the wider sense. In fact, there is no legal bases basis, nor an implicit EU competence on this matter that is derived from the competences attributed by the EU Treaties in the various spheres of substantive law.

Then, based on the distribution of competences individualized in the Treaty,[26] the Member States are responsible for endowing themselves with the proper instruments in order to *sanction* the respect for EU law.

The second element is the conditioning of the procedural competence of the Member States through the mechanism of the *effet utile* of the direct effect connected – as we will see[27] – to the obligation of consistent interpretation.[28]

This second element outlines the competence that has been, so far, indicated as an implicit competence of the EU on procedural matters in its attenuated form. The real nature of this competence is only apparent in the most recent decisions of the ECJ; those that we will consider as fitting in the second phase of the ECJ's jurisprudence on topics related to the procedural autonomy of the Member States. In fact, the ECJ defines the actual implications of this implicit EU competence on procedural matters in the attenuated form, which leads us to speak – as we will see – of a 'functionalized' procedural competence of the Member States. Indeed, the latter – as it will be examined in more detail[29] – retain a procedural competence that remains in a 'subservient function' in relation to their obligation to guarantee the effectiveness of the EU substantive law.

I will continue to refer to the notion of 'procedural autonomy' defined as such from now on. That of 'procedural competence' will be preferred only when it is necessary for a better argumentative clarification.[30]

---

[25]For the French version see Chap. 1, par. 1.1., note n. 5.

[26]See now explicitly in Art. 4.1. TFEU: "*In accordance with Article 5, competences not conferred upon the Union in the Treaties remain with the Member States*".

[27]In Chap. 3.

[28]On this, see below on para. 2.7.

[29]On this point, see Chap. 3, para. 3.2.

[30]In this sense, I do not agree therefore with the suggestion by W. van Gerven, *Of Rights, Remedies and Procedures*, p. 502, who proposes abandoning the term 'procedural autonomy' for that of 'procedural competence.'

2.4 The Direct Effect and the Primacy[31] of the EU Law Over the National Law: Main Aspects

Before concentrating on the specific aspects related to the *effet utile* of the direct effect and the obligation of consistent interpretation of the EU law, it is necessary, however, to briefly consider the concepts of direct effect and of primacy. In fact, they constitute in their reciprocate connection, '*The essential characteristics of the Community legal order.*'[32]

As is well-known, the direct effect consists of the capacity of the EU rule to create rights and duties "*directly and effectively in the hands of the individuals*", without the State having to exercise its intermediary function which consists of putting into place a formal procedure to recognize obligations and rights to individuals.[33]

Based on what has been clarified by the jurisprudence since the decision on *van Gend & Loos* – where the jurisprudence on the direct effect originated – all the EU provisions that are clear and precise and whose application does not require the enactment of further acts of execution or integration are endowed with such effect.[34] Nor is it necessary that these norms address individuals, as the direct effect also applies to the norms directed to Member States: the only relevant thing is, in fact, that the EU legal provision at stake is, due to its '*very nature... to produce direct effects in the legal relationship between Member States and their subjects.*'[35]

---

[31]The word "primacy" is used in "*Declaration n°17 concerning primacy*" annexed to the Lisbon Treaty. That's why I will use it here, instead of the word "supremacy" which (as I'm well aware) has till now been used by most English language doctrine as well as in the English versions of ECJ decisions.

[32]As the ECJ reminded us in its opinion of 14 December 1991. Opinion 1/91. *European Court reports* 1991 Page I-06079, where it is stated, precisely, that '*The essential characteristics of the Community legal order established as such are, in particular, its supremacy over the rights of the Member States and the direct effectiveness of a whole range of norms that apply to the citizens of those States as well as the States themselves.*' (para. 21).

[33]G. Tesauro, *Diritto comunitario*, p. 173. Author's translation. For a broader, rather recent study on several aspects pertaining to the direct effect, see the monographic volume by S. Amadeo, *Norme comunitarie, posizioni giuridiche soggettive e giudizi interni*, p. 3 ff. See also R. Kovar, *Immédiateté du droit communautaire*, p. 4 ff.

[34]It was stated in Judgement of the ECJ of 5 February 1963. Case 26/62. van Gend & Loos. *European Court reports* 1963 Page 00001, that: '*the wording of Article 12 contains a clear and unconditional prohibition which is not a positive but a negative obligation. This obligation, moreover, is not qualified by any reservation on the part of States which would make its implementation conditional upon a positive legislative measure enacted under national law.*'

[35]Judgement van Gend & Loos.

As is well-known, according to the interpretation given by the ECJ, the characteristics required for the purposes of the direct effect[36] are present in certain treaty provisions as well as in EU regulations[37] and decisions.[38] For the directives, however, it is also required that the date indicated in their transposition should have expired and they have not been implemented or they have been wrongly implemented.[39]

The primacy principle, implied in the logic of the jurisprudence of *van Gend & Loos*, was clearly identified by the ECJ in the judgement of *Costa v. Enel* of 1964. In this well-known decision the ECJ pointed out, quite unambiguously, that '*the law stemming from the treaty, an independent source of law, could not because of its special and original nature, be overridden by domestic legal provisions, however framed, without being deprived of its character as community law and without the legal basis of the community itself being called into question.*' And it drew from this premise the conclusion that '*the transfer by the states from their domestic legal system to the community legal system of the rights and obligations arising under the treaty carries with it a permanent limitation of their sovereign rights, against which a subsequent unilateral act incompatible with the concept of the community cannot prevail.*'[40] So, in case of conflict, contradiction or incompatibility between EU law and national law, the first necessarily prevails over the second.[41] This conclusion – as some scholars persuasively tell us – is the result of an '*existentielle*' exigency of EU law.[42]

The primacy is both a rule applied by the national courts to resolve a conflict between norms (domestic and EU ones) and a rule that applies to the legislature as well as the national public administration.[43]

Given previous comments (in para. 2.2.) about the absence, in the current treaty, of a proper legal basis for the adoption of EU laws in procedural matters – except for the case of the already mentioned directives on public procurement procedures[44]

---

[36]For an in-depth study see -in addition to G. Tesauro, *Diritto comunitario*; R. Alonso García, *Sistema Jurídico de la Unión Europea* and, more generally, the text books on EU law – the interesting works by S. Amadeo, *Norme comunitarie, posizioni giuridiche soggettive e giudizi interni*, Chap. III, p. 127 ff., and by O. Porchia, *I principi dell'ordinamento europeo. La cooperazione pluridirezionale*, p. 70 ff.

[37]According to and for the purposes of Art. 288.2 TFEU (*ex* Art. 249.2, TEC), which does not mean, moreover, that all the provisions of a regulation are bestowed with direct effect.

[38]As has been clarified since the Judgement of the ECJ of 6 October 1970. Case 9/70. Grad. *European Court reports* 1970 Page 00825, para. 5 ff.

[39]For an in-depth study, see G. Tesauro, *Diritto comunitario*, p. 180 ff.

[40]Judgement of the ECJ of 15 July 1964. Case 6/64. Costa v E.N.E.L. *European Court reports* 1964 Page 00585.

[41]A. Barav, *Primauté*, p. 855.

[42]Because, in the absence of primacy, it is void and, consequently, inexistent. In this sense, P. Pescatore, *L'Ordre juridique des Communautés européennes*, p. 227.

[43]For more details, see R. Alonso García, *Sistema Jurídico de la Unión Europea*, p. 218 ff.

[44]Council Directive 89/665/EEC of 21 December 1989 on the coordination of the laws, regulations and administrative provisions relating to the application of review procedures to the award of public supply and public works contracts, in *Official Journal L 395, 30/12/1989 P. 0033–0035* and

and for the other rare cases[45] of norms which add certain procedural rules to the regulation of specific areas of substantive law – there exists, indeed, a 'procedural competence of the Member States.' Therefore the primacy of the 'procedural' EU law cannot normally come into play in our reasoning about the limits of the so-called procedural autonomy of the Member States,[46] and, for the same reason, neither does the direct effect come into play here[47] but only, in an indirect way, precisely under the form of '*effet utile* of the direct effect.'

It is therefore necessary to concentrate on this last point.

2.5 *Effet Utile* of the Direct Effect and the Effectiveness of the EU Law: Effectiveness as the First External Limit of the Procedural Autonomy of the Member States

While – as said earlier – neither the primacy nor the direct effect of EU law come into play directly in relation to the procedural autonomy of the Member States,

Council Directive 92/13/EEC of 25 February 1992 coordinating the laws, regulations and administrative provisions relating to the application of EU rules on the procurement procedures of entities operating in the water, energy, transport and telecommunications sectors, in *Official Journal L 076, 23/03/1992 P. 0014–0020*, recently modified by the Directive 2007/66/EC of the European Parliament and of the Council of 11 December 2007 amending Council Directives 89/665/EEC and 92/13/EEC with regard to improving the effectiveness of review procedures concerning the award of public contracts, in *Official Journal of the European Union L 335, 20.12.2007 P.0031-0046*. On the 'old' directives see in particular M. Protto, *L'effettività della tutela giurisdizionale*, p. 112 ff.

[45]In this sense, in particular, certain directives on consumers' protection could be mentioned here. Particularly, Directive 98/27/EC of the European Parliament and of the Council of 19 May 1998 on injunctions for the protection of consumers' interests, in *Official Journal of the European Communities L 166, 11/06/1998 P. 0051-0055*; Council Directive 93/13/EEC of 5 April 1993 on unfair terms in consumer contracts, in *Official Journal L 095, 21/04/1993 P. 0029–0034*; Directive 2002/65/EC of the European Parliament and of the Council of 23 September 2002 concerning the distance marketing of consumer financial services and amending Council Directive 90/619/EEC and Directives 97/7/EC and 98/27/EC, in *Official Journal of the European Communities L 271, 9/10/2002 P. 0016-0024*. In this regard, see further G. Morbidelli, *La tutela giurisdizionale dei diritti nell'ordinamento comunitario*, p. 35 ff. (Chapter on 'La normativa comunitaria avente ad oggetto diretto istituti di tutela giurisdizionale'). See also the interesting reflections by K. Lenaerts, D. Gerard, *Decentralisation of EC Competition Law Enforcement: Judges in the Frontline*, p. 336 ff.

[46]In this sense s. Opinion of Mr Advocate-General Warner delivered on 30 November 1976. Cases 33/76 and 45/76. *Rewe* and *Comet* decisions. *European Court reports* 1976 Page 01989, in particular p. 2005.

[47]The conclusion that primacy and procedural autonomy are not antithetical terms and that neither the direct effect plays a role here is also addressed in S. Prechal, *Community Law in National Courts: The Lessons From Vam Schijndel*, p. 685 f.

except for very rare cases, they do come into play in an indirect way, through the mechanism of the *effet utile of the direct effect.*[48]

The need to guarantee the so-called '*effet utile*'[49] regards those norms of substantive law enacted by the EU legislator in the context of EU competences and which, even if endowed with the characteristics of the direct effect and primacy, however require a collaboration by the authorities of the Member States to be able to exercise their '*effet utile.*'[50] Or, in other words, in order to reach a full realization of their effects.[51]

Naturally, this requirement of full realization of the effects cannot be regarded as restricted solely to the rules of EU law with direct effect. It certainly concerns also the rules that do not have direct effect. Therefore – although in the language of the doctrine the expression '*effet utile*' is often used also in relation to this last purpose – it seems more appropriate to use the term 'effectiveness' *tout court*, which concerns both the requirement of the '*effet utile* of the direct effect' for the EU law bestowed with this attribute, and the requirement of full realization of their effects for those EU norms where it is not possible to speak of direct effect.

Therefore, the procedural autonomy of Member States understood as '*autonomous* choice of the means' directed towards the *sanctioning* of the respect for EU law comes up against an external limit in the exigency of guaranteeing the effectiveness of the norms of the EU substantive law. Then, it is not at all surprising that, in its *Rewe* jurisprudence, the ECJ has identified two essential limits to the procedural autonomy of Member States,[52] which we may henceforth call the two *Rewe* criteria.

The first – as we will see – [53] is the *equivalence* criterion, understood as the prohibition of unequal treatment in relation to similar actions of the national procedural system (herein, the first *Rewe* criterion). The second is precisely the *effectiveness* criterion, understood – in this first meaning – as the obligation not to

---

[48]The expression is taken from J. Mertens de Wilmars, *L'efficacité des différentes techniques nationales de protection juridique contre les violations du droit communautaire par les autorités nationales et les particuliers*, p. 381.

[49]On this matter, see among others J.-D. Mouton, *Effet utile*, p. 449 ff. and the case-law analyzed there.

[50]In this sense, J. Mertens de Wilmars, *L'efficacité des différentes techniques nationales de protection juridique contre les violations du droit communautaire par les autorités nationales et les particuliers*, p. 386. On this point, see the recent work by G. Martinico, *L'integrazione silente. La funzione interpretativa della Corte di giustizia e il diritto costituzionale europeo*, p. 81, who observes that the principle of direct effect means that it should be possible for the norm to be effectively applied and to produce the desired effects.

[51]In this sense, A. Tizzano, *La tutela dei privati nei confronti degli Stati membri dell'Unione europea*, c. 23.

[52]And in this sense it exercises what some authors have defined as a '*droit de regard*' over the national legal orders. S.A. Tizzano, *La tutela dei privati nei confronti degli Stati membri dell'Unione europea*, c. 24.

[53]In para. 2.8.

render impossible, in practice, the exercise of those rights that the national courts must protect (herein, the second *Rewe* criterion).[54]

Without having to review in detail the evolutionary stages followed by the ECJ's jurisprudence in this regard, it is sufficient here to emphasize how – despite what others argue[55] – in its current interpretation (which we will cover in Chapter 3 of this work) the second *Rewe* criterion constitutes in reality a truly 'obligation of result'[56] on the authorities of the Member States.[57] With it, procedural autonomy approaches the idea that is behind the use of the instrument of the EU directive[58] that – as is well-known – binds the Member State in relation to the result to be achieved, but leaves the choice of form and methods to the national authorities.[59]

The analogy under consideration is, in my opinion, illuminating since – as we shall see in Chapter 3 – the limitations that arise in the ECJ's jurisprudence regarding the procedural autonomy of Member States have been, from the beginning, directed to ensure the effectiveness of the EU law understood in the sense already explained: that is, as the ability to pursue the goal established by the norm of EU substantive law.[60] Therefore, one wonders if this analogy can be pushed to the limit to argue that the procedural rules in the wider sense should not only be interpreted in a way consistent

---

[54]Precisely, in *Rewe*, para. 5 of the grounds, the ECJ states that '... *in the absence of community rules on this subject, it is for the domestic legal system of each Member State to designate the courts having jurisdiction and to determine the procedural conditions governing actions at law intended to ensure the protection of the rights which citizens have from the direct effect of community law, it being understood that such conditions cannot be less favourable than those relating to similar actions of a domestic nature*' (first *Rewe* criterion) and that the conditions laid down by the domestic norms should not make it '*impossible in practice to exercise the rights which the national courts are obliged to protect.*' (second *Rewe* criterion).

[55]See for example S. Amadeo, *Norme comunitarie, posizioni giuridiche soggettive e giudizi interni*, p. 315, who notes that the principle of effectiveness should be understood here as having a very different meaning in relation to that of effet utile and, hence, as a requirement for minimum effectiveness.

[56]The expression '*obligation de résultat*' is taken from R. Kovar, *Droit communautaire et droit procédural national*, p. 234. The expression is picked up by A. Barav, *La plénitude des compétences du juge national en sa qualité de juge communautaire*, p. 9.

[57]In this sense, see also O. Dubos, *Les juridictions nationales, juge communautaire*, p. 252 ff., who refers to '*effet utile maximum de la norme communautaire.*'

[58]This analogy is brought to light already by R. Kovar, *Droit communautaire et droit procédural national*, p. 241. The idea has been picked up, more recently, by J. Cavallini, *Le juge national du provisoire face au droit communautaire*, p. 229 ff.

[59]Art. 288.3 TFEU (*ex* Art. 249.3 TEC). In this sense, I think that the observations made by certain authors, who affirm that within the EU legal order the procedural autonomy is -along with the uniformity and effectiveness requirements – an "*objective*" of the EU law, are completely misleading. Likewise, M. Accetto, S. Zleptnig, *The Principle of Effectiveness: Rethinking Its Role in Community Law*, p. 400 f.

[60]In this sense, see also O. Dubos, *Les juridictions nationales, juge communautaire*, p. 263 ff., who points out that '*L'idée d'effet utile de l'effect direct comme fondement de l'encadrement de l'autonomie procédurale n'est certes pas explicite dans la jurisprudence de la Cour, mais elle est bien présente.*'

with the EU order – as we shall see[61] – but also modified and replaced by provisions that enable the norms of EU substantive law to have full effects.[62]

2.6 *Continued.* The Effectiveness of Jurisdictional Protection as a Mere Corollary of the Requisite of Effectiveness of EU Law

Before going any further in our analysis, however, there is a point that needs clarification. This involves the relationship between the effectiveness of EU law and the effectiveness of jurisdictional protection. Indeed, many authors have written about this specific aspect.[63] In particular, it has been pointed out that the interventions of the ECJ regarding the procedural autonomy of Member States have always been primarily aimed at realizing the principle of effective judicial protection.[64] Or the starting point for a second phase of ECJ jurisprudence has been identified,[65] in which the emphasis is seen to have shifted from the effectiveness of EU law to the need for effective protection of the individual.[66]

In reality, from a careful analysis of the ECJ's jurisprudence in this field, it clearly emerges – in my opinion – that the primary objective of the Court is by no means the protection of individuals, but to ensure the effectiveness of EU law.[67]

---

[61]In next para. 2.7.

[62]As suggested moreover by W. van Gerven, *Bridging the gap between Community and National Laws: towards a principle of homogeneity in the field of legal remedies?*, p. 690 ff. (692). We come back to this point in the concluding remarks of Chap. 4, para. 4.7.

[63]See, in particular, the copious monographic work by S. Tarullo, *Il giusto processo amministrativo. Studio sull'effettività della tutela giurisdizionale nella prospettiva europea.*

[64]In this sense, see for example, G. Raiti, *La collaborazione giudiziaria nell'esperienza del rinvio pregiudiziale comunitario*, p. 345 f.

[65]Although not shared, the reading proposed by M. Accetto, S. Zleptnig, *The Principle of Effectiveness: Rethinking Its Role in Community Law*, p. 385 ff., is peculiar in this regard. They argue instead that the requirement of effectiveness of the EU law coincides with the principle of effective judicial protection only at an initial stage.

[66]In this sense, see M. Protto, *L'effettività della tutela giurisdizionale*, p. 1 ff. (9). In substantially analogue terms also, R. Caranta, *Effettività della garanzia giuisdizionale nei confronti della pubblica amministrazione e diritto comunitario: il problema della tutela cautelare*, p. 2554 ff. (2559); Id., *Diritto comunitario e tutela cautelare: dall'effettività allo "ius commune"*, p. 353 ff.; E. Chiti, *Misure cautelari positive e effettività del diritto comunitario*, p. 338 ff.; N. Trocker, *"Civil Law" e "Common Law" nella formazione del diritto processuale europeo*, para. 7 ff. See also Masucci, *La lunga marcia della Corte di Lussemburgo verso una tutela cautelare europea*, p. 1158 ff. In this regard, see moreover the critical reflections by A. Adinolfi, *La tutela giurisdizionale nazionale delle situazioni soggettive individuali conferite dal diritto comunitario*, p. 41 ff., on the possibility of achieve a harmonization, through the jurisprudence, of the inherent aspects of the judicial protection of the subjective situations recognized by the EU law to the individuals.

[67]As pointed out also by S. Tarullo, *Il giusto processo amministrativo. Studio sull'effettività della tutela giurisdizionale nella prospettiva europea*, p. 50 ff. In this regard, see also the broad

As has been consistently pointed out by many scholars, in fact, the EU interventions in the field of procedural autonomy are characterized by the prevailing concern to ensure, primarily, the *effet utile* of EU law.[68] Thus, the emphasis is placed on effective judicial protection only if the affirmation of EU law coincides with solutions that better protect individuals.[69]

In a case where there is no such coincidence – and where, therefore, the effectiveness of EU law requires a lower level of protection (which may exceptionally happen[70]) – the ECJ does not seem to hesitate to impose a lower level of judicial protection at the national level.[71]

Moreover, this is no surprise if we bear in mind the analogy of the system of judicial protection of the EU with the French system. The latter system of protection, unlike the German one, is ascribed to an objective approach to protection – instead of a subjective one.[72] Thus, the cases in which the ECJ's jurisprudence seems to guarantee the effective protection of individual rights are, in fact, cases in which the EU law has as a main goal the guaranteeing of rights: a coincidence, therefore, between objective judicial protection and individual rights.

This is the case – as we shall see – [73] in the jurisprudence related to the directives on equal treatment for men and women in the workplace and in relation to social security, where there is thus a coincidence between the *effet utile* of the direct effect and guaranteeing an EU standard of effective protection.

---

jurisprudential analysis of Th. Eilmansberger, *The relationship between rights and remedies in EC Law: in search of the missing link*, p. 1199 ff.

[68]D. De Pretis, *La tutela giurisdizionale amministrativa in Europa fra integrazione e diversità*, p. 29. In this sense, see also G. Morbidelli, *La tutela giurisdizionale dei diritti nell'ordinamento comunitario*, p. 46.

[69]This is the case, for example, in the recent Judgement of the ECJ, 25 July 2008. Case C-237/07. Janecek. *European Court reports* 2008 Page I-06221.

[70]It is the situation at stake, for example, in Judgement of the ECJ of 23 February 1994. Case C-236/92. Comitato di Coordinamento per la Difesa della Cava and others. *European Court reports* 1994 Page I-00483, where with its third question the national judge posed the following problem before the ECJ '*... Is a national court, when called on to protect "Community subjective rights" of individuals, under an obligation to disapply internal provisions -that are at variance with Community law – even where such "disapplication" may have disturbing effects on the Community public interest* [...]*?*' In this same sense, in my opinion, the Judgement of the ECJ of 21 January 1999. Case C-120/97. Upjohn. *European Court reports* 1999 Page I-00223, should also be read.

[71]See decisions quoted in the above note. In relation to them, see also for a more detailed analysis on this aspect D. De Pretis, *La tutela giurisdizionale amministrativa in Europa fra integrazione e diversità*, p. 29 ff.

[72]On this point see M. Fromont, *L'influence des droits française et allemande sur les conditions de recevabilité du recours en annulation devant la Court de justice des Communautés européens*, p. 47 ff. See also J. Ziller, *La dialectique du contentieux européen: le cas des recours contre les actes normatifs*, p. 446 ff. (449); M. Burgi, *Verwaltungsprozess und Europarecht*, p. 51 ff. (52). S. Prechal, *Community Law in National Courts: The Lessons From Vam Schijndel*, p. 706 seems instead to conclude, based on the analysis of a number of decisions by the ECJ, that the EU system combines elements of both of the systems alluded to.

[73]In particular, in Chap. 3, para. 3.2.3.

In this sense it can certainly be said – as has been done –[74] that, through the national courts, the citizen of the EU becomes an instrument in the process of implementation of EU law and the pursuit of its *effet utile*.[75]

So, in conclusion, as to the question of the alleged centrality, in the current phase of the ECJ's jurisprudence, of the right of individuals to effective judicial protection, I must share the reflection of those authors who, in this respect, note that we should not be dazzled by such appeals because the effectiveness of EU law is always the goal, while the effectiveness of the jurisdictional protection is the means.[76] Further, this is also supported by the most recent jurisprudence on this matter.[77]

And, in this respect, I think that nothing new should be expected after the entry into force of the Treaty of Lisbon,[78] whose provisions will rather have the effect of strengthening further the European Court of Justice in its task of 'functionalizing' the national courts to the requirements of effectiveness of the EU substantive law.[79]

---

[74]On this point, see R. Kovar, *Voies de droit ouvertes aux individus devant les instances nationales en cas de violation des normes et décision du droit communautaire*, p. 245 f. See also in particular M. Ruffert, *Rights and Remedies in European Community Law: A Comparative View*, p. 316; Ch. Callies, *Kohärenz und Konvergenz beim europäischen Individualrechtsschutz. Der Zugang zum Gericht im Lichte des Grundrechts auf effektiven Rechtsschutz*; para. V and the literature quoted there; Id., *Feinstaub im Rechtsschutz deutscher Verwaltungsgerichte. Europarechtliche Vorgaben für die Klagebefugnis vor deutschen Gerichten und ihre dogmatische Verarbeitung*, p. 2 ff. Also, M. Accetto, S. Zleptnig, *The Principle of Effectiveness: Rethinking Its Role in Community Law*, p. 392. Lastly, see P. Pescatore, *Il rinvio pregiudiziale di cui all'art. 177 del Trattato CEE e la cooperazione tra la Corte ed i giudici nazionali*, c. 43 ff.

[75]On this aspect, see moreover what was already stated by the ECJ in its jurisprudence in *van Gend & Loos* (Judgement of the ECJ of 5 February 1963, Case 26/62), where it is affirmed that: '*the vigilance of individuals concerned to protect their rights amounts to an effective supervision in addition to the supervision entrusted by Articles 169 and 170 to the diligence of the Commission and of the Member States*.' See also the ever pertinent reflections of S. Cassese, *Il sistema amministrativo europeo e la sua evoluzione*, p. 773, on the 'iron triangle' that is established between citizens, Commission and ECJ.

[76]G. Morbidelli, *La tutela giurisdizionale dei diritti nell'ordinamento comunitario*, p. 46. In the same vein see moreover also O. Dubos, *Les juridictions nationales, juge communautaire*, p. 308 ff.; S. Morettini, *L'effettività del diritto comunitario ed il processo amministrativo negli Stati membri*, para. 4.3; as well as S. Tarullo, *Il giusto processo amministrativo. Studio sull'effettività della tutela giurisdizionale nella prospettiva europea*, p. 51, who points out that '*it is not difficult to see that the principle of effectiveness of community law flashes in the background of the decisions of the Court of Justice also when it refers to the effectiveness of the judicial protection*.' (Author's translation). On this point, see however, the conclusions by S. Amadeo, *Norme comunitarie, posizioni giuridiche soggettive e giudizi interni*, p. 345 ff.

[77]In this regard, see the decision *Unibet* of 2007 that will be addressed in Chap. III, para. 3.1.

[78]S. Art. 19.1, *alinea* 2, TEU, and Art. 47 of the EU Charter of Fundamental Rights.

[79]On this point, see F. Picod, *Article I–29*, p. 385 ff., 394 f. See also the observations of M.P. Chiti, *La giurisdizione*, p. 357 f.

2.7 Procedural Autonomy, Effectiveness of EU Law and the Obligation of Consistent Interpretation: The Meeting/ Clashing Point Between EU Substantive Law and Procedural Competence of the Member States

Continuing our reasoning with regard to effectiveness, we must now deal with what many authors refer to as the third application layer, in the ECJ's jurisprudence, of the *effet utile* theory:[80] that related to the obligation of consistent interpretation. This is indeed – as we shall see in Chapter 3 – one of the most central aspects of the relationship between national law and EU law, and which helps to frame the issue about the limits of the procedural autonomy of the Member States.

Regarding the obligation for consistent interpretation, moreover, the close analogy once again clearly emerges – addressed earlier –[81] between the way the procedural autonomy of Member States should be understood and the idea behind the use of the instrument of the EU directive. In fact, in the most famous judgement in which the ECJ has explicitly stated the existence of this obligation of consistent interpretation, it is affirmed that, based on the provisions of Art. 189.3 EEC related to the directive, '*... although that provision leaves Member States to choose the ways and means of ensuring that the directive is implemented, that freedom does not affect the obligation imposed on all the Member States to which the directive is addressed, to adopt, in their national legal systems, all the measures necessary to ensure that the directive is fully effective, in accordance with the objective which it pursues.*'[82]

The obligation of consistent interpretation arises, therefore, in the jurisprudence of the ECJ, as the duty to interpret the norm of EU law in accordance with the objective that it pursues and in order to ensure full effect to the EU substantive law. In this way, it seeks to avoid those interpretations of the EU norm that would have the effect of reducing the '*effet pratique*,' or unduly restricting its scope of application, or even more, diminishing its *effet utile*.[83]

In the jurisprudence of the ECJ, however, the obligation of consistent interpretation has evolved from a mere requirement of interpretation of the EU norm according to '*the objective which it pursues*'[84] to '*the requirement that national law must be interpreted in conformity*' with the EU norm.[85]

---

[80]See J.-D. Mouton, *Effet utile*, p. 451.

[81]In para. 2.5.

[82]Judgement of the ECJ of 10 April 1984. Case 14/83. von Colson. *European Court reports* 1984 Page 01891, para. 15 of the grounds.

[83]In this sense, see J.-D. Mouton, *Effet utile*, p. 451, and the relevant jurisprudential references quoted there.

[84]Judgement of the ECJ of 10 April 1984. Case 14/83, para. 15.

[85]See in particular, Judgement of the ECJ of 13 November 1990. Case C-106/89. Marleasing. *European Court reports* 1990 Page I-04135, para. 9 of the grounds.

The obligation of consistent interpretation, understood in this wider meaning, has been subject to several developments in the jurisprudence of the ECJ[86] and has undergone an expansion that is highlighted in a paradigmatic way in the *Pupino* ruling.[87]

This obligation has reached a level of pervasiveness in the most recent jurisprudence, as evident in the *Pfeiffer* decision of 2004,[88] where the ECJ reiterates that '*The requirement for national law to be interpreted in conformity with Community law is inherent in the system of the Treaty, since it permits the national court, for the matters within its jurisdiction, to ensure the full effectiveness of Community law when it determines the dispute before it*;' and regarding its actual implications, it points out that it '*requires the national court to consider national law as a whole in order to assess to what extent it may be applied.*'[89]

The jurisprudential evolution in relation to the obligation of consistent interpretation therefore has amplified the content of this obligation in such a way that it has become the true meeting/clashing point between EU substantive law and the procedural competence of the Member States, as well demonstrated – and we will address it – in the much discussed decision in the *Lucchini* case of 2007.[90]

If applied in our specific context, the jurisprudence on the obligation of consistent interpretation involves the obligation, for the national court, to interpret the national (procedural) rules aimed at 'sanctioning' the observance of EU law in such a way as to pursue the purpose sought by the EU norm of substantive law, with respect to which the procedural autonomy of Member States has a necessarily subservient function.[91] This is an obligation that, in the most recent ECJ's jurisprudence on procedural autonomy of the Member States, adopts the form – as we shall

[86]See on this aspect, for all, the recent paper by G. Gaja, *L'esigenza di interpretare le norme nazionali in conformità con il diritto comunitario*, p. 133 ff. See also G. Tesauro, *Diritto comunitario*, p. 191 ff.; S. Amadeo, *Norme comunitarie, posizioni giuridiche soggettive e giudizi interni*, p. 211 ff. as well as A. Adinolfi, *The Judicial Application of Community Law in Italy*, p. 1335 ff. To this regard see the recent Judgement of the ECJ 16 July 2009. Case C-12/08. Mono Car Styling. *European Court reports* 2009 Page 00000, concerning the possibility to offset the lack of horizontal direct effect with the duty of consistent interpretation.

[87]As is well known, with this judgement the ECJ has extended it also to the so-called third pillar. See Judgement of the ECJ of 16 June 2005. Case C-105/03. Pupino. *European Court reports* 2005 Page I-05285, para. 43 of the grounds. On this decision, see E. Herlin-Karnell, *An exercise in effectiveness?*, p. 1181.

[88]As pointed out by G. Tesauro, *Diritto comunitario*, p. 193.

[89]Judgement of the ECJ of 5 October 2004. Joined cases C-397/01 to C-403/01. *Pfeiffer*. *European Court reports* 2004 Page I-08835, para.s 114 and 115 of the grounds. See also the previous jurisprudence. See as well, more recently, Judgement of the ECJ of 4 July 2006. Case C-212/04. *Adeneler*. *European Court reports* 2006 Page I-06057.

[90]Judgement of the ECJ of 18 July 2007. *Lucchini*. Case C-119/05. *European Court reports* 2007 Page I-06199, which will be extensively analyzed in Chap. 3, para. 3.4.

[91]As already observed by R. Kovar, *Droit communautaire et droit procédural national*, p. 251 ff. more than thirty years ago.

see –[92] of a real duty of 'functionalization' of the national law.[93] This obligation presents levels of such complexity and difficulty that it becomes an onerous and sometimes very unpleasant task for the national judge.

As I will try to argue in the conclusions of this second chapter,[94] although difficult and unpleasant, however it is a task that the national judge is not only obliged to accomplish but is further expected to accomplish in good faith, according to what can be inferred from the provision of Art. 4, third paragraph, TEU (*ex* Art. 10, TEC), as well as its interpretation by doctrine and jurisprudence.

2.8 The Second Limit to the Procedural Autonomy of Member States: The Non-discrimination Principle Understood as Equivalence Criterion and the Inapplicability, in This Sense, of a So-called Criterion of 'Vertical Equivalence'

The equivalence criterion[95] is based on the underlying idea – put forward in the *Rewe* decision – that the types of procedures for actions aimed at guaranteeing the protection of the recognized rights of individuals by EU norms cannot be less favourable than those for similar actions in the domestic procedural system.

In practice, however, there is the problem of knowing when we are faced with 'similar cases' that make the obligation of equivalence operative.[96] In this regard, the ECJ has recently reiterated that '*The principle of equivalence requires that the rule at issue be applied without distinction, whether the infringement alleged is of Community law or national law, where the purpose and cause of action are similar.*'[97] But it has then indicated that '*In order to determine whether the principle of equivalence has been complied with in the present case, the national court – which alone has direct knowledge of the procedural rules governing actions in the field of employment law – must consider both the purpose and the essential*

[92]In Chap. 3, para. 3.3.

[93]As already anticipated, it is placed in a 'subservient function' in relation to the requirement of effectiveness of the EU substantive law. In this sense see, lastly, the reflections by R. Kovar, *L'interprétation des droits nationaux en conformité avec le droit communautaire*, p. 381 ff., 386.

[94]Para. 2.10.

[95]On this aspect, see O. Dubos, *Les juridictions nationales, juge communautaire*, p. 269 ff. For a detailed study, see also A. Adinolfi, *La tutela giurisdizionale nazionale delle situazioni soggettive individuali conferite dal diritto comunitario*, p. 43 ff.; A. Biondi, *The European Court of Justice and certain national procedural limitations: not such a tough relationship*, p. 1274 ff.; T. Tridimas, *Enforcing Community Rights in National Courts: Some Recent Development*, p. 38 ff.

[96]On the problems related to this type of assessment see the critical observations of A. Biondi, *The European Court of Justice and certain national procedural limitations: not such a tough relationship*, p. 1274 ff.

[97]Judgement of the ECJ of 1 December 1998. Case C-326/96. Levez. *European Court reports* 1998 Page I-07835, para. 41.

characteristics of allegedly similar domestic actions' taking into account, likewise, '*... the role played by that provision in the procedure as a whole, as well as the operation and any special features of that procedure before the different national courts.*'[98]

To sum up, then, even if the ECJ has fully clarified in its jurisprudence that the equivalence criterion prohibits both direct and indirect discrimination, it has also stated that this principle cannot be interpreted in the sense that it obliges the Member States to extend the most favourable national regime to all actions based on EU law.[99]

The equivalence criterion as a limit to the procedural autonomy of the Member States has nothing to do with what in doctrine has been defined as the criterion of 'vertical equivalence,' a consequence of the equal rank of the legal orders.[100] It seems to me that the concern from which this idea of vertical equivalence derives is most linked to considerations of political opportunity (understood in terms of 'desirability' of such an equivalence),[101] rather than to considerations related to the specific theme, which is the object of our enquiry.[102] In fact, in our specific context the equivalence criterion is closely connected to the need to safeguard the direct effect and primacy of the substantive EU law, as well as to its effectiveness. These concerns do not exist with regard to the regime of the public acts of the EU.[103] In this latter context the rules of procedure play a quite different role, since there is no direct link (unlike in the case of national procedural norms) between these norms and the objective – which is essential in the EU system – to ensure an effective 'sanction' of the EU substantive law.

Even if, therefore, in the jurisprudence of the ECJ the standards of protection expected from the EU procedural law seem sometimes to be '*playing to a different*

---

[98]Para. 43 and 44 of the grounds in *Levez*. To this regard, see also Judgement of the ECJ of 10 July 1997. Case C-261/95. Palmisani. *European Court reports* 1997 Page I-04025.

[99]In this sense, see the last part of *Levez*, para. 42 of the grounds. For a detailed study, see T. Tridimas, *Enforcing Community Rights in National Courts: Some Recent Development*, p. 39 ff.

[100]In this vein, G. Greco, *Illegittimità comunitaria e pari dignità degli ordinamenti*, p. 513, who speaks of 'vertical' equivalence in the sense that the protection of the EU positions that can be fairly claimed by the Member States cannot be '*stronger or, any case, more favourable than that accorded by the community law itself*' (p. 513). In this sense, according to this author, a 'vertical' equivalence may subsist in the sense of '*equivalence as a result of the comparison between nationals and community regimes and remedies.*' (p. 515). Author's translation.

[101]In this sense, see R. Caranta, *Judicial protection against Member States: a new* Jus Commune *takes shape*, p. 726, who, without mentioning the issue of equal rank of the legal orders, refers to a 'vertical *ius commune*' ('*ius commune verticale*'). In a rather critical tone, P.J. Wattel, *Köbler, Cilfit and Welthgrove: we can't go on meeting like this*, in the para. with the suggestive title '*Those who live in glass houses should not throw stones*', p. 184 ff. See also S. Morettini, *L'effettività del diritto comunitario ed il processo amministrativo negli Stati membri*, para. 3.1.1, who speaks about a requirement of coherence of the systems based on '*political and judicial reasons.*'

[102]In this sense, I cannot understand the reasoning of A. Negrelli, *Il primato del diritto comunitario e il giudicato nazionale: un confronto che si poteva evitare o risolvere altrimenti*, p. 1236.

[103]As is underlined by M.P. Chiti, *Le peculiarità dell'invalidità amministrativa per anticomunitarietà*, p. 501 f.; Id., *Diritto amministrativo europeo*, p. 569.

tune'[104] if compared to those standards expected from the national legal orders, this asymmetry is not – in my opinion – a *vulnus* to the principle of equal rank of the legal orders. It is only the result of the absence, in the first case, of the concerns related to the direct effect and primacy of EU law that, under the reconstruction proposed here, seem instead quite central to the approach of the ECJ's jurisprudence on the question of the limits of the procedural autonomy of the Member States.

2.9 *Continued.* Equivalence Criterion and Obligation of Consistent Interpretation: Aligning the ECJ's Monopoly on the Interpretation of EU Law with the Exigency of Uniform Application. From Consistent Interpretation to a 'Uniform Procedural Law' Through the Mechanism of Uniform Interpretation? Critical Remarks

The obligation of consistent interpretation, as we have seen, requires '*above all the courts, to interpret their national law as consistent as possible with the provisions of the community law.*'[105] This includes, of course, procedural law. However, the jurisprudence of the ECJ has identified – as we shall see – the existence of a real monopoly of the ECJ itself in interpreting EU law. So, ultimately, it is the ECJ itself that must furnish – through the mechanism of interpretative preliminary ruling –[106] the binding interpretation in relation to the norms of EU law. As a consequence, this interpretation 'spins over' subsequently to the national legal system and limits the national courts' room for interpretation. Further, it demands that the national courts – through the mechanism of consistent interpretation – interpret their procedural domestic law in such a way as to be 'instrumental' in the pursuit of the objectives of substantive EU law, as interpreted by the ECJ.

---

[104]C. Kilpatrick, *The Future of Remedies in Europe*, p. 8. In this sense see also the observations of R. Caranta, *Judicial protection against Member States: a new* Jus Commune *takes shape*, p. 721 ff., who refers to the use of a '*double standard*' (p. 724). On the same line of reasoning see also S. Prechal, N. Shelkoplyas, *National Procedures, Public Policy and EC-Law. From Van Schijndel to Eco Swiss and Beyond*, p. 611.

[105]G. Tesauro, *Diritto comunitario*, p. 190 (Author's translation) and see futher the copious case law on this topic quoted there (note n. 284 ff.)

[106]In regard to the preliminary reference procedure see, for all, the well-known essay by P. Pescatore, *Il rinvio pregiudiziale di cui all'art. 177 del Trattato CEE e la cooperazione tra la Corte ed i giudici nazionali*, c. 26 ff. See also, for a more recent analysis, F. Sorrentino, *L'art. 177 del Trattato di Roma nel rapporto tra ordinamento comunitario e ordinamenti interni*, p. 737 ff.; A. Arnull, *The Evolution of the Court's Jurisdiction under Art. 177 EEC*, p. 129 ff.; C. Barnard, E. Sharpston, *The Changing Face of Article 177 References*, p. 1113 ff. Further, see the monographic volume by G. Raiti, *La collaborazione giudiziaria nell'esperienza del rinvio pregiudiziale comunitario*.

The absolute monopoly of the ECJ in relation to the interpretation of the EU law aims to ensure the *uniform interpretation* of the EU law throughout the Union. This is demonstrated unequivocally by the interesting ECJ jurisprudence that has been developed in relation to the interpretation of the national law 'modelled' in conformity with EU legislation.[107]

To this end, particularly in its jurisprudence in *Dzodzi* of 1990, the ECJ, after insisting that '*It does not appear either from the wording of Article 177 or from the aim of the procedure introduced by that article that the authors of the Treaty intended to exclude from the jurisdiction of the Court requests for a preliminary ruling on a Community provision in the specific case where the national law of a Member State refers to the content of that provision in order to determine rules applicable to a situation which is purely internal to that State*,' it specified – in regard to what here directly concerns us – that '*On the contrary, it is manifestly in the interest of the Community legal order that, in order to forestall future differences of interpretation, every Community provision should be given a uniform interpretation irrespective of the circumstances in which it is to be applied.*'[108]

This important (and criticized) jurisprudence[109] of the ECJ originates, therefore, from the primary need '*... to ensure that Community law has the same effect in all Member States of the Community in order to prevent divergences in the interpretation thereof in cases where the application of Community law is directly involved.*'[110]

The fact is, therefore, that in the ECJ's approach, the exigency of *uniform interpretation* of the EU law appears at this point of such importance as to prevail

---

[107]Namely, the national norms that either reproduce the text of a EU norm or refer directly to it even regarding a situation with no relevance for the EU law. For an in-depth analysis see the interesting paper by M.E. Bartoloni, *La competenza della Corte di giustizia ad interpretare il diritto nazionale "modellato" sulla normativa comunitaria*, p. 311 ff.

[108]Judgement of the ECJ of 18 October 1990. Joined cases C-297/88 and C-197/89. Dzodzi. *European Court reports* 1990 Page I-03763, para. 36 ff. of the grounds. In the same direction, see Judgement of the ECJ of 8 November 1990. Case C-231/89. Gmurzynska-Bscher. *European Court reports* 1990 Page I-04003, para. 24 of the grounds; Judgement of the ECJ of 17 July 1997. Case C-28/95. Leur-Bloem. *European Court reports* 1997 Page I-04161, para. 32 of the grounds; Judgement of the ECJ of 17 July 1997. Case C-130/95. Giloy. *European Court reports* 1997 Page I-04291, para. 28 of the grounds; Judgement of the ECJ of 16 June 1998. Case C-53/96. Hermès. *European Court reports* 1998 Page I-03603, para. 32 of the grounds; Judgement of the ECJ of 11 January 2001. Case C-1/99. Kofisa. *European Court reports* 2001 Page I-00207, para. 32 of the grounds; Judgement of the ECJ of 15 January 2002. Case C-43/00. Andersen. *European Court reports* 2002 Page I-00379, para. 18 of the grounds; Judgement of the ECJ of 16 March 2006. Case C-3/04. Poseidon. *European Court reports* 2006 Page I-02505, para. 16 of the grounds; Judgement of the ECJ of 14 December 2006. Case C-217/05. Confederación Española de Empresarios de Estaciones de Servicio. *European Court reports* 2006 Page I-11987, para. 20 of the grounds; Judgement of the ECJ of 11 December 2007. Case C-280/06. Philip Morris. *European Court reports* 2007 Page I-10893, para. 21 of the grounds.

[109]See, for all, the very harsh critique of H. Rasmussen, *Remedying the Crumbling EC Judicial System*, p. 1082 f.

[110]Judgement of the ECJ of 8 November 1990, Case C-231/89, para. 24.

also on the need to restrict an excessive expansion of the admissibility grounds of the interpretative preliminary ruling.[111]

Thus, it does not seem to be out of place to ask whether, based on the requirement of *uniform interpretation* and the mechanism – which we have just analyzed – of *consistent interpretation* of the national procedural law, in connection with the *equivalence criterion* applied *a contrario sensu*, it is possible to attain in practice (or at least get very close to) a 'uniform procedural law' within the territory of the European Union.

It is not denied that this interpretative option – which I will try to explain – can appear enticing to those who – like the author – for purely political and ideological reasons,[112] are in favour of greater harmonization of the national laws of the Member States.[113] However, as we shall see, the reasoning as it is carried out is wrong in its conclusions: that, despite its appearance, they are not at all the logical consequence of the applications of the mechanisms studied so far, even if applied in an extreme manner.

Hence, the partisans of the protection of diversity cannot but be reassured.

Let's see why.

It has been said – in para. 2.7. – that from the requirement of *consistent interpretation* of national law in relation to the objectives pursued by the EU law derives (as we will see better in Chapter 3, devoted to the analysis of the jurisprudence) a kind of obligation of 'functionalization' of the national law: in particular, of the national procedural norms in the wider sense, that must be interpreted so as to allow the pursuit of the purpose intended by the EU norm of substantive law.

---

[111]This expansion presents a number of problematic aspects as has been often pointed out in the Conclusions of the Advocates General in the decisions quoted above. On this point see also T. Tridimas, *Knocking on Heaven's door: Fragmentation, Efficiency and Defiance in the Preliminary Reference Procedure*, p. 9 ff., 34 ff.; *Contra* see moreover C. Barnard, E. Sharpston, *The Changing Face of Article 177 References*, p. 1127 ff.

[112]In this regard, to my mind come spontaneously the words of Jean Monnet at the end of his *Mémoires*, published in 1976 '*But time goes by, and Europe is still in a position in which it has already been... We cannot stop when around us the whole world is moving. Did not I say quite clearly that the Community we created is not an end in itself? It is a transformation process that continues, one from which our national forms of life emerged during an earlier historical phase. As our provinces yesterday, so today our people must learn how to live together under common rules and institutions freely accepted, if they want to achieve the desired progress and continue to dominate their destiny. The sovereign nations of the past are no longer the place where we can solve the current problems. And the Community itself is only a step towards the forms of organization of the world of tomorrow.*' (p. 461). Author's translation.

[113]It is in this perspective that the well-known essay of 1995 by W. van Gerven, *Bridging the gap between Community and National Laws: towards a principle of homogeneity in the field of legal remedies?*, p. 679 ff., should be read (and could also be appreciated). He concludes with a reference which should not leave any doubt about his 'ideological choice.' In fact, he refers to the founders of the modern comparative law and to their idea of creating a '*common law of mankind.*' And he concludes: '*Although it remains an enterprise with dubious chance of success, it must be tried over and over again, at least once in the lifetime of every new generation or lawyers. Let us try it again*' (p. 702).

It was added further that from the exigency of *uniform interpretation* derives such a strong monopoly of the ECJ on the interpretation of EU law that it subsists in any occasion where such law is applied – that is, even in situations that have only mere domestic relevance (and, therefore, are not relevant for the EU).

As a result of the interaction of these two mechanisms – and pushing through an application *a contratio sensu* of the *equivalence principle* – is it possible to argue that an increasing convergence of national procedural regimes, which goes beyond the exigency for *uniform application* of EU law in all Member States, is taking place, given that the application *a contrario sensu* of the equivalence principle (that is, an application of the principle of equality common to all the national legal orders) shall be understood in terms, now classic, of prohibition to 'discriminate' (in reverse) between situations that are only domestically relevant from those that are relevant[114] for the EU – in this case, in the application of procedural rules?

The answer is no, because there is something here that we must not overlook: namely, that in the absence of EU norms on procedural matters (that exist only in specific contexts[115]), the concept of procedural autonomy of the Member States understood in terms already explained (that is, as '*autonomous* choice of the means' directed to 'sanctioning' the observance of EU law) signifies, in the first instance, the appeal to existing resources within the national law.[116] Only when they do not exist or are totally inappropriate to be 'functionalized'[117] – and, therefore, in extreme cases –[118] suitable 'means' may be put into place. Moreover, their individualization is left to the discretion of the national legislator who can certainly take into consideration the system of 'means' within which the new instruments are introduced. In this way, there is no need to alter the 'intrinsic harmony' (the '*Paradise lost*' referred to in Chapt. 1) of the national procedural system through the insertion of elements totally unrelated to it or, even more, the replacement of fundamental institutions of the national procedural law with different institutions of a supposedly EU procedural law created by the jurisprudence.[119]

---

[114]On this point, see the essay by G. Greco, *Il diritto comunitario propulsore del diritto amministrativo europeo*, p. 88 f., where he speaks in this regard of an 'induced juridical effect' ('*effetto giuridico indotto*') of the EU norms.

[115]As the directives on public procurement procedures, for example, to which we will come back in Chap. 4. For other examples see in para. 2.4., note n. 45.

[116]As is admitted moreover by the most extremist authors. See, for example, J.S. Delicostopoulos, *Towards European Procedural Primacy in National Legal Systems*, p. 599 ff. (605).

[117]That is, as has been repeatedly reaffirmed, they should be interpreted in such a way as to allow the pursuit of the purpose intended in the EU norm of substantive law, in relation to which the procedural autonomy of the Member States is in a subservient function.

[118]See in this regard Chap. 3, para. 3.5.

[119]We will come back to this point in the concluding remarks of Chap. 4, para. 4.7.

2.10 The Procedural Autonomy of the Member States: Competence of the Member States in Procedural Matters and the Duty of Sincere Cooperation. Closing Remarks

To close the line of reasoning in relation to the procedural autonomy of the Member States – that, as argued, should be built around the principles and criteria that govern the relationship between national law and EU law – and before moving on to the analysis of jurisprudence on this matter, there still remains a fundamental issue to be addressed. That is, the provision of Art. 4, third paragraph, TEU (*ex* Art. 10, TEC), about the duty of sincere cooperation (*coopération loyale*) according to which "*Pursuant to the principle of sincere cooperation, the Union and the Member States shall, in full mutual respect, assist each other in carrying out tasks which flow from the Treaties. The Member States shall take any appropriate measure, general or particular, to ensure fulfilment of the obligations arising out of the Treaties or resulting from the acts of the institutions of the Union. The Member States shall facilitate the achievement of the Union's tasks and refrain from any measure which could jeopardise the attainment of the Union's objectives*".

As already noted at the time by *Mertens de Wilmars*,[120] this provision is in fact the legal basis for the system of articulation of the competences structured – as we have seen – over EU norms of substantive law and a national system of rules aimed at 'sanctioning' the observance of that EU substantive law.[121]

The obligation is therefore twofold: on the one hand, it is a matter of *ensuring the enforcement* of the EU norms; on the other, it is a matter of constantly verifying the suitability of the '*arsenal of national judicial protection*'[122] in relation to the main objective of ensuring the compliance with the EU law and refraining from adopting *measures* which could have the effect of weakening this arsenal and thus undermining the effectiveness of the EU law.

As has been persuasively observed by some scholars, it is not a mere, superfluous reproduction, within the Treaty on European Union of the international law

[120] J. Mertens de Wilmars, *L'efficacité des différentes techniques nationales de protection juridique contre les violations du droit communautaire par les autorités nationales et les particuliers*, p. 392. On this point, see also the observations of J.P. Jacqué, *Droit institutionnel de l'Union européenne*, p. 580 ff.

[121] For an in-depth analysis see, among others, M. Blanquet, *L'article 5 du Traité CEE. Recherche sur les obligations de fidélité des Etat membres de la Communauté européenne*, p. 1 ff.; A. Hatje, *Artikel 10 (Verpflichtung der Mitgliedstaaten)*, p. 314 ff.; C. Iannone, *Art. 10 TCE*, p. 219 ff.; M. Rossi, W. Kahl, *Grundsatz der loyalen Zusammenarbeit (Art. 10 EGV)*, cpv. 1 ff.; M. Zuleeg, *Art. 10: Verpflichtungen der Mitgliedstaaten*, p. 668 ff. See moreover A. Bleckmann, *Art. 5 EWG-Vertrag und die Gemeinschaftstreue*, p. 483 ff. For a recent study on some of the implications of this principle see lastly O. Porchia, *I principi dell'ordinamento europeo. La cooperazione pluridirezionale*, p 5 ff.

[122] The expression is borrowed from J. Mertens de Wilmars, *L'efficacité des différentes techniques nationales de protection juridique contre les violations du droit communautaire par les autorités nationales et les particuliers*, p. 392.

principle of *pacta sunt servanda*: rather, it is a provision that confers on the EU Treaty particular qualities in relation to an ordinary international law treaty.[123] The provision represents, therefore, the necessary and logical complement of the doctrine of primacy and direct effect.[124]

In addition to the influential opinions of some authors, it is the jurisprudence of the ECJ that has attributed a key role to this provision, as a qualified element to allow an evolution of the relationship between EU law and national laws. In particular, the ECJ has gradually revealed the nature of the norm as a source of '*obligations of result*'[125] whose meaning is not exhausted, then, with its implementation but which entails an obligation to act with the '*spirit of cooperation*[126] *to achieve the objectives of the community*,'[127] namely, an active and sincere cooperation.

From the provision of Art. 4.3, TEU derive obligations on both the national legislature and the administrative authority. And above all, on the national courts which become '*decentralized judges*' of the EU law to carry out its implementation.[128]

The latter, according to a correct interpretation of the concept of 'procedural autonomy,' must therefore use the *means* made available by their domestic law to *sanction* the observance of the EU law in order to ensure compliance with the two *Rewe* criteria of equivalence and (more importantly) effectiveness of EU substantive law.[129] This effectiveness can hardly be ensured without the active cooperation of the national courts given that the European Court of Justice, unlike the Supreme

[123]R. Quadri, *Articolo 5 CEE*, p. 51.

[124]See C. Nizzo, *L'art. 5 del Trattato CE e la clausola generale di buona fede nell'integrazione europea*, p. 381 ff. (382).

[125]Costantinesco is doubtful about the correctness of this construction. See V. Costantinesco, *L'art. 5 CEE. De la bonne foi à la loyauté communautaire*, p. 104. On this point see however A. Tizzano, *La tutela dei privati nei confronti degli Stati membri dell'Unione europea*, p. 20, as well as the recent reflections of C. Nizzo, *L'art. 5 del Trattato CE e la clausola generale di buona fede nell'integrazione europea*, note n. 19.

[126]Among the first, see Judgement of the ECJ of 10 December 1969. Joined cases 6 and 11–69. Commission of the European Communities v French Republic. *European Court reports* 1969 Page 00523, para.s 16 and 17 of the grounds; Judgement of the ECJ of 7 February 1973. Case 39–72. Commission of the European Communities v Italian Republic. *European Court reports* 1973 Page 00101, para. 25 of the grounds. On this point see A. Bleckmann, *Die Rechtsprechung des Europäischen Gerichtshof zur Gemeinschaftstreue*, p. 653 ff.; M. Zuleeg, *Art. 10: Verpflichtungen der Mitgliedstaaten*, p. 672 ff.

[127]So C. Iannone, *Art. 10 TCE*, p. 219 ff. (220). Author's translation. See the case law on this topic quoted there. In the same sense, see C. Nizzo, *L'art. 5 del Trattato CE e la clausola generale di buona fede nell'integrazione europea*, p. 381 ff.

[128]In this sense see A. Tizzano, *La tutela dei privati nei confronti degli Stati membri dell'Unione europea*, p. 17.

[129]In this sense see C. Iannone, *Art. 10 TCE*, p. 221.

Court of a federal system, does not have the tools to implement its decisions through forcible enforcement procedures.[130]

It is in this specific context that comes into play – as we will see in the next chapter – the central role developed in the jurisprudence of the ECJ of the obligation of consistent interpretation of the national law, to which we have referred to above. This is an obligation which should be interpreted as a duty, when necessary, to perform a rather 'manipulative' interpretation of the national law,[131] obviously, as long as the wording of the national norm allows the national judge this margin for manoeuvre and its consistent interpretation does not lead to a *contra legem* hermeneutic.[132]

In conclusion, my opinion[133] is that this obligation of consistent interpretation – so widely understood – represents an essential (and inescapable) realization of the duty of sincere cooperation that stems from Art. 4, third paragraph, TEU, which in turn, is the necessary and logical complement to the doctrine of primacy and direct effect.

As we shall see in the next chapter, specifically devoted to the analysis of the ECJ's jurisprudence, although the concept of 'manipulative interpretation' could be inferred from the context outlined here, the ECJ is satisfied, in fact, with something less. From the specific context of those decisions that have helped to better outline the limits of the procedural autonomy of the Member States, it is possible to deduce therefore, in my opinion, a different concept: that of 'functionalization of the national procedural competence'. This concept indeed seems more suitable to describe the essence of the phenomenon since it focuses attention on the ultimate aim (of the primacy and effectiveness of the EU substantive law), without trampling too much on the aspect (which is rather central in the concept of 'manipulative interpretation') related to the use of a national procedural tool for (more or less) different purposes to which it was designed to serve.

---

[130]As explicitly pointed out by P. Mengozzi, *L'applicazione del diritto comunitario e l'evolversi della giurisprudenza della Corte di giustizia nella direzione di una chiamata dei giudici nazionali ad assicurare una efficace tutela dei diritti da esso attribuiti ai cittadini degli stati membri*, p. 32 f. In this perspective, therefore, the positions of certain scholars, who affirm the ECJ's identification as a 'Supreme Court of the Union,' should be considered very carefully. In this sense, T. Tridimas, *Knocking on Heaven's door: Fragmentation, Efficiency and Defiance in the Preliminary Reference Procedure*, p. 36. On this point, see also the reflections of K. Lenaerts, T. Corthaut, *Towards an Internally Consistent Doctrine of Invoking Norms of EU Law*, p. 502 f.

[131]The expression 'manipulative' is transposed from the language used with respect to a certain type of judgements of the Italian Constitutional Court. On this point see, for all, R. Romboli, *Il ruolo del giudice in rapporto all'evoluzione del sistema delle fonti ed alla disciplina dell'ordinamento giudiziario*, *passim*.

[132]As in fact is noted by R. Kovar, *L'interprétation des droits nationaux en conformité avec le droit communautaire*, p. 394, '*La Cour convient qu'une juridiction nationale ne peut pas être obligée d'en venir à une interprétation* contra legem.' On this point, see the observations of S. Amadeo, *Norme comunitarie, posizioni giuridiche soggettive e giudizi interni*, p. 219 ff.

[133]Some authors trace the obligation of consistent interpretation back to the principle of sincere cooperation. See, in particular, G. Tesauro, *Diritto comunitario*, p. 219; A. Hatje, *Artikel 10 (Verpflichtung der Mietgliedstaaten)*, p. 323 ff.; J.V. Louis, Th. Ronse, *L'ordre juridique de l'Union européenne*, p. 147. See also V. Atripaldi, *Leale cooperazione comunitaria ed obbligo degli stati al riesame degli atti amministrativi definitivi contrari al diritto comunitario*, p. 886 f.

Chapter 3
The Jurisprudence of the ECJ on the Procedural Autonomy of Member States: Analysis of the Fundamental Judgements

...... they themselves decreed
Their own revolt, not I: if I foreknew
Foreknowledge had no influence on their fault
Which had no less proved certain unforeknown.
So without least impulse or shadow of fate, [120]
Or aught by me immutably foreseen
They trespass, authors to themselves in all,
Both what they judge and what they choose; for so
I formed them free, and free they must remain,
Till they enthrall themselves: I else must change [125]
Their nature, and revoke the high decree
Unchangeable, eternal, which ordained
Their freedom: they themselves ordained their fall.

(John Milton, Paradise Lost, Book III)

3.1 Introductory Premise

As already stated in the first Chapter, the chapter that follows consists of an analysis of the ECJ's decisions, which have been issued as a result of references for a preliminary ruling under Art. 267, TFEU (*ex* Art. 234, TEC).[1] These have been selected because of their specific relevance for the argumentation on the procedural autonomy of the Member States that I wish to outline here. Till now, there are a number of academic works that have considered the issue of the so-called procedural autonomy from the (national or comparative) perspective of national procedural legislations. The aim has been almost always to explain, as thoroughly as possible, all the decisions of the EU judges which have dealt with one or the other

[1]For this particular reason, in this chapter the judgements of the ECJ will be indicated with quotes that mention the extended parties. The national court which has made the referral will be also indicated.

D.-U. Galetta, *Procedural Autonomy of EU Member States: Paradise Lost?*,
DOI 10.1007/978-3-642-12547-8_3,

aspects of this topic.[2] In so doing, however, the authors were almost obliged to choose a classic line of argumentative reasoning, that is, the grouping of the decisions of the ECJ on the basis of the topic of procedural relevance on which these decisions were more or less concentrated: the time limit for submitting an appeal, precautionary protection and so on.

The aim of the present study is, instead, quite different, as I do not at all claim to be exhaustive. On the contrary, I have made a selection from the ECJ's jurisprudence and the analysis of the chosen decisions that follows is mainly aimed at highlighting the rationale that – according to my intuition – underlies all of the interventions of the ECJ on the issue of procedural autonomy. In this perspective, limiting the analysis of the decisions of the ECJ only to the specific context of the judicial administrative law process would not have much point. The scope of this study is, in fact, necessarily much broader as it is intended to cover all the measures which – as has already been mentioned more than once[3] – are more generally related to the power that rests with the authorities of the Member States to 'sanction' the observance of the European law.

3.2 The First Phase of the ECJ's Jurisprudence on the Procedural Autonomy of the Member States: The Two 'Rewe Criteria' and the Obligation of Consistent Interpretation as an Instrument to Guarantee the Effectiveness of EU Law

The first phase of the jurisprudence of the ECJ regarding the procedural autonomy of the Member States starts with the well-known decision on the *Rewe* case, of 1976, where the ECJ explains the two famous 'Rewe criteria' of equality of treatment and effectiveness as general limits to the procedural autonomy of the Member States.[4]

The entire first phase of the jurisprudence is based, therefore, as we shall see, on the application of the two *Rewe* criteria, which were also gradually improved in their connection to the obligation of consistent interpretation. In this context, it is possible to identify a number of differences – in terms of the incisiveness of the supervision of the ECJ in practice – which depend, not so much on the sectors of intervention,[5] but on the weight of the EU interests at stake and, more particularly,

---

[2]The most recent example of this traditional way of carrying out research is the extensive and well-documented comparative study of 2008 by M. Eliantonio, *Europeanisation of Administrative Justice? The influence of ECJ's Case Law in Italy, Germany and England.*

[3]In Chap. 1 and Chap. 2.

[4]To which I have referred in Chap. 2.

[5]As argued by M. Dougan, *National Remedies before the Court of Justice*, *passim*; C. Kilpatrick, *The Future of Remedies in Europe*, p. 14 ff.; and, in a much more dubitative way by G. de Burca,

on the relevance of these interests for the pursuit of the objectives set by the Treaty. The subdivision into paragraphs seeks, therefore, to account for this element that, from time to time, gathers together or singles out the individual decisions under examination.[6]

3.2.1 Procedural Autonomy of the Member States and National Norms Limiting the Repeatability of Amounts Obtained in Conflict with EU Provisions: The Explanation and Specification of the Two 'Rewe Criteria' by the ECJ

The analysis of the most important ECJ jurisprudence on the procedural autonomy of the Member States cannot but start within the context in which the first fundamental decision on this topic was issued: namely, the dispute over the procedural rules that limit the repeatability of amounts of money unduly paid to a Member State where the payment is contrary to EU rules in the sphere of competition and taxation, but also and fundamentally to those EU rules aimed at ensuring the free movement of goods, services or capital and, thereby, the establishment of the common market. This objective was one of the fundamental aims of the Treaty under Art. 2, TEC.

In the well-known decision in the *Rewe* case of 16 December 1976[7] the ECJ identified for the first time the two external limits to the procedural autonomy of the Member States. They are – as already explained – the two '*Rewe* criteria:' the *equivalence* criterion and the *effectiveness* criterion, understood in this first formulation as a minimum threshold of effectiveness.[8]

On this premise, the context in which the *Rewe* decision is framed is characterized by a constant attitude on the part of the ECJ, which has never really departed from the supervisory model outlined in this first and most important decision. In this particular case, the ECJ had to consider the compatibility of the time-limits set by

A. Ryall, *The ECJ and Judicial Review of National Administrative Procedure in the Field of the EIA*, p. 159.

[6]In this sense, I completely share the recent reflections by N. Bassi, *Mutuo riconoscimento e tutela giurisdizionale. La circolazione degli effetti del provvedimento amministrativo straniero fra diritto europeo e protezione degli interessi del terzo*, p. 94, on the need to perform an evaluation of the trends of the EU jurisprudence 'as a whole,' instead of making 'manipulative extractions' from it.

[7]Judgement of the ECJ of 16 December 1976. Rewe-Zentralfinanz eG and Rewe-Zentral AG v Landwirtschaftskammer für das Saarland. Reference for a preliminary ruling: Bundesverwaltungsgericht – Germany. Case 33-76. *European Court reports* 1976 Page 01989.

[8]In this sense, C. Blumann, L. Dubouis, *Droit institutionnel de l'Unione européenne*, p. 404. On this point, see also S. Hegels, *EG-Eigenverwaltungsrecht und Gemeinschaftsverwaltungsrecht. Europäisches Verwaltungsrecht für den direkten und den indirekten Gemeinschaftsrechtsvollzug*, p. 61 ff.

the national legislation for the annulment of the administrative act and reimbursement of the sum improperly paid to the national administration with EU law.[9] In this regard, the ECJ merely stated that '...*in the present state of community law there is nothing to prevent a citizen who contests before a national court a decision of a national authority on the ground that it is incompatible with community law from being confronted with the defence that limitation periods laid down by national law have expired, it being understood that the procedural conditions governing the action may not be less favourable than those relating to similar actions of a domestic nature.*'[10]

In the contemporary decision in the *Comet* case,[11] which presents many similarities, the ECJ returned to the very same arguments already presented in the *Rewe* judgement and reached the same conclusions on the assumption that the laying down of time-limits for submitting an appeal '...*with regard to actions of a fiscal nature is an application of the fundamental principle of legal certainty protecting both the tax-payer and the administration concerned.*'

The *Just* decision came four years later, on 27 February 1980,[12] and addresses, once again, the procedural limitations imposed by national law on the possibility of requesting the repayment of amounts claimed (in this case, charges levied)[13] in contravention to EU law and which, again, represents a potential obstacle to the aim of establishing the internal market.[14] Also here the ECJ, recalling its previous jurisprudence in *Rewe* and *Comet*, has recognized that it is '...*compatible with community law to lay down reasonable limitation periods in the interests of legal certainty which protects both the tax-payer and the administration concerned;*'[15] and thus, they meet the two conditions referred to in the *Rewe* decision.

Another important decision in this context is the *San Giorgio* judgement of 1983.[16] In this case, however, the dispute was not – unlike the three cases examined

[9]That in this specific case consisted of charges for phytosanitary inspections regarded by the Court as equivalent to custom duties.

[10]Para. 6 of the grounds in *Rewe*.

[11]Judgement of the ECJ of 16 December 1976. Comet BV v Produktschap voor Siergewassen. Reference for a preliminary ruling: College van Beroep voor het Bedrijfsleven – Netherlands. Case 45–76. *European Court reports* 1976 Page 02043. On both decisions, *Rewe* and *Comet*, see the comment by R. Kovar, *Droit communautaire et droit procédural national*, p. 230 ff. See also P. Kalbe, *Gemeinschaftsrecht und nationale Rechtsbehelfsfristen* p. 360 ff.; A. Marzano, *Sulla ripetibilità delle somme indebitamente corrisposte per tasse di effetto equivalente ai dazi doganali*, p. 71 ff.

[12]Judgement of the ECJ of 27 February 1980. Hans Just I/S v Danish Ministry for Fiscal Affairs. Reference for a preliminary ruling: Østre Landsret – Denmark, Case 68–79. *European Court reports* 1980 Page 0501.

[13]Namely, taxation of spirits.

[14]The alluded Treaty norm is, specifically, Art. 95, EEC, now Art. 110, TFEU.

[15]Para. 22 of the grounds in *Just*.

[16]Judgement of the ECJ of 9 November 1983. Amministrazione delle Finanze dello Stato v SpA San Giorgio. Reference for a preliminary ruling: Tribunale civile e penale di Trento – Italy. Case 199/82. *European Court reports* 1983 Page 03595.

above – over the limitation periods laid down by the national law in order to request a repayment of the sums unduly paid, but on the burden of proof prescribed in this regard by the national procedural law. The central question on this regard is therefore the first one: the question formulated by the national judge to the ECJ on whether a Member State is legitimately entitled to subordinate the refund of the tax to the proof that it has not been passed[17] to other persons.[18] In this regard, the ECJ provided a response very much in line with the *Rewe* criteria stating that in principle there is no incompatibility with the EU law, but that "*... any requirement of proof which has the effect of making it virtually impossible or excessively difficult to secure the repayment of charges levied contrary to community law would be incompatible with community law*".[19]

Fourteen years later the *Fantask* decision of 1997[20] was once again related to the time limits laid down by the national law for the repayment of charges levied in breach of the directive on free movement of capital. Also in this case the ECJ, after recalling its previous jurisprudence,[21] merely noted that '*...Community law, as it*

[17]A related issue, regarding the national norms on illicit enrichment, is dealt with by the ECJ in two contemporary decisions: Judgement of the ECJ (Third Chamber) of 10 July 1980. Amministrazione delle finanze dello Stato v Ariete SpA. Reference for a preliminary ruling: Corte d'appello di Torino – Italy. Case 811/79. *European Court reports* 1980 Page 02545, and Judgement of the ECJ (Third Chamber) of 10 July 1980. Amministrazione delle finanze dello Stato v Sas Mediterranea importazione, rappresentanze, esportazione, commercio (MIRECO). Reference for a preliminary ruling: Corte suprema di Cassazione – Italy. Case 826/79. *European Court reports* 1980 Page 02559, which outcomes are identical (see, in particular, para. 13 ff.). On the question of the compatibility with the EU law of the national norms related to undue increase in wealth that has the effect of limiting the protection of rights guaranteed by the EU law (and, consequently, its effectiveness), see in particular the following interesting decisions: Judgement of the ECJ of 20 September 2001. Courage Ltd v Bernard Crehan and Bernard Crehan v Courage Ltd and Others. Reference for a preliminary ruling: Court of Appeal (England and Wales) (Civil Division) – United Kingdom. Case C-453/99. *European Court reports* 2001 Page I-06297 and Judgement of the ECJ (Third Chamber) of 13 July 2006. Vincenzo Manfredi v Lloyd Adriatico Assicurazioni SpA (C-295/04), Antonio Cannito v Fondiaria Sai SpA (C-296/04) and Nicolò Tricarico (C-297/04) and Pasqualina Murgolo (C-298/04) v Assitalia SpA. Reference for a preliminary ruling: Giudice di pace di Bitonto - Italy. Joined cases C-295/04 to C-298/04. *European Court reports* 2006 Page I-06619.

[18]See para. 11 of the grounds in *San Giorgio*.

[19]Para.s 14 of the grounds in *San Giorgio*.

[20]Judgement of the ECJ of 2 December 1997. Fantask A/S e.a. v Industriministeriet (Erhvervministeriet). Reference for a preliminary ruling: Østre Landsret – Denmark. Case C-188/95. *European Court reports* 1997 Page I-06783.

[21]In para. 48 of the grounds in *Fantask* it is stated: '*The Court has ... acknowledged, in the interests of legal certainty which protects both the taxpayer and the authority concerned, that the setting of reasonable limitation periods for bringing proceedings is compatible with Community law. Such periods cannot be regarded as rendering virtually impossible or excessively difficult the exercise of rights conferred by Community law, even if the expiry of those periods necessarily entails the dismissal, in whole or in part, of the action brought (see, in particular, Case 33/76 Rewe v Landwirtschaftskammer Saarland [1976] ECR 1989, para. 5, Case 45/76 Comet v Produktschap voor Siergewassen [1976] ECR 2043, para.s 17 and 18, and Case C-261/95 Palmisani v Istituto Nazionale della Previdenza Sociale [1997] ECR I-0000, para. 28).*'

now stands, does not prevent a Member State which has not properly transposed the Directive from resisting actions for the repayment of charges levied in breach thereof by relying on a limitation period under national law which runs from the date on which the charges in question became payable, provided that such a period is not less favourable for actions based on Community law than for actions based on national law and does not render virtually impossible or excessively difficult the exercise of rights conferred by Community law.'[22] This is despite the precedent of the *Emmott* case,[23] which has triggered much debate among many scholars, and which we will analyze in detail later in this chapter.[24]

3.2.2 Procedural Autonomy of the Member States and National Norms that Prevent the Recovery of Aid Paid in Violation of EU Law: The First Phase of the ECJ's Jurisprudence on This Matter

To assess the ECJ's position on the issues covered in our analysis, another important area to look at is related to the recovery of aid paid in violation of EU law. Here, it emerges quite clearly that the issue of procedural autonomy of the Member States extends beyond purely judicial administrative law process matters.

Almost all the decisions that we will see here, in fact, deal with issues that concern, in a more general sense – and to use the terminology used by *Mertens de Wilmars*, that has been already recalled many times – the '*pouvoir de sanction*' of the national law in relation to the compliance with EU norms. Thus, these decisions refer both to judicial administrative law process in the strict sense and to those rules which are not strictly related to process but relate more generally – with regard to the Member States submitting a preliminary reference – to the whole of national rules concerning legal disputes.[25]

---

[22]Para. 52 of the grounds in *Fantask*.

[23]I do not share, in this sense, the reflections of T. Tridimas, *Enforcing Community Rights in National Courts: Some Recent Development*, p. 43, where he observes that '*Fantask gave a fatal blow to Emmott*.' In fact, as we shall see, it is a matter of giving different responses to situations that are framed differently rather than a matter of contradictions and abandonment of a jurisprudential trend. The ECJ's approach, therefore, remains consistent.

[24]Particularly, in next para. 3.2.3.

[25]As already mentioned (Chap. 2, para. 2.3.), J. Mertens de Wilmars, *L'efficacité des différentes techniques nationales de protection juridique contre les violations du droit communautaire par les autorités nationales et les particuliers*, p. 390, who notes that in this regard we should refer to '*… tout l'ensemble des règles formelles ou substantielles qui, dans chaque Etat membre, ordonnent l'ensemble des divers contentieux nationaux*.'

In the first decision that is relevant in this specific context, the judgement on the *Milchkontor* case of 1983,[26] the national referring judge asked the ECJ to respond to the following question: '... *whether community law ... directly authorizes the competent national authorities to demand repayment of aids unduly paid, so that the substantive conditions for a right of recovery are exhaustively set out in that provision, or whether recovery is governed by the rules and procedures laid down by national legislation; if it is, the court wishes to know what limits are placed on the application of national law.*'[27] In concrete terms, the issue was related to the relationship between the revocation powers of national administrations and the protection of the legitimate expectations of the beneficiaries of unduly-paid EU aid.[28] The ECJ will return frequently to this matter. The response of the ECJ – even in relation to different issues and context – does not move away from the two criteria established in the *Rewe* jurisprudence in the sense that '...*in the absence of provisions of community law disputes concerning the recovery of amounts unduly paid under community law must be decided by national courts pursuant to their own national law subject to the limits imposed by community law inasmuch as the rules and procedures laid down by national law must not have the effect of making it virtually impossible to implement community regulations and national legislation must be applied in a manner which is not discriminatory compared to procedures for deciding similar but purely national disputes.*'[29]

In this case, however, there is an important variation in relation to the case-law examined in the previous chapter as the ECJ, in the course of its reasoning, addresses an important point in relation to the question of the procedural autonomy of the Member States when its expressly observes that '... *the application of national law must not affect the scope and effectiveness of community law*' and adds that '...*that would be the case in particular if the application of national law made it impossible in practice to recover sums irregularly granted.*'[30] So, on the one hand, it is certainly not possible for the national law to concede a discretionary power to the administration in order to decide whether or not to demand the return of EU funds improperly or illegally granted because '...*the duty to recover such sums...* [*is*] *impose*[*d*] *on the national administration* [*by the community law*].'[31] On the other hand – as regards the specific problem posed by § 48 of the German law on administrative procedure (*Verwaltungsverfahrensgesetz – VwVfG*) which

[26]Judgement of the ECJ (Fifth Chamber) of 21 September 1983. Deutsche Milchkontor GmbH and others v Federal Republic of Germany. References for a preliminary ruling: Verwaltungsgericht Frankfurt am Main – Germany. Joined cases 205 to 215/82, *European Court reports*, 1983, Page 02633.

[27]Para. 15 of the grounds in *Milchkontor*.

[28]In this sense, see moreover my recent work: *La tutela dell'affidamento nella prospettiva del diritto amministrativo italiano, tedesco e comunitario: un'analisi comparata*, p. 757 ff.

[29]Para. 19 of the grounds in *Milchkontor*.

[30]Para. 22 of the grounds in *Milchkontor*.

[31]Para. 22 of the grounds in *Milchkontor*.

provides a special form of protection of legitimate expectations[32] – even if the ECJ stresses that '... *the principles of the protection of legitimate expectation and assurance of legal certainty are part of the legal order of the community*' and that '... *the fact that national legislation provides for the same principles to be observed in a matter such as the recovery of unduly-paid community aids cannot, therefore, be considered contrary to that same legal order,*' it recalls that in balancing the different conflicting interests '... *the interests of the community [should] be taken fully into consideration.*'[33] For now the ECJ stops here, but with this last statement – that explicitly links here to the first *Rewe* criterion, the equivalence criterion[34] – it lays down the basis for more insightful decisions on this particular problem that will follow a decade later.[35]

The decision in the *Huber* case of 2002,[36] while in line with the *Milchkontor* jurisprudence, goes a further step forward in relation to the obligation of consistent interpretation. While, in fact, the ECJ reaffirms that '... *Community law does not preclude the application of the principles of the protection of legitimate expectations and legal certainty in order to prevent the recovery of aid part-financed by the Community which has been wrongly paid, provided that the interest of the Community is also taken into consideration,*' it then adds however a further element to its line of reasoning stating, that '*The application of the principle of the protection of legitimate expectations assumes that the good faith of the beneficiary of the aid in*

---

[32]Para. 2 of § 48 VwVfG in fact states that: "*Ein rechtswidriger Verwaltungsakt, der eine einmalige oder laufende Geldleistung oder teilbare Sachleistung gewährt oder hierfür Voraussetzung ist, darf nicht zurückgenommen werden, soweit der Begünstigte auf den Bestand des Verwaltungsaktes vertraut hat und sein Vertrauen unter Abwägung mit dem öffentlichen Interesse an einer Rücknahme schutzwürdig ist. Das Vertrauen ist in der Regel schutzwürdig, wenn der Begünstigte gewährte Leistungen verbraucht oder eine Vermögensdisposition getroffen hat, die er nicht mehr oder nur unter unzumutbaren Nachteilen rückgängig machen kann* "(An unlawful administrative act granting a one-off or ongoing financial benefit or a benefit that is divisible or which is a prerequisite of it, cannot be withdrawn when the beneficiary has relied on the existence of the administrative act and its expectations, prior to balancing the public interest on the withdrawal, and is worthy of protection. Legitimate expectation, as a rule, is worthy of protection if the recipient has made use of the benefits or has adopted a provision on its assets that can no longer be cancelled or can only be cancelled at the cost of unacceptable drawbacks) – Author's translation. The exceptions to this rule which follow in para. 2, are omitted here.

[33]Para.s 30–32 of the grounds in *Milchkontor*.

[34]In fact, in para. 32 of the grounds in *Milchkontor* it is stated: '... *the principle that national legislation must be applied without discrimination compared to purely national procedures of the same kind requires the interests of the community to be taken fully into consideration in the application of a provision which, like the first sentence of Para. 48(2) of the Verwaltungsverfahrensgesetz, requires the various interests in question... to be weighed up against one another before the decision is revoked ...*'

[35]On this point, see next para. 3.3.2. This aspect is noted also by E. Grabitz, *Europäisches Verwaltungsrecht. Gemeinschaftsrechtliche Grundsätze des Verwaltungsrechts*, p. 1789 ff. On this point, see also M. Burgi, *Verwaltungsprozess und Europarecht*, p. 50.

[36]Judgement of the ECJ (Fifth Chamber) of 19 September 2002. Republik Österreich v Martin Huber. Reference for a preliminary ruling: Oberster Gerichtshof – Austria. Case C-336/00. *European Court reports* 2002 p. I-07699.

question is established.'[37] This is so since, in fact, the principle of protection of legitimate expectations, as formulated in the EU jurisprudence, requires a prior enquiry on the good faith of the beneficiary of the aid in relation to the regularity of the aid itself.[38] Thus, the procedural autonomy of the Member States here faces a limit as the eventual derogations of the principle that imposes on the national court the duty to sanction the breach of the obligations imposed by the EU law – in this case, the recovery of the aids paid – should be re-interpreted in the light of the requirement of effectiveness of the EU law. As a result, these derogations should be interpreted restrictively. When evaluating the conflicting interests, the EU interest (in this case, to recover the aid) should be taken into due account. The re-interpretation resulting from the EU jurisprudence of the general principles of law (like, for example, the protection of legitimate expectations) applicable to the balancing of interests to be undertaken by the national court, should also be taken into due account.[39]

3.2.3 Procedural Autonomy of the Member States and Obligation of Consistent Interpretation: The Particular Case of the Directives on Equal Treatment for Men and Women in the Workplace and in Relation to Social Security

In line with our earlier observations there are a number of important decisions by the ECJ concerning the specific issue of the conflict between national and EU procedural norms aimed at achieving the fundamental principle of equality between men and women in the context of the workplace and social security.[40] Due to its

[37] Para. 59 of the grounds in *Huber*.

[38] In the EU jurisprudence the schema of protection of legitimate expectations was, in fact, copied from the German model of protection, according to which the verification of the subsistence of an expectation, understood in a subjective sense (*Vertrauen*) and, consequently, of the good faith in subjective sense is an essential element in the legal reasoning concerning the protection of legitimate expectations. For an in-depth analysis, see my recent work *La tutela dell'affidamento nella prospettiva del diritto amministrativo italiano, tedesco e comunitario: un'analisi comparata*, p. 757 ff.

[39] In this regard, I refer to the *feedback* phenomenon of the principles and institutions developed by the EU jurisprudence on the national legal orders of the Member States. Under this mechanism principles and institutions borrowed from the legal orders of the Member States suffer, when passing through the EU jurisprudence, changes that are often very substantial (almost a "change of nature"). As a consequence, this makes the next implementation stage very difficult, even for those Member States from which they were originally borrowed. These remarks can already be found in D.U. Galetta, *Principio di proporzionalità e sindacato giurisdizionale nel diritto amministrativo*, p. 5 ff.

[40] To this regard, see the sectoral study by C. Kilpatrick, *Turning Remedies Around: A Sectoral Analysis of the Court of Justice*, p. 143.

importance, this principle was explicitly considered in Art. 2 of the EC Treaty (see now in Art. 3 par. 3, TEU).

In response to a preliminary reference that, in essence, sought to clarify the compatibility of the norms of the Irish *Sex Discrimination Order* with the Directive 76/207/EEC (on the implementation of the principle of equal treatment for men and women), in its decision in the *Johnston* case of 1986,[41] the ECJ stated that the procedural rules at issue in the case – which established a burden of proof with the consequence of depriving the interested party from pleading the rights conferred by the directive before the courts – could be contrary to the objectives set by the Directive. As a result, it was necessary to interpret those rules in a way that allows the accomplishment of objectives set by the Directive and, thereby, the effectiveness of the EU law.

In my opinion, the fact that in the *Johnston* case the ECJ made explicit reference to the right to an effective judicial remedy should not be overstated.[42] In fact, this does not represent the beginning of a second phase in the ECJ's jurisprudence, characterized by a shift from an emphasis on the effectiveness of EU law to the requirement of an effective protection of the individual.[43] Rather – as already explained above[44] – it is a case of the coincidence between the *effet utile* of the direct effect and the guarantee of a EU standard of effective protection, as is clear from the wording of the sixth question reformulated by the ECJ: '*... the sixth question... raises the point whether community law, and more particularly Directive No. 76/207, requires the Member States to ensure that their national courts and tribunals exercise effective control over compliance with the provisions of the directive and with the national legislation intended to put it into effect.*'[45] What counts, therefore, is the compliance with the objectives set by the Directive, that is, the effectiveness of the EU law. In this sense, from our point of view (that of the procedural autonomy of the Member States and its limits), the fact that it confers individuals certain rights through provisions with such characteristics that made them directly enforceable – rights that, consequently, could be pleaded and enforced before a national court – represents a purely accidental element and that

---

[41]Judgement of the ECJ of 15 May 1986. Marguerite Johnston v Chief Constable of the Royal Ulster Constabulary. Reference for a preliminary ruling: Industrial Tribunal, Belfast (Northern Ireland) – United Kingdom. Case 222/84. *European Court reports* 1986 Page 01651.

[42]Para. 13 ff. of the grounds in *Johnston*. G. Morbidelli, *La tutela giurisdizionale dei diritti nell'ordinamento comunitario*, p. 46, observes in this regard that '*there is no need for dazzling with such arguments*' given that '*the pole star of the whole reasoning is always represented by the effet utile.*' Author's translation.

[43]As is argued, instead, by certain authors. In this sense, for example, M. Protto, *L'effettività della tutela giurisdizionale*, p. 1 ff. (9); N. Trocker, *"Civil Law" e "Common Law" nella formazione del diritto processuale europeo*, para. 7 ff.

[44]See Chap. 2, para. 2.6.

[45]Para. 13 of the grounds in *Johnston*.

does not alter the core of the problem.[46] Given that we are dealing with a directive here, and not with a regulation, the primacy principle eventually comes into play only in relation to norms with characteristics that meet the criteria set out by the ECJ in its jurisprudence on norms with direct effect.[47] Regarding the rest of the provisions, it is necessary to refer instead to the effectiveness of the EU law and to the obligation of consistent interpretation of the norms of the national law (in this case, the evidence rules of the *Sex Discrimination Order*) with respect to the objectives pursued by the Directive.[48]

Five years later, and again in relation to equality between men and women in the context of workplace and social security, the ECJ took another crucial step in its jurisprudence on procedural autonomy of the Member States with the well-known decision in the *Emmott* case of 1991.[49] However, when considered in depth, this is a new and deserved tribute by the ECJ to the effectiveness of the EU law and to the obligation of consistent interpretation of the norms of national law.

In this case, the problem concerned the expiry of the time limit laid down by the national law to initiate a proceeding aimed at protecting the rights recognized by the provisions with direct effect of Directive 79/7/EEC, on the progressive implementation of the principle of equal treatment for men and women in matters of social security. It is important to emphasize this aspect of the matter because, in this specific case, the problem arose particularly from the combination of two factors: first, that the directive had not been properly transposed by the Social Welfare (no. 2) Act, 16 July 1985, and, second, that, according to the domestic procedural

---

[46]In para. 17 of the grounds in Johnston it is affirmed that '*...Article 6 of the directive requires Member States to introduce into their internal legal systems such measures as are needed to enable all persons who consider themselves wronged by discrimination "to pursue their claims by judicial process." It follows from that provision that the Member States must take measures which are sufficiently effective to achieve the aim of the directive and that they must ensure that the rights thus conferred may be effectively relied upon before the national courts by the persons concerned.*'

[47]See, in particular, regarding the Directive, the Judgement of the ECJ of 4 December 1974. Yvonne van Duyn v Home Office. Reference for a preliminary ruling: High Court of Justice, Chancery Division – United Kingdom. Case 41–74. *European Court reports* 1974 Page 01337.

[48]This is clearly apparent when reading para. 53 of the grounds in Johnston, where the ECJ specifies that '*in this context it should be observed first of all that, as the Court has already stated in its judgements... the Member States' obligation under a directive to achieve the result envisaged by that directive and their duty under Article 5 of the Treaty to take all appropriate measures, whether general or particular, to ensure the fulfilment of that obligation, is binding on all the authorities of Member States including, for matters within their jurisdiction, the courts. It follows that, in applying national law, and in particular the provisions of national legislation specifically introduced in order to implement directive no 76/207, national courts are required to interpret their national law in the light of the wording and the purpose of the directive in order to achieve the result referred to in the third para. of Article 189 of the EEC Treaty. It is therefore for the Industrial Tribunal to interpret the provisions of the Sex Discrimination Order, and in particular Article 53(1) thereof, in the light of the provisions of the directive, as interpreted above, in order to give it its full effect.*'

[49]Judgement of the ECJ of 25 July 1991. Theresa Emmott v Minister for Social Welfare and Attorney General. Reference for a preliminary ruling: High Court – Ireland. Case C-208/90. *European Court reports* 1991 Page I-04269.

law, the period for initiating a proceeding in order to assert those rights had expired. These rights – by virtue of the direct effect of the Directive's norms where they were included – could have been invoked before the national judge starting from the expiry date to transpose the Directive – that is, 23 December 1984. However, the provisions of the national norms to transpose the Directive did not enter into force until various dates in 1986. Only later did the ECJ intervene with two decisions, affirming the direct effect of the Directive's norms improperly transposed.[50] In this case, thus, from the combination of these two factors seemed to emerge – and aside from what will be explained in Chapter 4 of this work – the impossibility of the applicant to assert his rights. Regarding the preliminary question, as submitted by the Irish Supreme Court, the lack of effectiveness of the EU law therefore became absolute and incontrovertible. Far from declaring that the periods laid down by the national law for initiating proceeding should not be applied,[51] the much-discussed decision of the ECJ merely stated that: '... *until such time as a directive has been properly transposed, a defaulting Member State may not rely on an individual's delay in initiating proceedings against it in order to protect rights conferred upon him by the provisions of the directive and that a period laid down by national law within which proceedings must be initiated cannot begin to run before that time.*'[52] Once again,[53] then, the ECJ is not disputing the time limit laid down by the national law to initiate a proceeding. The problem is, rather, that there is an obligation to interpret the national procedural norms regarding the starting date for this time limit in accordance with the requirement of effectiveness of the EU law, when (as in this case) the EU law in practice takes the form of a directive not correctly transposed into the national law and partly self-executing.[54] There is no problem then – and no real *vulnus* of the procedural autonomy of the Member States – but, rather, a useful clarification of the obligations of the Member States under Art. 288 paragraph 3, TFEU (*ex* Art. 249 paragraph 3, TEC),[55] and on the actual value of the principle of direct effect of norms contained in expired directives.[56]

---

[50]See para.s 5 and 6 of the grounds in *Emmott*.

[51]In this sense, the broad interpretation of the meaning of this decision by certain authors is not justified, and neither are the related critiques. See, for example, E.M. Barbieri, *Norme comunitarie self-executing e decorrenza dei termini di prescrizione e decadenza*, p. 73 ff.

[52]Para. 23 of the grounds in *Emmott*.

[53]As in the *Johnston* case, already considered.

[54]The expression of 'self-executing directive' is used here as a matter of convenience but it only partly reflects the real meaning of the phenomenon. On this aspect, see moreover what was already explained in Chap. 2.

[55]As rightly pointed out by J. Cavallini, *Le juge national du provisoire face au droit communautaire*, p. 237 ff.

[56]It is interesting in fact – in relation to this specific aspect – the specifications of the ECJ in para. 20 of the grounds in Emmott where it affirms that '*Only in specific circumstances, in particular where a Member State has failed to take the implementing measures required or has adopted measures which are not in conformity with a directive, has the Court recognized the right of persons affected thereby to rely, in judicial proceedings, on a directive as against a defaulting Member State. This minimum guarantee, arising from the binding nature of the obligation imposed*

Apart from the fact that – as we shall see[57] – it originated from a preliminary reference that could well have been avoided, if re-read in this perspective the *Emmott* judgement does not seem to me to represent an isolated and highly invasive jurisprudence of the procedural autonomy of the Member States at all – as has instead been often stressed by many scholars.[58] In fact, the two subsequent decisions of the ECJ on similar issues – the decisions on the *Steenhorst-Neerings* and the *Johnson* cases – are in a line of absolute continuity with respect to the jurisprudence in *Emmott*, as (re)interpreted here.[59]

With the *Steenhorst-Neerings* decision of 1993[60] – again on the interpretation of Art. 4, no 1, of the Directive 79/7/EEC – after expressly recalling the two *Rewe* criteria on procedural autonomy of the Member States,[61] the ECJ points out that these criteria are met '...*[by a] national rule restricting the retroactive effect of a claim for benefits for incapacity for work*.'[62] This is because of the fact that – unlike what has been highlighted with regard to the *Emmott* case – here there is no conflict between the (procedural) norm of the national law at issue and the requirement of effectiveness of the (substantive) EU law, since '... *the rule described in the question referred for a preliminary ruling in this case does not affect the right of individuals to rely on Directive 79/7 in proceedings before the national courts*

---

on the Member States by the effect of directives, cannot justify a Member State absolving itself from taking in due time implementing measures appropriate to the purpose of each directive.'

[57]In Chap. 4, para. 4.3.3.

[58]In this respect, see the arguments and literature quoted in J. McKendrick, *Modifying Procedural Autonomy: Better Protection for Community Rights*, p. 576 ff. (*Emmott criticised*). See also, in particular, L. Flynn, *Whatever Happened to Emmott? The Perfecting of Community Rules on National Time-Limits*, p. 51 ff., who defines the *Emmott* jurisprudence as '*an aberration in the Court's jurisprudence*' (p. 62) and A. Arnull, *The European Union and its Court of Justice*, p. 300 ff.

[59]Of a contrary opinion, J. McKendrick, *Modifying Procedural Autonomy: Better Protection for Community Rights*, p. 565 ff., who departs from an analysis – in my opinion, misleading – of the outcomes that the *Emmott* jurisprudence would produce, to finally suggest a return to *Emmott* (p. 586). In the same line, L. Flynn, *Whatever Happened to Emmott? The Perfecting of Community Rules on National Time-Limits*, p. 51 ff. See also T. Tridimas, *Enforcing Community Rights in National Courts: Some Recent Development*, p. 41 ff.

[60]Judgement of the ECJ of 27 October 1993. H. Steenhorst-Neerings v Bestuur van de Bedrijfsvereniging voor Detailhandel, Ambachten en Huisvrouwen. Reference for a preliminary ruling: Raad van Beroep 's-Hertogenbosch – Netherlands. Case C-338/91. *European Court reports* 1993 Page I-05475.

[61]In fact, in para. 15 of the grounds in Steenhorst-Neerings it is stated that '...*the right to claim benefits for incapacity for work under the same conditions as men conferred on married women by the direct effect of Article 4(1) of Directive 79/7 must be exercised under the conditions determined by national law, provided that, as the Court has consistently held, those conditions are no less favourable than those relating to similar domestic actions and that they are not framed so as to render virtually impossible the exercise of rights conferred by Community law.*'

[62]Para. 16 of the grounds in *Steenhorst-Neerings*.

against a defaulting Member State. It merely limits the retroactive effect of claims made for the purpose of obtaining the relevant benefits'.[63]

The same conclusions are reached by the ECJ later in the *Johnson* judgement of 1994[64] on a similar case.[65]

Instead, the ECJ reached rather different conclusions in the *Levez* decision of 1998,[66] concerning the interpretation of Directive 75/117/EEC, on the approximation of the laws of the Member States relating to the application of the principle of equal pay for men and women.

In theory, the problem here was quite similar to that already addressed by the ECJ in its decisions on *Steenhorst-Neerings* and *Johnson*. In fact, insofar as these cases are similar the ECJ merely reaffirms that '... *a national rule under which entitlement to arrears of remuneration is restricted to the two years preceding the date on which the proceedings were instituted is not in itself open to criticism*'.[67] There is, however, a substantial difference between the *Levez* case and the two other decisions mentioned above as '*In the present case, the order for reference states that Mrs Levez was late in bringing her claim because of the inaccurate information provided by her employer in December 1991 regarding the level of remuneration received by men performing like work to her own*'.[68] As a consequence, '... *to allow an employer to rely on a national rule such as the rule at issue would, in the circumstances of the case before the national court, would be manifestly incompatible with the principle of effectiveness*' since '... *the application of the rule at issue is likely, in the circumstances of the present case, to make it virtually impossible or excessively difficult to obtain arrears of remuneration in respect of sex discrimination*'.[69]

This last assertion of the ECJ, which may seem so *tranchant* and restrictive of the procedural autonomy of the Member States, can however be better understood when reading the conclusions of the Advocate General which shows that the national procedural law actually recognizes that the British labour judge has '... *a power of extension when implementing the procedural rules applying to similar domestic actions.*' Consequently – the Advocate General affirms – '... *should it prove possible in fact for the courts, in the context of claims for pay arrears based*

---

[63]Para. 21 of the grounds in *Steenhorst-Neerings*.

[64]Judgement of the ECJ of 6 December 1994. Elsie Rita Johnson v Chief Adjudication Officer. Reference for a preliminary ruling: Court of Appeal (England) – United Kingdom. Case C-410/92. *European Court reports* 1994 Page I-05483.

[65]The ECJ states, in fact, in para. 30 of the grounds in Johnston that '*the national rule which adversely affects Mrs Johnson's action before the Court of Appeal is similar to that at issue in Steenhorst-Neerings. Neither rule constitutes a bar to proceedings; they merely limit the period prior to the bringing of the claim in respect of which arrears of benefit are payable.*'

[66]Judgement of the ECJ of 1 December 1998. B.S. Levez v T.H. Jennings (Harlow Pools) Ltd. Reference for a preliminary ruling: Employment Appeal Tribunal, London – United Kingdom. Case C-326/96. *European Court reports* 1998 Page I-07835.

[67]Para. 20 of the grounds in *Levez*.

[68]Para. 27 of the grounds in *Levez*.

[69]Para. 32 of the grounds in *Levez*.

on provisions of domestic law, particularly employment law, to take account of circumstances such as deceit on the part of the employer in order to relax the legal time-limit, that course of action should also be open in the present case if the principle of equivalence is not to be breached.'[70] That is why, therefore, the decision under examination also fits, without forcing it, into the framework of the two *Rewe* limits to the procedural autonomy of the Member States – and it is mainly the equivalence criterion that comes into play here. Moreover, this is confirmed by the answer given by the ECJ to the second preliminary question submitted in the *Levez* case, related to the influence, in this specific context, of the fact that in the national law there was still an alternative remedy not exhausted by the applicant for the reasons mentioned above.[71]

3.3 The Second Phase of the ECJ's Jurisprudence on the Procedural Autonomy of the Member States: From the Obligation of Consistent Interpretation to Functionalized Procedural Competence

The second phase of the ECJ jurisprudence on procedural autonomy of the Member States starts off with the well-known *van Schijndel* decision of 1995.[72] This second phase is characterized by the fact that the ECJ, taking the obligation of consistent interpretation – upon which the jurisprudence of the first phase is also based – to its extreme consequences, starts to outline the boundaries of a real duty of the national court to 'functionalize' the means made potentially available by the domestic law to pursue the primary goal of ensuring the effectiveness of the EU law. This duty to 'functionalize' the means made available by the national procedural law, in a broad

[70] Opinion of Mr Advocate General Léger delivered on 12 May 1998. B.S. Levez v T.H. Jennings (Harlow Pools) Ltd. Reference for a preliminary ruling: Employment Appeal Tribunal, London – United Kingdom. Case C-326/96. *European Court reports 1998 Page I-07835*, Para. 98.

[71] In fact, in para. 35 of the grounds in Levez it is stated: '*the United Kingdom Government argues that, on the facts, Mrs Levez could, in proceedings before the County Court, successfully have claimed full compensation for the damage suffered on account of the fact that her employer's deceit had prevented her from bringing a claim under the Act. She could have relied in such proceedings both on the Act and on the deceit committed by her employer, and the rule at issue would not have applied.*' To this end, and wholly consistent with the co-jurisdictional model that is the basis of the preliminary ruling mechanism, it concludes that: '*In view of the foregoing, the answer must be that Community law precludes the application of a rule of national law which limits an employee's entitlement to arrears of remuneration or damages for breach of the principle of equal pay to a period of two years prior to the date on which the proceedings were instituted, even when another remedy is available, if the latter is likely to entail procedural rules or other conditions which are less favourable than those applicable to similar domestic actions*' and that '*It is for the national court to determine whether that is the case.*' (Para. 53 of the grounds).

[72] In this sense, see the interesting analysis of S. Prechal, N. Shelkoplyas, *National Procedures, Public Policy and EC-Law. From Van Schijndel to Eco Swiss and Beyond*, p. 589 ff.

sense, to 'sanction' the EU law is therefore – according to the argument proposed here – nothing else but a further extension of the obligation of consistent interpretation.[73] Moreover, such an extension is the consequence of the elevation of the 'standards of effectiveness' of the EU law required from the Member States, put into operation after the Maastricht Treaty of 1992. As it was stated in Declaration No. 19 of the Intergovernmental Conference, adopted in the Maastricht Treaty, '*the Conference, while recognizing that it must be for each Member State to determine how the provisions of Community law can best be enforced in the light of its own particular institutions, legal system and other circumstances, but in any event in compliance with Article 189 of the Treaty establishing the European Community, considers it essential for the proper functioning of the Community that the measures taken by the different Member States should result in Community law being applied with the same effectiveness and rigour as in the application of their national law.*'[74] This greater rigour is confirmed also by the introduction in the text of Art. 171 (now Art. 260, TFEU) of the possibility to impose penalty payments on non-compliant Member States by the ECJ.[75]

3.3.1 The 'Functionalization' of the Concept of 'National Rules of Public Policy'

The *van Schijndel* decision of 1995[76] signals a crucial break point in the jurisprudence of the ECJ on procedural autonomy of the Member States.[77] It represents, in fact, the transitional moment from a jurisprudence that was mainly confined to identify – by reference to the two *Rewe* criteria – the correct lanes between which the procedural autonomy of the Member States should be placed to a jurisprudence that is, instead, more 'proactive,' in the sense that the ECJ, with the indispensable

[73]On this point, see Chap. 2, para. 2.10.

[74]Declaration on the implementation of Community law, adopted in the Maastricht Treaty of 1992, which can be accessed at http://eur-lex.europa.eu/en/treaties/dat/11992M/htm/11992M.html#0102000039. On this point, see S. Magiera, *Die Durchsetzung des Gemeinschaftsrechts im europäischen Integrationsprozeß*, p. 173 ff. (178 s.); O. Dubos, *Les juridictions nationales, juge communautaire*, p. 292 ff.

[75]On this aspect, see S. Magiera, *Die Durchsetzung des Gemeinschaftsrechts im europäischen Integrationsprozeß*, p. 181 and – more recently – A. Tizzano, *Qualche riflessione sul contributo della Corte di Giustizia allo sviluppo del sistema comunitario*, p. 152, that points out how Member States can no longer rely on a "sort of impunity" even in case of crushing infringements of their obligations under EU law.

[76]Judgement of the ECJ of 14 December 1995. Jeroen van Schijndel and Johannes Nicolaas Cornelis van Veen v Stichting Pensioenfonds voor Fysiotherapeuten. References for a preliminary ruling: Hoge Raad – Netherlands. Joined cases C-430/93 and C-431/93. *European Court reports* 1995 Page I-04705.

[77]In this regard, see the comment by S. Prechal, *Community Law in National Courts: The Lessons From Vam Schijndel*, p. 681 ff.

help of the referring court, goes as far as to identify, within individual national legal orders, those means that are best suited to pursue the goal of effectiveness of the EU law, which remains the central concern of the ECJ. Even in this changed context, it is still the national court – within the sphere of distribution of competences that characterizes the system of cooperation between courts of which the preliminary ruling procedure is its maximum expression – that must be the guarantor of the functioning of the '*systéme national de sanction*'[78] aimed at ensuring the effectiveness of EU law. As a consequence, it must observe in practice the rulings contained in the judgements of the ECJ and adapt them to the specific circumstances of the case.[79]

The *van Schijndel* case was about the interpretation due to various provisions of the Treaty and, in particular, the need for the national court to eventually apply *ex officio* these provisions in a pending case before it in order to assess their compatibility with the national norms, even if those provisions have not been invoked by the party having an interest in its application. In this regard, after analyzing the pertinent norms of the Dutch legislation, the ECJ merely states – in relation to the first preliminary question – that '*The competition rules mentioned by the national court are binding rules, directly applicable in the national legal order. Where, by virtue of domestic law, courts or tribunals must raise of their own motion points of law based on binding domestic rules which have not been raised by the parties, such an obligation also exists where binding Community rules are concerned.*'[80] However, in relation to the second preliminary question,[81] it specifies that '*the answer to the second question must be that Community law does not require national courts to raise of their own motion an issue concerning the breach of provisions of Community law where examination of that issue would oblige them to abandon the passive role assigned to them by going beyond the ambit of the dispute defined by the parties themselves and relying on facts and circumstances other than those on which the party with an interest in application of those provisions bases his claim.*'[82] This is, therefore, a solution that respects the national procedural competence, since the obligation to raise legal considerations of its own based on a binding EU norm subsists only if the court, according to its own national

[78]This expression is taken from J. Mertens de Wilmars, *L'efficacité des différentes techniques nationales de protection juridique contre les violations du droit communautaire par les autorités nationales et les particuliers*, p. 392.

[79]On this point, see the interesting observations of V. Cerulli Irelli, *Trasformazioni del sistema di tutela giurisdizionale nelle controversie di diritto pubblico per effetto della giurisprudenza europea*, p. 449 s.

[80]Para. 13 of the grounds in *van Schijndel*.

[81]This is the second preliminary question, in para. 12, 2), of the grounds in *van Schijndel*: '*If Question (1) must in principle be answered in the affirmative, does that answer also apply if in so doing the court would have to abandon the passive role assigned to it since it would be required (a) to go beyond the ambit of the dispute defined by the parties and/or (b) to rely on facts and circumstances other than those on which the party with an interest in application of those provisions relies in order to substantiate his claim?*'

[82]Para. 22 of the grounds in *van Schijndel*.

procedural law, is obliged to proceed in the same way in the case when, in a similar situation of domestic law, a binding national norm that has not been invoked by the interested party comes to its attention. This is, thus, a very direct application of the first *Rewe* criterion regarding the prohibition of discrimination between similar situations of the national law.[83] As a matter of fact, at the end of paragraph 13 of the grounds in *van Schijndel*, the ECJ explicitly refers to paragraph 5 of the grounds in *Rewe* which – as we have seen[84] – precisely addresses this first principle.

Rather than a source of concern, this jurisprudence seems to me worthy of admiration because of its balance[85] and, at the same time, originality in emphasizing the idea of a duty of the national court (in its role of decentralized EU court)[86] to 'functionalize' the means already made available in its domestic law to allow the achievement of the goal of effectiveness of the EU law. However, as the answer to the second preliminary question shows, this does not mean relinquishing the dispositive principle *tout court* by going beyond the ambit of the dispute as defined by the parties.[87] If such a possibility is not envisaged in the national procedural order, even by way of exception, it will be impossible to 'functionalize' – namely, to interpret the national procedural norms in such a way as to make it possible to pursue the purpose intended in the EU norm of substantive law. This is because the 'functionalization,' as is apparent from this decision, is only possible where a device is already available in the national law – as in this case, the obligation for the national court to raise *ex officio* legal considerations based on a national norm which is binding.

This trend was explicitly confirmed by the ECJ shortly later in the *Kraaijeveld* judgement of 1996[88] and also by the decision on the *Eco Swiss* case four years later, in 1999.[89] This decision – despite appearances – is in absolute continuity with the

[83]However, of a different opinion is, for example, J. McKendrick, *Modifying Procedural Autonomy: Better Protection for Community Rights*, p. 582 ff., who criticises this decision as an expression of a '*purposive approach*' that may lead, in his opinion, to a complete unpredictability of the outcomes of the cases before the ECJ. See also R. Caranta, *Impulso di parte e iniziativa del giudice nell'applicazione del diritto comunitario*, c. 1289 ff.

[84]See above Chap. 2, para. 2.5, note 54.

[85]As pointed out by S. Prechal, N. Shelkoplyas, *National Procedures, Public Policy and EC-Law. From Van Schijndel to Eco Swiss and Beyond*, p. 594 ff., "*the Court's interference with the Dutch rules at issue was less dramatic than some might have expected*" (p. 596).

[86]On this point, see A. Tizzano, *La tutela dei privati nei confronti degli Stati membri dell'Unione europea*, c. 17.

[87]This conclusion is also reached by O. Dubos, *Les juridictions nationales, juge communautaire*, p. 331.

[88]Judgement of the ECJ of 24 October 1996. Aannemersbedrijf P.K. Kraaijeveld BV e.a. v Gedeputeerde Staten van Zuid-Holland. Reference for a preliminary ruling: Raad van State – Netherlands. Case C-72/95. *European Court reports* 1996 Page I-05403.

[89]Judgement of the ECJ of 1 June 1999. Eco Swiss China Time Ltd v Benetton International NV. Reference for a preliminary ruling: Hoge Raad – Netherlands. Case C-126/97. *European Court reports* 1999 Page I-03055.

van Schijndel jurisprudence. The issue at stake in this case was to evaluate whether a national court that must decide on the possible annulment of an arbitration award should grant the application if it considers that the decision of the arbitration award is contrary to Art. 105 TFEU (*ex* Art. 85 TEC), '*... although, under domestic procedural rules, it may grant such an application only on a limited number of grounds, one of them being inconsistency with public policy, which, according to the applicable national law, is not generally to be invoked on the sole ground that, because of the terms or the enforcement of an arbitration award, effect will not be given to a prohibition laid down by domestic competition law.*'[90] The response of the ECJ – which clearly follows the trend of the 'functionalization' of the norms of national law that are, according to the arguments of the referring court, potentially instrumental to achieving the effectiveness of the EU substantive law – is focused here on the idea of 'national rules of public policy.'[91] In fact, in the following paragraphs of the decision, it is stated that '*... Article 85 of the Treaty constitutes a fundamental provision which is essential for the accomplishment of the tasks entrusted to the Community and, in particular, for the functioning of the internal market. The importance of such a provision led the framers of the Treaty to provide expressly, in Article 85(2) of the Treaty, that any agreements or decisions prohibited pursuant to that Article are to be automatically void.*

It follows that where its domestic rules of procedure require a national court to grant an application for annulment of an arbitration award where such an application is founded on failure to observe national rules of public policy, it must also grant such an application where it is founded on failure to comply with the prohibition laid down in Article 85(1) of the Treaty.'[92] This is because the relevance, in terms of the national rules of public policy, of the norms on competition law should be inferred from the general framework of the EU law and not, conversely, from the national law.

It follows that, again, there is no request to introduce *ex novo* procedural solutions (in the broad sense) that are entirely new, but only a request directed to the national court – in accordance with the duty of sincere cooperation (*coopération loyale*) laid down in Art. 4, paragraph 3, TEU (*ex* Art. 10, TEC) – [93] to assess all the

[90]Para. 31 of the grounds in *Eco Swiss*.

[91]It must be stressed that the expression used by the ECJ in its working language, French, is '*règles nationales d'ordre public,*' that corresponds to the Dutch expression (Dutch is here the language of the proceeding) '*nationale regels van openbare orde*'. The expression "*national rules of public policy*" used in the English version has, in this sense, a partially different meaning. On this concept and its critics, and for an in-depth analysis see, moreover, S. Prechal, N. Shelkoplyas, *National Procedures, Public Policy and EC-Law. From Van Schijndel to Eco Swiss and Beyond*, p. 600 ff.; A.P. Komninos, *Case C-126/97, Eco Swiss*, p. 459 ff., 471 ff.

[92]Para.s 36 and 37 of the grounds in *Eco Swiss*.

[93]See Chap. 2, para. 2.10.

possible courses of action available in the national law. The national court, then, should 'functionalize' when needed the legal tools made available by the national law for the resolution of cases that show, from a EU law perspective, similarities with the basic problem that gave rise to the preliminary reference.[94]

Neither does the ECJ require a 'functionalization' that goes beyond reasonable limits, as demonstrated by the recent decision in *van der Weerd*, of 2007.[95] Here the referring court submitted a number of preliminary questions on the interpretation of Directive 85/511/EEC and the possible need to raise *ex officio* issues related to its violation that were not raised by the parties of the dispute. However, with great sense of balance, the ECJ stresses that, although the Dutch court has jurisdiction under its national law to raise *ex officio* issues related to the violation of national rules of public policy, as regards the principle of equivalence '*...The provisions of Directive 85/511 which are at issue do not occupy a similar position within the Community legal order.*'[96] Therefore, this case is not comparable to the previous one, where the norms of competition law of the Treaty were under consideration and, hence, norms of such importance from a EU law perspective that could be regarded as equal to national rules of public policy.[97]

In conclusion, thus, at least with regard to this first *tranche* of cases, this practice of the ECJ does not seem to me to justify criticism. The 'functionalization' of procedural norms (in the broad sense), on the one hand, is a creative and necessary solution in order to confine the procedural competence of the Member States within the limits identified by the two *Rewe* criteria and ensure with it, despite the lack of EU procedural norms, the effectiveness of the EU substantive law. On the other hand, as we have seen, so far it has not crossed the boundaries of a 'reasonable functionalization.'

---

[94]On this point, see however the observations of S. Prechal, N. Shelkoplyas, *National Procedures, Public Policy and EC-Law. From Van Schijndel to Eco Swiss and Beyond*, p. 598 s.

[95]Judgement of the ECJ (Fourth Chamber) of 7 June 2007. J. van der Weerd and Others (C-222/05), H. de Rooy sr. and H. de Rooy jr. (C-223/05), Maatschap H. en J. van 't Oever and Others (C-224/05) and B.J. van Middendorp (C-225/05) v Minister van Landbouw, Natuur en Voedselkwaliteit. Reference for a preliminary ruling: College van Beroep voor het bedrijfsleven – Netherlands. Joined cases C-222/05 to C-225/05. *European Court reports* 2007 Page I-04233.

[96]Since, it continues, '*They govern neither the conditions in which procedures relating to the control of foot-and-mouth disease may be initiated nor the authorities which have the power, within their area of responsibility, to determine the extent of the rights and obligations of individuals.*' Para. 29–30 of the grounds in *van der Weerd.*

[97]See C. Rodríguez Iglesias, *Sui limiti all'autonomia procedimentale e processuale degli Stati membri nell'applicazione del diritto comunitari*, p. 19. On the need for a clarification by the ECJ in relation to the nature of the national rules of public policy, see S. Prechal, *Community Law in National Courts: The Lessons From Vam Schijndel*, p. 702 ff. (704).

3.3.2 *The 'Functionalization' of the Norms Concerning the 'Revocation' of Illegitimate Administrative Acts*

We have to verify now if what was said at the end of the preceding paragraph, also applies to those decisions, all of them very recent, which outline the boundaries of a 'EU functionalization' of the internal norms that bestow the administration with power to 'revoke' illegitimate administrative acts.[98]

The question lies outside the very specific context of procedural law but – according to what has been repeatedly stated – also concerns the broader topic of the '*pouvoir de sanction*' of the national law with regard to compliance with the EU norms and, therefore, the topic of the procedural autonomy of the Member States.

Before moving on to the analysis of the judgements of the ECJ relevant to this specific context, though, a terminological clarification is needed. This is related to the fact – already noted elsewhere by the author[99] – that there is a lack of linguistic equivalence between the terminology used by the ECJ and the corresponding conceptual categories in the national legislation to which the ECJ itself refers. The ECJ, in fact, almost always uses the term 'revocation' in relation to both genuine revocation and to what, in the Italian legislation (as well as the French and German ones), would be classified as "annulment *ex officio*". On this basis – and even if the decisions that follow, as we shall see, concern the exercise of the power to *ex officio* annulment in the strict sense, from now on in this book the term 'revocation' will always be used in order to remain faithful to the language used by the ECJ in most of the decisions under examination.

The decision in the *Alcan* case of 1997[100] originated from a reference for a preliminary ruling of the German Federal Administrative Court which, in essence, requested the ECJ if and to what extent it is necessary to 'functionalize' the national revocation proceeding – as regulated in § 48 VwVfG[101] – in order to recover an aid that was declared incompatible with the EU law by a decision of the Commission. From the point of view of the national law the issue was related to the need to

---

[98]On this jurisprudence, see in particular, D. Ritleng, *Le retrait des actes administratifs contraires au droit communautaire*, p. 237 ff.

[99]Specifically, see D.U. Galetta, *Autotutela decisoria e diritto comunitario*, p. 41 ff., for a detailed analysis on this specific matter and for the literature quoted there.

[100]Judgement of the ECJ of 20 March 1997. Land Rheinland-Pfalz v Alcan Deutschland GmbH. Reference for a preliminary ruling: Bundesverwaltungsgericht – Germany. Case C-24/95. *European Court reports* 1997 Page I-01591.

[101]The first question, in para. 20 of the grounds in *Alcan*, is in fact the following: '*Is the competent authority obliged, by reason of the requirement to apply national law in such a way that "the recovery required by Community law is not rendered practically impossible and the interests of the Community are taken fully into consideration", to revoke, in accordance with a final, binding decision of the EC Commission ordering recovery, the aid decision in question even if the authority has allowed the preclusive time-limit which exists for that purpose under national law in the interest of legal certainty to elapse?*'. On this point, see in particular the observations by J. Schwarze, *Europäische Rahmenbedingungen für die Verwaltungsgerichtsbarkeit*, p. 251 s.

protect what, according to § 48 VwVfG as interpreted by the German administrative courts, constituted a legitimate expectation of the recipient of the aid. In fact, in the interpretation of the German administrative courts, to the extent that the unlawfulness of the aid was attributable to the competent authority, its revocation was contrary to the principle of good faith in relation to the recipient of the aid. And it is precisely on this point that the ECJ intervened by requiring the national court to interpret the norm of the national law on 'revocation' in accordance with the main exigency of effectiveness of the EU law. The ECJ's conclusion is in fact that '*Community law requires the competent authority to revoke a decision granting unlawful aid, in accordance with a final decision of the Commission declaring the aid incompatible with the common market and ordering recovery, even where such recovery is excluded by national law because the gain no longer exists, in the absence of bad faith on the part of the recipient of the aid.*'[102] But beyond the 'strong' ruling, the premise on which this is based is the decisive element. In fact, the ECJ indicates that '*the recipient of the aid cannot claim that it had a legitimate expectation that the aid was lawful. The recipient's obligation to ensure that the procedure set out in Article 93(3) of the Treaty has been complied with cannot, in fact, depend on the conduct of the State authorities.*'[103]

There is, therefore, no correspondence between the situation of the recipient of the aid and the situation in which, according to the EU law, there is a legitimate expectation.

So, to sum up, as a result of the obligation of consistent interpretation, on the one hand, and of the application of the second *Rewe* criterion,[104] on the other, it is necessary to re-read the concept of legitimate expectation in a way that is compatible with the EU law. This must be done by 'functionalizing' the 'revocation' proceeding under § 48 VwVfG since '*In circumstances such as those in the main proceedings, failure to revoke the decision granting aid would seriously and adversely affect the Community interest and render practically impossible the recovery required by Community law.*'[105]

On lines similar to the *Alcan* jurisprudence, seven years later we find the *Delena Wells* decision of 2004,[106] which is about the requirement to functionalize – in

[102]Para. 54 of the grounds in *Alcan*.

[103]Para. 41 of the grounds in *Alcan*.

[104]On which basis, it is recalled, the national procedural norms should not make it '*impossible in practice to exercise the rights which the national courts are obliged to protect.*'

[105]Para. 42 of the grounds in *Alcan*. In this sense, the bitter critique by R. Scholz does not seem to me justified at all in *Zum Verhältnis vom europäischen Gemeinschaftsrecht und nationalem Verwaltungsverfahrensrecht. Zur Rechtsprechung des EuGH im Fall, "Alcan"*, p. 261 ff., when he speaks of an 'overflow of competences' by the ECJ and calls for a decision on this matter by the German Federal Constitutional Court.

[106]Judgement of the ECJ (Fifth Chamber) of 7 January 2004. The Queen, on the application of Delena Wells v Secretary of State for Transport, Local Government and the Regions. Reference for a preliminary ruling: High Court of Justice (England & Wales), Queen's Bench Division (Administrative Court) – United Kingdom. Case C-201/02. *European Court reports* 2004 Page I-00723.

terms of the 'functionalized' procedural competence of the Member States – the tools made available by national law in order to ensure the effectiveness of EU law. Here, among the many preliminary questions posed, the English referring judge essentially asked the ECJ to provide guidelines about the way in which the national public administrations should make use of the special revoking powers, provided for them by their national legal order, in order to eliminate national administrative acts that were contrary to EU law. In this regard, the ECJ after reminding that '... *under the principle of cooperation in good faith laid down in Article 10 EC the Member States are required to nullify the unlawful consequences of a breach of Community law*' and that '*Such an obligation is owed, within the sphere of its competence, by every organ of the Member State concerned,*' explains that '... *it is for the competent authorities of a Member State to take, within the sphere of their competence, all the* [*necessary*] *general or particular measures*' and that '*Such particular measures include, subject to the limits laid down by the principle of procedural autonomy of the Member States, the revocation or suspension of a consent already granted.*'[107]

The reasoning outlined in the *Delena Wells* ruling is drawn on and deepened by the ECJ in its January 2004 decision of *Kühne & Heitz*.[108] The request of the Dutch court was specifically about the implications arising from the principle of cooperation under Art. 10, TEC (now Art. 4.3 TEU), and sought to clarify if '*Under Community law ... in the circumstances described in the grounds of this decision, an administrative body* [*is*] *required to reopen a decision which has become final in order to ensure the full operation of Community law.*'[109] In this sense, the question aimed at clarifying how far it was possible to push the duty to 'functionalize' the power to 'revoke' recognized in the Dutch national law.

In this regard, the ECJ affirmed that legal certainty is included among the general principles recognized by the EU law and that this principle entails, as a rule, that there is no obligation to review an administrative decision which has become final.[110] However, it then states that if it is necessary – as in the present case – to take into account the interpretation of a EU provision given in the meantime by the ECJ, the principle of cooperation under Art. 10, TEC, must be interpreted in such a way that it requires an administrative body, to which such a request is directed, to review its final administrative decision (in order to take into account the interpretation of the relevant provision given in the meantime by the ECJ) if these four conditions are present:

---

[107]Para.s 64 and 65 of the grounds in *Delena Wells*.

[108]Judgement of the ECJ of 13 January 2004. Kühne & Heitz NV v Produktschap voor Pluimvee en Eieren. Reference for a preliminary ruling: College van Beroep voor het bedrijfsleven – Netherlands. Case C-453/00. *European Court reports* 2004 Page I-00837.

[109]Para. 19 of the grounds in *Kühne & Heitz*.

[110]Para. 24 of the grounds in *Kühne & Heitz*.

a. It has the power, under national law, to reopen that decision;
b. The decision in question has become final as a result of a judgement of a national court ruling at final instance;
c. The judgement is, in the light of a decision given by the ECJ subsequent to it, based on a misinterpretation of EU law which was adopted without a question being referred to the ECJ for a preliminary ruling;
d. The person concerned complained to the administrative body immediately after becoming aware of that decision of the ECJ.[111]

The practical implications of this jurisprudence for the national administrative law have been already mentioned elsewhere.[112] What is important here is to reiterate, in particular, only the first condition identified by the ECJ. In our reasoning, this means that it is not necessary to impose new "legal tools" unknown to the national law, but rather to simply require the use of those that already exist and potentially expand their scope to encompass situations that are relevant for the EU where the problem of ensuring the effectiveness of the EU law is at stake. Therefore, it is only a functionalization of the "legal tools" available in the national law and not the imposition of new ones,[113] which is absolutely in line with the two *Rewe* criteria and the obligation of consistent interpretation of the EU law in a broader sense.

Therefore, there is no contradiction between the jurisprudence of *Delena Wells* and *Kühne & Heitz*, and the subsequent decision of the ECJ in *i-21-Arcor* of 2006,[114] on the interpretation of certain provisions of Directive 97/13/EC on a common framework for general authorizations and individual licences in the field of telecommunications services.

In this case, the applicants sought the repayment of amounts wrongly collected by the German financial authority since they were based on an unlawful fee assessment under the above mentioned Directive. However, according to German procedural law, the time-limits to contest the already mentioned fee assessment had expired. So the only possible alternative was their revocation by the national administration, under and for the purposes of § 48 VwVfG. The preliminary question – as redefined by the ECJ – was therefore about '*... the relationship between Article 11(1) of Directive 97/13 and Paragraph 48 of the Law on Administrative Procedure, as interpreted by the Bundesverwaltungsgericht*'.[115]

[111]Para. 28 of the grounds in *Kühne & Heitz*.

[112]See D.U. Galetta, *Autotutela decisoria e diritto comunitario*, p. 39 ff.

[113]I do not share the observations of A. Arnull, *Case C-432/05, Unibet*, p. 1773 ff. (even if they are about a judgement partly different from that being considered here) and his opinion about the alleged trends followed by the ECJ on issues of 'procedural autonomy.' Of the same opinion as the author, see moreover E. Picozza, *Diritto amministrativo e diritto comunitario*, p. 309.

[114]Judgement of the ECJ (Grand Chamber) of 19 September 2006. i-21 Germany GmbH (C-392/04) and Arcor AG & Co. KG (C-422/04) v Bundesrepublik Deutschland. Reference for a preliminary ruling: Bundesverwaltungsgericht – Germany. Joined cases C-392/04 and C-422/04. *European Court reports* 2006 Page I-08559.

[115]Para. 50 of the grounds in *i-21*.

In this regard, the ECJ refers primarily to the *Kühne & Heitz* jurisprudence noting that '*In accordance with the principle of legal certainty, Community law does not require that administrative bodies be placed under an obligation, in principle, to reopen an administrative decision which has become final upon expiry of the reasonable time-limits for legal remedies or by exhaustion of those remedies*'[116] but that however '*there could be a limit to this principle in certain cases.*'[117] Accordingly, the ECJ focuses on the particularities of the case under examination. And, after highlighting the differences between the case in question and the *Kühne & Heitz* one[118] – and recalling the two *Rewe* criteria as a limit to the procedural autonomy of the Member States,[119] the ECJ identifies the criterion which the referring judge should consider in order to resolve the dispute. In this regard, it states that, '... *if the national rules applicable to appeals impose an obligation to withdraw an administrative act that is unlawful under domestic law, even though that act has become final, where to uphold that act would be "downright intolerable",*[120] *the same obligation to withdraw must exist under equivalent conditions in the case of an administrative act which does not comply with Community law,*'[121] since '*Where, pursuant to rules of national law, the authorities are required to withdraw an administrative decision which has become final if that decision is manifestly incompatible with domestic law, that same obligation must exist if the decision is manifestly incompatible with Community law.*'[122]

This is essentially an application of the first *Rewe* criterion (equivalence principle),[123] re-read in the light of the obligation to functionalize the procedural tools offered by the national law to ensure the effectiveness of the EU law.[124] This is a duty of functionalization that however, once again, does not go too far, because

[116]Para. 51 of the grounds in *i-21*.

[117]Para. 52 of the grounds in *i-21*.

[118]Particularly, the ECJ notes that '*The case giving rise to the judgement in Kühne & Heitz, however, was entirely different from those at issue in the main proceedings. Whilst the undertaking Kühne & Heitz NV had exhausted all legal remedies available to it, i-21 and Arcor did not avail themselves of their right to appeal against the fee assessments issued to them.*' (Para. 53 of the grounds in *i-21*).

[119]Para. 57 of the grounds in *i-21*.

[120]In this regard, in para. 8 of the grounds in *i-21*, it is stated as an explanation that '*...according to German case-law, the administrative authority has discretion in principle, pursuant to Para. 48 of the Law on Administrative Procedure, to withdraw an unlawful administrative act which has become final. That discretion may, however, be extinguished if to uphold the act in question would be "downright intolerable" in respect of public policy, good faith, fairness, equal treatment or manifest unlawfulness.*' The act of withdrawal would then be in this case dutiful.

[121]Para. 63 of the grounds in *i-21*.

[122]Para. 69 of the grounds in *i-21*.

[123]As pointed out also by M.P. Chiti, *L'effettività della tutela giurisdizionale tra riforme nazionali e influenza del diritto comunitario*, p. 491.

[124]On this point, see the reflections by B. Marchetti, *Sul potere di annullamento d'ufficio, la Corte ribadisce l'autonomia procedurale degli Stati membri, ma si sbilancia un po'*, p. 1139 ff. This point, however, is not picked up at all by M. Ludwigs, *Die Arcor-Entscheidung des EuGH: Ein Beitrag zur Stärkung der mitgliedstaatlichen Verfahrensautonomie*, p. 549 ff.

ultimately it is for '... *the national court to ascertain whether legislation which is clearly incompatible with Community law, such as that on which the fee assessments at issue in the main proceedings are based, constitutes manifest unlawfulness within the meaning of the national law concerned. If that is the case, it is for the national court to draw the necessary conclusions under its national law with regard to the withdrawal of those assessments.*'[125]

Finally, the recent decision in the *Kempter* case of February 2008 lies within the same context.[126] Here the German referring judge first asked the ECJ if the 'revocation' of an administrative decision that has become final by virtue of a judgement of a court of final instance was necessary only if the claimant had invoked the EU law within the judicial proceeding of domestic law which he had initiated against that decision. In response to this first question, after stating that '... *a preliminary ruling is based on a dialogue between one court and another, the initiation of which depends entirely on the national court's assessment as to whether a reference is appropriate and necessary,*'[127] and referring to its previous jurisprudence on this matter, the ECJ merely reaffirms that '*It is to be noted that, while Community law does not require national courts to raise of their own motion a plea alleging infringement of Community provisions where examination of that plea would oblige them to go beyond the ambit of the dispute as defined by the parties, they are obliged to raise of their own motion points of law based on binding Community rules where, under national law, they must or may do so in relation to a binding rule of national law.*'[128] In this sense, the *Kempter* jurisprudence is in line with the jurisprudence already analyzed in the previous paragraph.[129]

Instead, with regard to the second preliminary question posed, the referring judge sought to understand how far the 'functionalization' of the national 'revocation' proceeding should be pushed, specifically in relation to the possibility of subjecting such 'revocation' to certain time-limits. To better understand this part of the decision it is necessary, however, to refer to the original version of the *Kempter* decision, because its incorrect translation into English (and Italian) could lead to a misinterpretation of the meaning of the question posed. The preliminary question is not actually '*whether Community law imposes a limit in time for making an application for review of an administrative decision that has become final*' but, instead, if it is possible to identify within the EU law the existence of a time limit regarding the revocation application.[130] This allows us to fully understand the

[125]Para. 72 of the grounds in *i-21*.

[126]Judgement of the ECJ (Grand Chamber) of 12 February 2008. Willy Kempter KG v Hauptzollamt Hamburg-Jonas. Reference for a preliminary ruling: Finanzgericht Hamburg – Germany. Case C-2/06. *European Court reports* 2008 Page I-00411.

[127]Para. 42 of the grounds in *Kempter*.

[128]Para. 45 of the grounds in *Kempter*. On this, see the observations of E. Cannizzaro, *Sui rapporti fra sistemi processuali nazionali e diritto dell'Unione europea*, p. 460 ff.

[129]Para. 3.3.1.

[130]"*Mit seiner zweiten Frage möchte das vorlegende Gericht im Wesentlichen wissen, ob das Gemeinschaftsrecht die Möglichkeit, einen Antrag auf Überprüfung einer bestandskräftigen*

consistency of the response of the ECJ with the previous rulings examined here. In fact, it merely points out that although the EU law does not *provide*[131] for any time limit for submitting an application to review an administrative decision that has become final, however – in the context of their procedural competence – '*The Member States... remain free to set reasonable time-limits for seeking remedies, in a manner consistent with the Community principles of effectiveness and equivalence.*'[132] There is, therefore, once again, a procedural competence of the Member States, although 'functionalized' within the limits imposed by the two *Rewe* criteria and the obligation of consistent interpretation.

3.4 The Most Recent Decisions by the ECJ on *Res Judicata* Reinterpreted in the Light of the Jurisprudential Trend Identified So Far

As a conclusion to this analysis of the core decisions of the ECJ on the procedural autonomy of the Member States it is worthwhile examining, in particular, those recent decisions of the ECJ which deal with the issue of *res judicata* and have attracted so much debate in doctrine. The specific goal of this analysis is to verify whether the interpretation trends described above are confirmed or denied by this recent jurisprudence.

Chronologically, the first decision on this point[133] is the *Köbler* judgement of 2005.[134] While focused specifically on the issue of Member States' liability for the

Verwaltungsentscheidung zu stellen, in zeitlicher Hinsicht beschränkt". Para. 47 of the grounds in *Kempter* in the version of the language of the proceedings. In this regard, it is worth noting that in relation to the EU judgements the authentic text is that of the language of the proceedings. For a detailed analysis on this point, see D.U. Galetta and Jacques Ziller, *Il regime linguistico della Comunità*, in M.P. Chiti and G. Greco (eds.), *Trattato di diritto amministrativo europeo* (coord. by G.F. Cartei and D.U. Galetta), Giuffrè, Milan, 2nd. Ed., 2007, General Part, Vol. II, p. 1067 ff.

131 Also here the English translation is not accurate as the expression used by the ECJ is "... *die Möglichkeit, einen Antrag auf Überprüfung einer bestandskräftigen Verwaltungsentscheidung zu stellen, durch das Gemeinschaftsrecht in zeitlicher Hinsicht nicht beschränkt wird*" (Para. 56 of the grounds in *Kempter*). The misleading expression in the English version '*Community law does not impose any specific time-limit*' does not appear anywhere (highlighting added).

132 Para. 60 of the grounds in *Kempter*.

133 Moreover, as it as been underlined, the decision in *Köbler* should be read in connection with the *Eco Swiss* judgement of 1999. See on this point C. Consolo, *La sentenza Lucchini della Corte di giustizia: quale possibile adattamento degli ordinamenti processuali interni e in specie del nostro?*, p. 226 s.

134 Judgement of the ECJ of 30 September 2003. Gerhard Köbler v Republik Österreich. Reference for a preliminary ruling: Landesgericht für Zivilrechtssachen Wien – Austria. Case C-224/01. *European Court reports* 2003 Page I-10239.

violation of EU law,[135] it contains a reflection on the value of the *res judicata* worth recalling. In fact, the ECJ notes that '... *although considerations to do with observance of the principle of res judicata or the independence of the judiciary have caused national legal systems to impose restrictions, which may sometimes be stringent, on the possibility of rendering the State liable for damage caused by mistaken judicial decisions, such considerations have not been such as absolutely to exclude that possibility.*'[136]

This logical step in the Court's reasoning – which is better illustrated in the conclusions of the Advocate General – [137] shows that this reasoning is again based on an application of the two *Rewe* criteria (equivalence and effectiveness) linked to the obligation of consistent interpretation. It also shows that the combination of these three elements may lead to the 'functionalization' of those national procedural norms that, by providing for exceptions to the general rule (in this context, the principle of *res judicata*), makes it impossible for the Member States to rely on the rule in question, as absolute and binding, within the meaning and the effects of the principle of sincere cooperation under Art. 4.3 TEU (*ex* Art. 10, TEC). Hence, it is not possible to honestly 'yell' at the breakdown of coherence of the national procedural order.[138]

Nor is there any contradiction – from my point of view – between the reasoning of the *Köbler* jurisprudence and the later decision in the *Kapferer* case of 2006.[139] In this latter case too, the preliminary question was, among other things, about the value to be attributed to the *res judicata*.

The preliminary reference in *Kapferer* revolved round the already analysed *Kühne & Heitz* judgement of 2004.[140] With this judgement the ECJ had concluded that, in consideration of the specific circumstances of the case and under specific conditions – first of all under the condition that the administrative body under national law had the power to reopen a decision which had become final – the principle of *res judicata* was not an obstacle to the possibility for the national administrative body to reopen a final decision and review it in order to take account

[135]This topic is certainly related to the one considered here, but it will not be addressed in detail. In this regard, the reflections by S. Amadeo, *Norme comunitarie, posizioni giuridiche soggettive e giudizi interni*, p. 263 ff., are interesting and its reading is helpful for understanding why the issue of liability, though largely relevant, can be left out in the specific context of the present analysis. For a detailed analysis of the issue see, among others, M.P. Chiti, *Diritto amministrativo europeo*, p. 129 ff., 634 ff.

[136]Para. 48 of the grounds in *Köbler*.

[137]Opinion of Mr Advocate General Léger delivered on 8 April 2003. Gerhard Köbler v Republik Österreich. Reference for a preliminary ruling: Landesgericht für Zivilrechtssachen Wien – Austria. Case C-224/01. *European Court reports* 2003 Page I-10239, particularly, para.s 95 ff.

[138]The *Paradise Lost* – as my provocative title suggests – that, evidently, has never existed as such.

[139]Judgement of the ECJ (First Chamber) of 16 March 2006. Rosmarie Kapferer v Schlank & Schick GmbH. Reference for a preliminary ruling: Landesgericht Innsbruck – Austria. Case C-234/04. *European Court reports* 2006 Page I-02585.

[140]Judgement of the ECJ of 13 January 2004. See in previous para. 3.3.2.

of the interpretation of the relevant provision of EU law given in the meantime by the ECJ.

This is why in the *Kapferer* judgement the Austrian Landesgericht of Innsbruck referred the following question to the ECJ for a preliminary ruling: '*...Is the principle of cooperation enshrined in Article 10 EC to be interpreted as meaning that, in the circumstances stated in the judgement of the Court of Justice in Case C-453/00 Kühne & Heitz, a national court is also obliged to review and set aside a final judicial decision if the latter should infringe Community law? Are there any other conditions applicable to the review and setting aside of judicial decisions in contrast to administrative decisions?*'.[141] And it therefore offered the ECJ a good opportunity to clarify that, in answering this question, the key reasoning is based on the obligation of consistent interpretation in connection with the equivalence and the effectiveness criterion.

Let's see how this reasoning is developed here by the ECJ.

After recalling the paragraph of *Köbler* where the importance of the principle of *res judicata* is reaffirmed,[142] the ECJ concludes that '*Having regard to the foregoing considerations, the answer to Question 1(a) must be that the principle of cooperation under Article 10 EC does not require a national court to set aside its internal rules of procedure in order to review and set aside a final judicial decision if that decision should be contrary to Community law.*'[143] However, precisely '*the foregoing considerations*' are of relevance in the present case since – as pointed out by the Court earlier – if '*By laying down the procedural rules for proceedings designed to ensure protection of the rights which individuals acquire through the direct effect of Community law, Member States must ensure that such rules are not less favourable than those governing similar domestic actions (principle of equivalence) and are not framed in such a way as to render impossible in practice the exercise of rights conferred by Community law (principle of effectiveness)*' with regard to the case under examination '*However, compliance with the limits of the power of the Member States in procedural matters has not been called into question in the dispute in the main proceedings as regards appeal proceedings*'[144]. In as far "*it is apparent from the reference for a preliminary ruling that that condition*" – namely the first

[141]Para. 18 of the grounds in *Kapferer*.

[142]I refer here to para. 38 in *Köbler*, where while making reference to the previous jurisprudence in *Eco Swiss* (quoted above), the Court observes that '*In that regard the importance of the principle of res judicata cannot be disputed... In order to ensure both stability of the law and legal relations and the sound administration of justice, it is important that judicial decisions which have become definitive after all rights of appeal have been exhausted or after expiry of the time-limits provided for in that connection can no longer be called in question.*'

[143]Para. 24 of the grounds in *Kapferer*.

[144]Para. 22 of the grounds in *Kapferer*.

condition of the *Kühne & Heitz* judgement, according to which that body should be empowered under national law to reopen that decision[145] – "*has not been satisfied*".[146] This is why in this specific case the obligation of consistent interpretation cannot be used – together with the equivalence and the effectiveness criterion – in order to functionalize the national procedural law.

This line of reasoning is a fundamental premise in order to analyze the *Lucchini* decision of 2004[147] with the right approach.[148]

First of all, it is necessary to note that the decision under examination is framed in the specific context of the EU jurisprudence on recovery of unlawful State aids.[149] As for the peculiarities of the case, the preliminary reference of the Council of State (*Consiglio di Stato*) arose from the contradiction identified between the decision of the Administrative Tribunal (*Tribunale amministrativo regionale – TAR*), which was appealed before it, and the Commission's Decision 90/555/EEC. Lucchini SPA had appealed before the *Tribunale amministrativo* of the Lazio Region (TAR Lazio) against the decree by which it was requested by the national administration to return an aid which was contrary to EU law and, in particular, with a decision of the Commission never challenged by the applicant. The *TAR* of Lazio granted Lucchini's appeal and concluded that the public authorities' powers to revoke their own invalid acts on the ground that they are unlawful or contain substantive errors were limited in the present case by the right to the payment of aid established by the Rome Court of Appeal (*Corte d'appello di Roma*) in a final judgement.

It is worth anticipating that – in the author's opinion – the ECJ, in its decision in *Lucchini*, did not deviate at all from its interpretative trends: it simply took them to their extreme consequences,[150] given the particular gravity of the situation created in this case[151] and the fact that we were dealing not only with a severe and open

---

[145]The decision the ECJ is referring to, is the decision over competence by the "Bezirksgericht". And according to national law the national judge has no power to reopen that decision. See point 13 of the grounds in *Kapferer*.

[146]Para. 23 of the grounds in *Kapferer*.

[147]Judgement of the ECJ (Grand Chamber) of 18 July 2007. Ministero dell'Industria, del Commercio e dell'Artigianato v Lucchini SpA. Reference for a preliminary ruling: Consiglio di Stato – Italy. Case C-119/05. *European Court reports* 2007 Page I-06199.

[148]In this sense, see the observations by M.P. Chiti, *Diritto amministrativo europeo*, p. 574.

[149]As pointed out by C. Kremer, *Effektuierung des europäischen Beihilferechts durch die Begrenzung der Rechtskraft*, p. 726 ff. (729), who also identifies an element of continuity between *Lucchini* and the decisions of the ECJ related to the functionalization of the provision in § 48 *VwVfG* (this element clearly emerges in the analysis of the jurisprudence outlined here by the author). In this sense, see also D. Ritleng, *Le retrait des actes administratifs contraires au droit communautaire*, p. 247 s.

[150]For the confirmation of the fact that such a result, in a case like this, could be inferred at least from *Kühne & Heitz*, see the inspiring reflections by G. Morbidelli, *Corte Costitituzionale e Corti europee: la tutela dei diritti (dal punto di vista della Corte del Lussemburgo)*, p. 285 ff.

[151]This is rightly pointed out, among others, by the observations submitted by the Dutch government, which are summarized in the conclusions of the Advocate General, in para.s 25 and 26

infringement of EU law but also – as has been underlined by the most influent doctrine – with a "mindful disregard".[152]

In fact, when responding to the question posed by the *Consiglio di Stato*, essentially, on how to resolve the conflict between the exigency to implement a decision of the Commission that was never challenged and the need to respect the principle of *res judicata*, the ECJ focuses, first of all, on the specific issue of the national norm on *res judicata*.[153] In so doing, it rightly points out that there was actually a problem of interpreting the scope of this norm by the national court.[154] The obligation of consistent interpretation comes into play in the ECJ's argument here, according to which '*... it is for the national courts to interpret, as far as it is possible, the provisions of national law in such a way that they can be applied in a manner which contributes to the implementation of Community law.*'[155] In addition to this obligation of consistent interpretation – the Court continues – the national court has '*a duty to give full effect*' to the provisions of the EU law. This should be linked to the fact that '*... the assessment of the compatibility of aid measures or of an aid scheme with the common market falls within the exclusive competence of the Commission*' (and that, as a result, the final decision by the national civil court challenged here was built upon a subject over which there is no national competence[156]). In the present case, the consequence of this can only be that '*Community law precludes the application of a provision of national law, such as Article 2909 of the Italian Civil Code, which seeks to lay down the principle of res judicata in so far as the application of that provision prevents the recovery of State aid granted in*

(Opinion of Mr Advocate General Geelhoed delivered on 14 September 2006. Ministero dell'Industria, del Commercio e dell'Artigianato v Lucchini SpA. Reference for a preliminary ruling: Consiglio di Stato – Italy. Case C-119/05. *European Court reports* 2007 Page I-06199). On this point, see also the observations of M.P. Chiti, *Le peculiarità dell'invalidità amministrativa per anticomunitarietà*, p. 484, 492 ff.

[152]An infringement of EU law, which was "*sicuramente consapevole*". G. Tesauro, *Diritto* comunitario, p. 209. Author's translation. This opinion is shared, for example, by A. Biondi, *Case C-119/05, Lucchini*, p. 1467, who uses in this regard the expression "*blatant disregard*".

[153]On this point, see for all the sharp observations of G. Mari, *La forza di giudicato delle decisioni dei giudici nazionali di ultima istanza nella giurisprudenza comunitaria*, p. 1051 ff., and the literature and jurisprudence quoted there on the intangibility of *res judicata*.

[154]In fact, in para. 59 of the grounds in *Lucchini* it is stated that '*According to the national court, Article 2909 of the Italian Civil Code precludes not only the reopening, in a second set of proceedings, of pleas in law which have already been expressly and definitively determined but also precludes the examination of matters which could have been raised in earlier proceedings but were not. One of the consequences of such an interpretation of that provision may be that effects are attributed to a decision of a national court which exceed the limits of the jurisdiction of the court in question as laid down in Community law. It is clear, as the Consiglio di Stato has observed, that the effect of applying that provision, interpreted in such a manner, in the present case would be to frustrate the application of Community law in so far as it would make it impossible to recover State aid that was granted in breach of Community law.*'

[155]Para. 60 of the grounds in *Lucchini*.

[156]Para.s 61 and 62 of the grounds in Lucchini. In this sense, see D. Simon, *Lex exigences de la primauté du droit communautaire; continuité ou métamorphoses?*, p. 13.

breach of Community law which has been found to be incompatible with the common market in a decision of the Commission which has become final.'[157]

A few brief observations about this judgement are at this point necessary in order to understand what exactly the Court of Justice has asked of the national court here.

Regarding the procedural autonomy of the Member States, it is necessary to emphasize, first of all, that it is not the primacy of the EU law that comes into play here,[158] but rather – as we have seen – the obligation of consistent interpretation connected with the exigency of effectiveness of the EU law. If, in fact, the substantive regulation in matters of aids concerns the EU legislator, the Member States[159] remain responsible for the establishment of the national system of sanctions – understanding this expression in a broad sense – aimed at pursuing the specific objective of ensuring the effectiveness of the EU substantive law in force on the specific matter. As there is no EU law that regulates these procedural aspects, in the broad sense, then, in this context, there cannot be a problem of primacy[160]: in this respect, the primacy referred to by the ECJ in the grounds of *Lucchini* should be understood as related to the substantive law on aids and not to procedural matters, [161] the described situation not being changed by the fact that we are dealing here with a case of direct EU administration.[162]

The procedural competence of the Member States, which instead is at issue here, finds its limit in the fact that the implementation of national procedural norms – whatever these may be[163] – cannot lead to the result of making the EU norms wholly ineffective[164]: this is a clearly unacceptable result from the perspective of

[157]Para. 63 of the grounds in *Lucchini*.

[158]Based on the reasoning already explained in Chap. 2, para. 2.4. In any case many authors refer here instead to a primacy problem. For example E. Fontana, *Intorno a qualche limite ordinamentale all'attuazione del diritto comunitario*, p. 2569 ff., para. 4; L. Raimondi, *Atti nazionali inoppugnabili e diritto comunitario tra principio di effettività e competenze di attribuzione*, p. 773 ff.

[159]'*In the absence of provisions of community law disputes concerning the recovery of amounts unduly paid under community law must be decided by national courts pursuant to their own national law.*' Para. 19 of the grounds in *Milchkontor,* quoted in para. 3.2.2. note n. 26.

[160]As was already explained in Chapter 2, para. 2.2., as a matter of fact the Member States's procedural competence disappears only in the rare cases of adoption of EU procedural law.

[161]In this regard, see D. Simon, *Autorité de chose jugée de l'arrêt d'une juridiction nationale devenu définitif*, p. 13.

[162]Because even in case of direct EU administration the adoption of a EU "procedural law" to substitute the national procedural law is an exception to the rule of procedural competence of Member States. See further in Chapter 2, para. 2.2.

[163]Obviously, this does not apply to criminal law where this problem has its specific configuration since the concerns about the effectiveness of EU substantive law are necessarily overruled by the exigency of certainty of the law. This is well illustrated moreover in the Judgement of the ECJ in the famous *Berlusconi* case (Judgement 3 May 2005, Joined cases C-387/02, C-391/02 and C-403/02, *European Court reports* 2005 Page I-03565).

[164]In this sense, see the observations of K. Lenaerts, *The Rule of Law and the Coherence of the Judicial System of the European Union*, p. 1649 s. and particularly note 146.

the EU law[165] since the national court has an obligation to interpret the national law in conformity with the EU law. This means that – in relation to the preliminary question posed by the national court in the present case – the interpretation of the provision in Art. 2909 of the Italian Civil Code cannot be such as to prevent the activation of the national public administration, through its own 'revocation' power, to remove the obstacle that can stand in the way of the effectiveness of the EU law. And if, in terms of procedural domestic law, this should represent an unavoidable step in order to allow the 'revocation' of the aid by the Administration[166] (and, hence, the effectiveness of EU law), it is still necessary to 'functionalize' the national procedural norms on matters of revocation of the *res judicata*[167] by providing for an expansion of the reasons for extraordinary revocation. [168] This is because – as we have already seen[169] – when taken to its extreme consequences '*... the principle of interpretation in conformity with Community law ... requires the referring court to do whatever lies within its jurisdiction, having regard to the whole body of rules of national law*' to ensure that the EU law '*is fully effective.*'[170]

[165]Borrowing Consolo's words, this is the reason of the '*harshness with which this lesson is taught.*' (Author's translation) See C. Consolo, *La sentenza Lucchini della Corte di giustizia: quale possibile adattamento degli ordinamenti processuali interni e in specie del nostro?*, p. 234. The more that – as noted by D. Simon, *Autorité de chose jugée de l'arrêt d'une juridiction nationale devenu définitif*, p. 14 – the violation is completely '*flagrant.*' See also the observations of V. Cerulli Irelli, *Trasformazioni del sistema di tutela giurisdizionale nelle controversie di diritto pubblico per effetto della giurisprudenza europea*, p. 460 s.

[166]As V. Cerulli Irelli seems to believe in *Trasformazioni del sistema di tutela giurisdizionale nelle controversie di diritto pubblico per effetto della giurisprudenza europea*, p. 463.

[167]As the Advocate General states in his conclusions quoted above, it is not a coincidence in this respect that '*It is evident from comparative research, however, that, despite the major importance to be attached to res judicata, its effect is not absolute. The various national legal systems permit exceptions to res judicata, albeit subject to strict conditions. This may be the case, for example, in the event of fraud or if a flagrant breach of fundamental rights is committed in the judgement which has become inviolable.*' (para. 37). In relation to the limits of the intangibility of the *res judicata*, see the reflections of C. Consolo, *La sentenza Lucchini della Corte di giustizia: quale possibile adattamento degli ordinamenti processuali interni e in specie del nostro?*, p. 231 ff. See also C. Malinconico, *Il recupero degli aiuti di Stato tra preclusioni processuali nazionali e limiti alla proposizione d'ufficio del ricorso pregiudiziale alla Corte di* giustizia, p. 805 ff.; R. Colonna, *Giudicato e jus superveniens retroattivo: un'armonizzazione difficile*, p. 257 ff.; G. Montedoro, *Il giudizio amministrativo fra annullamento e disapplicazione (ovvero dell' "insostenibile leggerezza" del processo impugnatorio)*, p. 527 ff.

[168]See Art. 395 Italian Civil Procedure Code (c.p.c.). On this point, see C. Consolo, *La sentenza Lucchini della Corte di giustizia: quale possibile adattamento degli ordinamenti processuali interni e in specie del nostro?*, p. 235 ff. See also C. Kremer, *Gemeinschaftsrechtliche Grenzen der Rechtskraft*, p. 491 s.

[169]In Chap. 2, para. 2.7.

[170]Judgement of the ECJ of 5 October 2004. *Pfeiffer*. Joined cases C-397/01 to C-403/01. *European Court reports* 2004 Page I-08835, para.s 113 ff. and, in particular, para. 118 of the grounds.

Re-read in this light, I consider that the ECJ's decision in the *Lucchini* case does not deserve all the severe criticisms directed at it.[171] And if this decision could have been avoided, it is because – as I will try to argue in the fourth chapter[172] – the preliminary reference could have been avoided; or at least the question submitted to the ECJ should have had a different formulation.

In recent times the ECJ has once again stated in a preliminary ruling on a question concerning the stability of *res judicata* in its judgement in the *Olimpiclub*[173] case.

The problem here at stake concerned the (new) approach followed by national judges in interpreting the meaning of Art. 2909 of the Italian Civil Code when referred to taxation matters.[174] In particular, the question referred was whether the need to ensure "*stability of the law and legal relations*"[175] could justify such a wide interpretation of *res judicata* if the consequence were a lack of effectiveness of substantive law in the field of value added tax (VAT).

If we consider the whole situation, in my opinion the answer of the ECJ could not have been different. Actually the point is that "*... as the national court itself points out – not only does the interpretation in question prevent a judicial decision that has acquired the force of res judicata from being called into question, even if that decision entails a breach of Community law; it also prevents any finding on a fundamental issue common to other cases, contained in a judicial decision which has acquired the force of res judicata, from being called into question in the context of judicial scrutiny of another decision taken by the relevant tax authority in respect of the same taxpayer or taxable person, but relating to a different tax year*". With the consequence that "*... if ever the judicial decision that had become final were based on an interpretation of the Community rules concerning abusive practice in the field of VAT which was at odds with Community law, those rules would continue*

---

[171]Very harsh critiques, but that still leave the interpreter 'the benefit of the doubt,' as those by V. Cerulli Irelli, *Trasformazioni del sistema di tutela giurisdizionale nelle controversie di diritto pubblico per effetto della giurisprudenza* europea, p. 472 ff. As well as harsh critiques *tout court* such as those of A. Negrelli, *Il primato del diritto comunitario e il giudicato nazionale: un confronto che si poteva evitare o risolvere altrimenti*, p. 1128 ff. (who sketches apocalyptic scenarios – precisely, of *Paradise lost* – of distortion of the principles and foundations of the national procedural law) and of G. Petrillo, *Il "caso Lucchini": il giudicato nazionale cede al diritto comunitario* p. 431 ff.

[172]See Chap. 4, para. 4.3.3.

[173]Judgement of the ECJ (Second Chamber) of 3 September 2009. Amministrazione dell'Economia e delle Finanze and Agenzia delle entrate v Fallimento Olimpiclub Srl. Reference for a preliminary ruling: Corte Suprema di Cassazione – Italy. Case C-2/08. *European Court reports 2009*. With regard to the problem of *res judicata* the ECJ again stated in the same way in its Judgement (First Chamber) of 6 October 2009. Asturcom Telecomunicaciones SL v Cristina Rodríguez Nogueira. Reference for a preliminary ruling: Juzgado de Primera Instancia no 4 de Bilbao – Spain. Case C-40/08. European Court reports 2009 Page 00000.

[174]Since the judgement of the United Chambers of the Italian Supreme Court of Cassation of 16 June 2006, n. 13916, in *Foro italiano*, 2007, I, c. 493 ff.

[175]So the terminology used in para. 22 of the grounds in *Olimpiclub*.

to be misapplied for each new tax year, without it being possible to rectify the interpretation".[176] It is therefore evident that such an interpretation of Art. 2909 of the Italian Civil Code would constitute such an obstacle to the application of EU substantial law in the field of VAT, that it cannot be justified[177] by the need of ensuring stability of the law (*i.e.* legal certainty).

It is therefore necessary to reconsider the (new) interpretation of Art. 2909: as the duty of sincere cooperation of Art. 4.3, TEU (*ex* Art. 10, TEC) entails an obligation for national judges to interpret their national procedural law in a way such as to 'sanction' in the best possible way the respect of the EU law by assuring the respect of the equivalence criterion and, first of all, of the *effectiveness* criterion.

In this connection, attention should be drawn to the fact that the judgement of the "Suprema Corte di Cassazione" recalled by the referring judge[178] follows an interpretation of Art. 2909 of the Italian Civil Code in the sense of "ultra-activeness of *res judicata*"[179] that is not at all certain. The principle of the discreteness of final judgements – to which the Italian courts adhered for a long time and in accordance with which each tax year remains separate from other tax years – is actually stated in Art. 7 of Decree n. 917/86.[180] And even if this provision is specifically referred to income taxation for natural persons the duty of consistent interpretation entails the duty for national judges to refer back to their previous interpretation of Art. 2909 based on an analogical interpretation of Art. 7 of Decree n. 917/86 for the field of VAT. This step – in my opinion – represents for national judges a concrete application of that generic duty of sincere cooperation stated in Art. 4.3, TEU (*ex* Art. 10, TEC).[181]

As a matter of fact – and to conclude – if the principle of *res judicata* is surely a fundamental one "*both for the Community legal order and for the national legal*

[176]Grounds 29 s. of *Olimpiclub* judgement.

[177]When balancing the weight of colliding principles it is the test of proportionality which must be used. Therefore the limitation of the one principle in order to satisfy the needs related to the opposing principle must be limited to what is strictly necessary (test of necessity). See D.U. Galetta, *Le Principe de proportionnalité*, p. 357 ff.

[178]See ground 3.5. of the judgement 13916/06.

[179]In as far as "*. . . not only does the interpretation in question prevent a judicial decision that has acquired the force of res judicata from being called into question, even if that decision entails a breach of Community law; it also prevents any finding on a fundamental issue common to other cases, contained in a judicial decision which has acquired the force of res judicata, from being called into question in the context of judicial scrutiny of another decision taken by the relevant tax authority in respect of the same taxpayer or taxable person, but relating to a different tax year*" (Grounds 29 s. of *Olimpiclub* judgement).

[180]Art. 7 para. 1 of the Presidential Decree (D.P.R.) of 22 decembre 1986 no 917 approving the consolidated text of the law on income tax, Ordinary Supplement to GURI No 302 of 31 December 1986 – ("*L'imposta è dovuta per anni solari, a ciascuno dei quali corrisponde un'obbligazione tributaria autonoma*").

[181]See Chapter 2, para 2.10.

systems",[182] as it ensures "*stability of the law and legal relations*",[183] nevertheless we are dealing here with constellations where there was a conflict between two different "stabilities of law": in as far as it was also the obligation to assure the effectiveness of EU law which was at stake and, therefore, the "stability" of EU law.[184]

3.5 The Specific Case of the National Procedural Norms Which Are an Obstacle to the Functioning of the Mechanism of Cooperation Between Courts Under Art. 267 TFEU (*ex* Art. 234 TEC): A Duty to "Disapply"[185] the National Procedural Norms in the Absence of Primacy? Concluding Remarks

The decisions analyzed so far, once placed in their specific context, do not lead – as explained – to such interpretative outcomes that would overturn the basic rule of procedural autonomy of the Member States conditioned, from time to time, by the application of the two *Rewe* criteria and the obligation of consistent interpretation of EU law. The outcome arising from the application of these three correctives is, at worst, a result of mere 'functionalization' of the procedural competence of the Member States with respect to the main objective of ensuring the effectiveness of EU law. In the decisions examined so far, there is no (explicit or implicit) requirement by the ECJ to replace the existing national procedural norms with norms that meet the criteria eventually specified by it.[186]

Therefore, we find ourselves almost always within that framework – well described by Advocate General Warner in his opinion in the *Rewe/Comet* case – of interaction between national law and EU law on the basis of a mechanism where '*... community law and national law operate jointly, where the second one is applied wherever the scope of application of the first one ends, in the sense that it rules the consequences.*'[187]

In this general context, the analysis of those cases – very particular ones indeed – in which the application of the national procedural norm, in addition to undermining

[182]Paragraph 22 of the grounds in *Olimpiclub*.

[183]S. para. 22 of the grounds in *Olimpiclub*.

[184]See D.U. Galetta, *Riflessioni sulla più recente giurisprudenza comunitaria in materia di giudicato nazionale*, p. 981.

[185]As I have already pointed out, the term 'disapply' is not an English word (the proper term is 'not to apply'). However, it appears in several decisions of the ECJ . That's why I have decided to use it in this para.

[186]In this perspective, I do not share the reflections of R. Caranta, *L'ampliamento degli strumenti di tutela cautelare e la progressiva "comunitarizzazione" delle regole processuali nazionali*, p. 2555 ff.

[187]Opinion of Mr Advocate General Warner delivered on 30 November 1976. Cases 33–76 and 45–76. *Rewe* and *Comet* decisions. *European Court reports* 1976 Page 01989 [Unofficial translation].

the effectiveness of the EU law, would result in preventing the functioning of the mechanism of cooperation between national judges and the ECJ designed in the old Art. 234, TEC, deserves separate consideration. For these particular cases – and in the absence of a problem of primacy of EU procedural norms – the ECJ seems to go beyond the idea of 'functionalization' of the national procedural law when it asks the national court to "disapply" *tout court* those national procedural rules that prevent the proper functioning of the mechanism of preliminary ruling designed by Art. 267, TFEU (*ex* Art. 234, TEC).

It is not a coincidence, therefore, that the decisions that will be examined below are the judgements of the ECJ most discussed in the doctrine addressing the issue of the so-called procedural autonomy of the Member States. So far, at least to my knowledge, there have been no attempts to bring them under the same interpretative framework. But I think that only by so doing it is possible to interpret their real meaning in terms of the limitations on the procedural autonomy of the Member States.

The first significant one – certainly well known among the experts – is the *Factortame* decision of 1990.[188] The preliminary questions behind the reference by the House of Lords – that, ultimately, concerned the extension of the power of national courts to grant interim protection when rights conferred by the EU law are involved – are too well known to merit further analysis.[189] Instead, one aspect that has not been adequately emphasized in the literature is the connection between the ruling of the ECJ in the *Factortame* case and the mechanism of Art. 267, TFEU.[190] The ECJ states here in fact that '... *the full effectiveness of Community law would be ... impaired if a rule of national law could prevent a court seised of a dispute governed by Community law from granting interim relief in order to ensure the full effectiveness of the judgement to be given on the existence of the rights claimed under Community law*' and this entails a consequence that '*a court which in those circumstances would grant interim relief, if it were not for a rule of national law, is obliged to set aside that rule.*'[191] Its reasoning continues then with this important clarification: '*That interpretation is reinforced by the system established by Article 177 of the EEC Treaty whose effectiveness would be impaired if a national court, having stayed proceedings pending the reply by the Court of Justice to the question referred to it for a preliminary ruling, were not able to grant interim relief until it*

---

[188]Judgement of the ECJ of 19 June 1990. The Queen v Secretary of State for Transport, ex parte: Factortame Ltd and others. Reference for a preliminary ruling: House of Lords – United Kingdom. Case C-213/89. *European Court reports* 1990 Page I-02433. On this, see in particular the reflections of J. Schwarze, *Der Beitrag des Europäischen Gerichtshofs zur Europäisierung des Verwaltungsrechts*, p. 427 ff.

[189]In this regard, see for all, P. Craig, *Sovereignty of the United Kingdom Parliament after Factortame*, p. 221 ff.

[190]See though O. Dubos, *Les juridictions nationales, juge communautaire*, p. 289 ff., who explicitly notes the connection with old Art. 234, TEC, but he connects it to the onset of a so-called third generation dispute.

[191]Para. 21 of the grounds in *Factortame*.

delivered its judgement following the reply given by the Court of Justice.'[192] As emerges, in fact, from a detailed analysis of the grounds of this decision, the exigency (as mentioned in paragraph 21 above) to "disapply" the national legislation that prevents, in this case, the granting of precautionary measures is connected both to the requirement of effectiveness of EU law (embodied in this case by the Treaty norms violated by the British regulation governing the registration of fishing vessels)[193] and to the exigency of not frustrating the cooperation mechanism designed by Art. 267, TFEU. This is because, in the case under analysis, to apply the British procedural domestic legislation – that prevented the adoption of precautionary measures to suspend the application of Parliament acts – would be tantamount to frustrating the purpose of the preliminary reference itself, which aimed at identifying the scope of the rights claimed by the applicant based on EU norms with direct effect.[194] The decision of the ECJ over Art. 267, TFEU (*ex* Art. 234, TEC) would intervene in a situation where the applicant's rights – and, therefore, the effectiveness of the EU law – were already irreversibly compromised. In fact, as is apparent from reading the facts of the case, if the applicant had not been granted a precautionary measure suspending the application of national norms (which were pleaded to be incompatible with EU law), then the vessels of the applicant would have been denied the right to fish with effect from the 1st of April 1989. Then, the response of the ECJ to the preliminary reference would have been completely useless in the light of the cooperation between national judge and EU judge, and only relevant for possible future cases.[195]

A situation similar in substance to the one described above was created, shortly afterwards, in the *Zuckerfabrik* case of 1991[196] and – in relation to the link between

---

[192]Para. 22 of the grounds in *Factortame*.

[193]In this sense, it is stated in para. 8 of the grounds in Factortame: '*On 4 August 1989 the Commission brought an action before the Court under Article 169 of the EEC Treaty for a declaration that, by imposing the nationality requirements laid down in Section 14 of the 1988 Act, the United Kingdom had failed to fulfil its obligations under Articles 7, 52 and 221 of the EEC Treaty.*'

[194]In fact, para.s 10 and 11 of the grounds in Factortame state that '*Since those vessels were to be deprived of the right to engage in fishing as from 1 April 1989, the companies in question, by means of an application for judicial review, challenged the compatibility of Part II of the 1988 Act with Community law. They also applied for the grant of interim relief until such time as final judgement was given on their application for judicial review.*' Therefore, '*In its judgement of 10 March 1989, the Divisional Court of the Queen' s Bench Division... decided to stay the proceedings and to make a reference under Article 177 of the EEC Treaty for a preliminary ruling on the issues of Community law raised in the proceedings.*'

[195]While the ECJ, instead, has always been very clear in stressing the importance of the binding value of its response to a preliminary reference. Because of that, it cannot be considered as a mere request for an advisory opinion. For an in-depth analysis on this point, see M.E. Bartoloni, *La competenza della Corte di giustizia ad interpretare il diritto nazionale "modellato" sulla normativa comunitaria*, p. 311 ff. (318).

[196]Judgement of the ECJ of 21 February 1991. Zuckerfabrik Süderdithmarschen AG v Hauptzollamt Itzehoe and Zuckerfabrik Soest GmbH v Hauptzollamt Paderborn. References for a preliminary ruling: Finanzgericht Hamburg and Finanzgericht Düsseldorf – Germany. Joined

precautionary powers of the national courts and the practical utility of the preliminary reference – in the subsequent *Atlanta* case of 1995.[197] These cases therefore, have similar outcomes with regard to the responses provided by the ECJ to the preliminary questions posed by the two German courts.

The ECJ returns five years later to the issue of the centrality of the preliminary ruling procedure as a mechanism for cooperation between courts – aimed ultimately to ensure maximum effectiveness of the EU law – and the need to set aside national procedural norms that prevent its operation with the *Peterbroeck* decision in 1995.[198] This decision has generated intense debate,[199] similar to that produced by the *Factortame* decision.

The problem in this case was related to issues already raised several times before the ECJ. In particular, it was about national procedural provisions that established time limits for appeals. These provisions prevented the national court from considering of its own motion pleas related to the incompatibility with the EU law, when the applicant could no longer invoke these pleas due to the expiration of the time limits. In this regard, after recalling the principle of sincere cooperation under old Art. 10, TEC, and the two *Rewe* criteria as the limits to the procedural autonomy of the Member States,[200] the ECJ focused on the peculiarities of the case under analysis. In fact, it stressed that '*Whilst a period of 60 days so imposed on a litigant is not objectionable per se, the special features of the procedure in question must be emphasized*;' indeed, as is inferred from reading the facts of the case, '*. . . the Cour d' Appel is the first court which can make a reference to the Court of Justice since the Director before whom the first-instance proceedings are conducted is a member of the fiscal authorities and, consequently, is not a court or tribunal within the meaning of Article 177 of the Treaty*.'[201] Allowing therefore in the case under examination the application of the national procedural norms would have ultimately

cases C-143/88 and C-92/89. *European Court reports* 1991 Page I-00415. On this decision, see for all the comment by G. Tesauro, *Tutela cautelare e diritto comunitario*, p. 131 ff. Particularly, note – in support of the thesis advocated here – the fact that he too observes that '*the most relevant point of the decision is the new and broader interpretation of Art. 177 of the Treaty*.' Author's translation.

[197]Judgement of the ECJ of 9 November 1995. Atlanta Fruchthandelsgesellschaft mbH and others v Bundesamt für Ernährung und Forstwirtschaft. Reference for a preliminary ruling: Verwaltungsgericht Frankfurt am Main – Germany. Case C-465/93. *European Court reports* 1995 Page I-03761.

[198]Judgement of the ECJ of 14 December 1995. Peterbroeck, Van Campenhout & Cie SCS v Belgian State. Reference for a preliminary ruling: Cour d'appel de Bruxelles – Belgium. Case C-312/93. *European Court reports* 1995 Page I-04599.

[199]Among others, see in particular the comments of E.M. Barbieri, *Poteri del giudice amministrativo e diritto comunitario*, p. 692 ff.; Id., *Poteri dei giudici nazionali e situazioni giuridiche soggettive di diritto comunitario*, p. 144 ff.; A. Russo, *E'sempre più "diffuso" il controllo di conformità al diritto comunitario ad opera del giudice nazionale?*, p. 701 ff.

[200]See para. 12 of the grounds in *Peterbroeck*.

[201]Para.s 16 and 17 of the grounds in *Peterbroeck*.

the effect of preventing the reference for a preliminary ruling[202] and '*The Court has also held that a rule of national law preventing the procedure laid down in Article 177 of the Treaty from being followed must be set aside*'[203] with the consequence – at this point obvious – that '... *the question submitted by the Cour d' Appel, Brussels, must therefore be that Community law precludes application of a domestic procedural rule whose effect, in procedural circumstances such as those in question in the main proceedings, is to prevent the national court, seised of a matter falling within its jurisdiction, from considering of its own motion whether a measure of domestic law is compatible with a provision of Community law when the latter provision has not been invoked by the litigant within a certain period.*'[204]

And it is in relation to the obstacle posed by the national norm to the activation of the mechanism of preliminary ruling that the ECJ provides its most relevant precedent, the last remaining decision to be examined here. This is the *Rheinmühlen* decision of 1974[205] – thus, 20 years earlier. This is a ruling fundamental to the complete understanding of the rationale behind the decisions just examined because – in relation to a preliminary question specifically related to the interpretation of paragraph 2 of Art. 177, EEC – essentially, it was about the relationship between the procedural competence of the Member States and the potential ability of a national procedural norm to be an obstacle to the functioning of the mechanism of preliminary ruling.[206] Indeed, the norm of §126 paragraph 5 of the German *Finanzgerichtsordnung* at stake here stated that, if a proceeding for "*Revision*" (which is a proceeding aiming at "quashing" the decisions of lower courts)[207] against a decision of the *Finanzhof* was considered to be founded, with the consequence that the

[202]A reinterpretation of the *Peterbroeck* decision in this sense is proposed also by C. Schepisi, *Sull' applicabilità d' ufficio delle norme comunitarie da parte dei giudici nazionali*, p. 811 ff.

[203]Para. 13 of the grounds in *Peterbroeck*.

[204]Para. 21 of the grounds in *Peterbroeck*.

[205]Judgement of the ECJ of 16 January 1974. Rheinmühlen-Düsseldorf v Einfuhr- und Vorratsstelle für Getreide und Futtermittel. Reference for a preliminary ruling: Bundesfinanzhof – Germany. Case 166-73. *European Court reports* 1974 Page 00033.

[206]The *Rheinmühlen* decision is also interpreted by Advocate General Warner in this sense in his conclusions of 30 November 1976, Case 33/76 (*Rewe* and *Comet* decisions), particularly, p. 2004.

[207]This is not the same as a the "appeal on a point of law" of common law systems. In order to understand what a "system of cassation" ("quashing") is, I suggest reading the explanation referred to the French system (which is very similar to the German one, to which the *Rheinmühlen* decision refers) in Bell/Boyron/Whittacker, *Principles of French Law*, Oxford University Press, 1998, p. 3 s., 85, where they explain: "*the* Cour de Cassation *is concerned with ensuring the proper application of law to the facts as found by the* juges du fond. ... *Thus the* Cour de Cassation *does not re-decide cases submitted to it (having corrected the legal rules to be applied) but rather, as its name indicates, quashes the decision of lower courts. In this perspective, it appears rather as a court of review than one hearing appeals on point of law*" (p. 85).

decision of the *Finanzhof* was "quashed" by the *Bundesfinanzhof* and the case referred for decision to another *Finanzhof*,[208] this latter court of first instance would have to be bound in its decision on the points of law by the rulings of the court superior to it (the *Bundesfinanzhof*).[209] This resulted, in this case, in the impossibility for the *Finanzhof*, to which the dispute had been referred for decision from the *Bundesfinanzhof*, to submit a preliminary reference to the ECJ – as he would have wanted – in order to request the interpretation of the provisions of Regulation No. 19/62/EEC, on which the solution of the dispute referred to him depended. Therefore, the procedural autonomy of the Member States deals here – in a very direct way – with the functioning of the mechanism of the preliminary ruling.

Therefore – and fully consistent with the subsequent decisions that have just been discussed[210] – with the decision in *Rheinmühlen* of 1976, the ECJ has already identified, in substance (and even if not expressly stated in these terms), the obligation of the national court to "disapply", where appropriate, national procedural norms even in the absence of primacy. In this sense, the ECJ affirms, '*. . . a rule of national law whereby a court is bound on points of law by the rulings of a superior court cannot deprive the inferior courts of their power to refer to the Court questions of interpretation of community law involving such rulings*' since '*If inferior courts were bound without being able to refer matters to the Court, the jurisdiction of the latter to give preliminary rulings and the application of community law at all levels of the judicial systems of the Member States would be compromised.*'[211]

The motivation of the *Rheinmühlen* decision is so clear in its concise insight[212] that it seems to me unnecessary – at this point – to indulge in further explanations.

It seems therefore clear to me that the last decisions examined here are isolated cases in the context of the diverse ECJ jurisprudence on the procedural autonomy of the Member States. In fact, in all of them the concern with the primacy and the

---

[208]§ 126, para. 3, of *Finanzgerichtsordnung* (FGO) of 6 October 1965 (in *BGBl.* I, p. 1477 ff. and in http://www.juris.de) states: "*Ist die Revision begründet, so kann der Bundesfinanzhof*

1. in der Sache selbst entscheiden oder

2. das angefochtene Urteil aufheben und die Sache zur anderweitigen Verhandlung und Entscheidung zurückverweisen".

[209]In fact § 126, para. 5, of *Finanzgerichtsordnung* (FGO) states: "*Das Gericht, an das die Sache zur anderweitigen Verhandlung und Entscheidung zurückverwiesen ist, hat seiner Entscheidung die rechtliche Beurteilung des Bundesfinanzhofs zugrunde zu legen*". This is again in line with the "philosophy" of this review procedure, which aims at ensuring the unity of law, avoiding different interpretations from different lower courts. S. again Bell/Boyron/Whittacker, *Principles of French Law*, p. 3 s.

[210]And, in my opinion, even with the more recent decision of the ECJ in the *Cartesio* case (Judgement of the ECJ of 16 December 2008, case C-210/06, *European Court reports 2008*, Page I-09641). For a (partially) different point of view see R. Alonso García, *Cuestión prejudicial comunitaria y autonomía procesal nacional: a propósito del asunto Cartesio, STJCE de 16 de diciembre de 2008 (C-210/06)*, p. 197 ff.

[211]Para. 4 of the grounds in *Rheinmühlen*.

[212]In this sense, the observations of G. Raiti, *La collaborazione giudiziaria nell'esperienza del rinvio pregiudiziale comunitario*, p. 282 ff., when he speaks of the 'ambiguity' of the *Rheinmühlen* jurisprudence, should not be misinterpreted.

effectiveness of EU law is reinforced by the even greater concern to prevent the operation of national procedural rules from annihilating the essential mechanism for the development of EU law, represented by the reference to the ECJ for a preliminary ruling. This is even more so if we take into account the fact that the Commission has always preferred to refrain from appealing, in this regard, to the action of non-fulfilment under Art. 258 TFEU (*ex* Art. 226, TEC), because it considers that it is not the most suitable instrument to ensure the correct application of Art. 267 TFEU (*ex* Art. 234, TEC) on the preliminary ruling procedure.[213]

In conclusion, then, the outcome arising from the jurisprudence analyzed here – which is based on the 'explosive' combination of the requirements of primacy and effectiveness of EU substantive law, with the exigency of imposing the use of the interpretative preliminary ruling procedure without using the infringement procedure under Art. 258 TFEU (*ex* Art. 226 TEC) – seems to me quite evident: a real obligation to "disapply", in a particular case, the national procedural norms may arise as final result, even in the absence of the primacy of EU procedural law (which does not exist), from the combination of the duties of the Member States, under Art. 4.3, TFEU (*ex* Art. 10, TEC), in this specific context where not even a 'functionalization' of the national procedural norms may be in practice sufficient or feasible.[214] And if this is still not enough, the 'positive' obligation to adopt the necessary and appropriate procedural measures to ensure the realization of the result of substantive law imposed by the EU norms arises – as seen clearly in the *Factortame* case.

---

[213]As referred by G. Raiti, *La collaborazione giudiziaria nell'esperienza del rinvio pregiudiziale comunitario*, p. 303. On this point see also the observations of O. Dubos, *Les juridictions nationales, juge communautaire*, p. 638 ff.; A. Hatje, *Artikel 10 (Verpflichtung der Mietglied-staaten)*, p. 329.

[214]In this specific perspective should also be framed the Judgement of the ECJ of 9 March 1978. Amministrazione delle Finanze dello Stato v Simmenthal SpA. Reference for a preliminary ruling: Pretura di Susa – Italy. Case 106/77. *European Court reports* 1978 Page 00629. In this case, where there was a conflict between '...*certain rules of community law and a subsequent national law, namely the said law no 1239/70,*' the Pretore di Susa has stated that '...*according to recently decided cases of the Italian Constitutional Court (Judgements No 232/75 and No 205/76 and Order No 206/76), the question whether the law in question was unconstitutional under Article 11 of the Constitution must be referred to the Constitutional Court itself.*' (para.s 5 and 6 of the grounds). Therefore, he asked the ECJ if this interpretation was compatible with the Treaty norms and with the ECJ's jurisprudence on the matter. To this question – as is known – the Court responded that the need for the national court with jurisdiction over the dispute to refer the case to the Constitutional Court in this regard was '...*incompatible with those requirements which are the very essence of community law*' like any other procedural mechanism of the domestic law '...*which might impair the effectiveness of community law by withholding from the national court having jurisdiction to apply such law the power to do everything necessary at the moment of its application to set aside national legislative provisions which might prevent community rules from having full force and effect.*' Further, it notes that '*This would be the case in the event of a conflict between a provision of community law and a subsequent national law if the solution of the conflict were to be reserved for an authority with a discretion of its own, other than the court called upon to apply community law, even if such an impediment to the full effectiveness of community law were only temporary.*' (Para.s 22–23 of the grounds).

Chapter 4
The Procedural Autonomy of the Member States: Judges and Legislators. Conclusions

So spake the false dissembler unperceived
For neither Man nor Angel can discern
Hypocrisy, the only evil that walks
Invisible, except to God alone,
By his permissive will, through Heaven and Earth [685]
(John Milton, Paradise Lost, Book III)

4.1 Primacy of EU Substantive Law and Procedural Autonomy of the Member States: The Difficult Role of the ECJ

The close connection between the primacy of EU substantive law and procedural autonomy of the Member States – that some scholars have defined in terms of '*lien consubstantiel*'[1] – has clearly become apparent from the analysis conducted so far. From this analysis has also clearly emerged the need to constantly seek a balance between these two elements, which are certainly inseparable[2] and, at the same time, in constant tension with each other.

As the analysis of the jurisprudence conducted in Chapter 3 has allowed us to verify, the primacy of EU substantive law and the procedural autonomy of the Member States can be seen as the two extremes of an elastic band, which can be extended – and, in case of need, very much so – but which has, however, an inevitable breaking point.

---

[1]In this sense, R. Kovar, *La contribution de la Cour de justice à l'édification de l'ordre juridique communautaire*, p. 49.

[2]As also pointed out by Advocate General Warner in his opinion on 30 November 1976. Cases 33-76 and 45-76. *Rewe* and *Comet* decisions. *European Court reports* 1976 page 01989, p. 2000 ff. and particularly p. 2003 f.

D.-U. Galetta, *Procedural Autonomy of EU Member States: Paradise Lost?*,
DOI 10.1007/978-3-642-12547-8_4,

This explains – or should explain – why when considering these problems, the ECJ's jurisprudence often faces an almost impossible task: namely, to avoid breaking the elastic band when the Member States keep pulling it[3]...

The argumentative 'twirls' exercised by the ECJ, especially in its *obiter dicta*, should be framed, therefore, in this context. Even if they may be questionable – sometimes, perhaps, unnecessary – they denote, though, the constant efforts by the ECJ not only to find balanced solutions, but also to justify these solutions in the best way it can. As a matter of fact, these solutions end up being constant, as far as the outcomes of the balancing made is concerned. In fact, the ECJ adopts – as I tried to highlight in Chapter 3 – a very consistent approach in its jurisprudence. But this is a consistency that is not always easy to identify because it is based on a combination of several factors and does not emerge in an obvious way unless one considers the overall framework of reference within which the ECJ decides. This framework of reference is constituted by both legal and factual elements that characterize the case under analysis[4] and the framework of relationships between national law and EU law that serves as a setting in each case (namely, the principles and criteria that govern the relations between national law and EU law, mentioned in Chapter 2).

An example – certainly not the only one, but the most recent and discussed by the Italian doctrine – of the perennial tension of the elastic band that holds together procedural autonomy and primacy is the often recalled *Lucchini* case.[5] According to some scholars, this is already a case of breaking the elastic band because the ECJ had allegedly sacrificed the procedural autonomy of the Member States to the primacy of EU substantive law, by skipping a fundamental principle of the Italian national procedural order: namely, the principle of *res judicata*.

Apart from the fact that – as has been said[6] – this decision should not be misunderstood in relation to its impact in practice,[7] the truth is that, in this as in other cases, the responsibility is rather of the referring court which – as we shall see[8] – could and should have avoided submitting the preliminary reference in those terms.[9] But even beyond this point, I think that neither in the *Lucchini* judgement,

[3]See the recent reflections of ECJ judge Th. von Danwitz, *Funktionsbedingungen der Rechtsprechung des Europäischen Gerichten*, p. 769 ff., who explains how the often "blatant and stubborn disregard" of their obligation by the Member States has influenced the ECJ's attitude (p. 772).

[4]This is not criticisable given that the judge should try to reach the solution adjusted to law for each individual case. As recently stressed by Cassese, *Quando gli ordinamenti si scontrano. Dal dialogo alla cooperazione tra le Corti*, p. 79. On this aspect see also the observations of R. Caranta, *La tutela giurisdizionale (italiana, sotto l'influenza comunitaria)*, p. 1042.

[5]See in particular Chap. 3, para. 3.4.

[6]See Chap. 3, para 3.4.

[7]See for all the reflections of K. Lenaerts, *The Rule of Law and the Coherence of the Judicial System of the European Union*, p. 1649 f. and in particular note No. 146.

[8]In para. 4.3.

[9]On this specific issue, a partially different evaluation of the Lucchini story is proposed, though, by M.P. Chiti, *Le peculiarità dell'invalidità amministrativa per anticomunitarietà*, p. 493, who refers to it as the search for a 'dialogue' between the *Consiglio di Stato* and ECJ.

nor in the many other decisions discussed in Chapter 3, is there a 'change of route' by the ECJ towards increasing invasions against the procedural autonomy of the Member States. Rather, it seems to me that many recent decisions confirm the opposite and reaffirm, therefore, the willingness of the Court to maintain as balanced an approach as possible.[10] This is even so, despite the continued and repeated attempts by national courts to make the ECJ say things that are beyond the task assigned to the ECJ and sometimes, more generally, the jurisdiction of EU law *tout court*.[11]

An example of the balance exercised by the ECJ is seen in the decisions where the Court, when questioned on issues such as the extension of the supervisory and decisional powers of the judge,[12] has deliberately 'declined' the invitation to intervene on matters that had little to do with the concern to ensure the effectiveness of EU law and much, instead, with an attempt of the national courts to use the preliminary ruling procedure to introduce through the window (of EU jurisprudence) those questions than cannot be brought in through the door (an intervention of the national legislator to strengthen the decision-making and supervisory powers of the national court with respect to acts of the administration). I refer, in particular, to the famous *Upjohn* jurisprudence of 1999. In this case the British court asked the ECJ '*...whether Directive 65/65 and, more generally, Community law require the Member States to establish a procedure for judicial review of national decisions revoking marketing authorisations for proprietary medicinal products, whereby the national courts and tribunals having jurisdiction are empowered to substitute their assessment of the facts, and, in particular, of the scientific evidence relied on in support of the revocation decision, for the assessment made by the national authorities competent to revoke such authorisations.*'[13] And the ECJ responded with a negative answer.[14]

Another relevant and more recent example of the balanced approach by the ECJ is represented by the *Unibet* decision of 2007.[15] Here the Swedish referring court asked the ECJ, essentially, whether the principle of effective judicial protection should be interpreted as requiring the existence, in the legal order of a Member State, of a free-standing action for an examination as to whether

[10]On this point, see also the case law analyzed in G. Raiti, *La collaborazione giudiziaria nell'esperienza del rinvio pregiudiziale comunitario*, in particular, p. 412 ff. and his reflections on the matter.

[11]On this point, see para. 4.3.

[12]For an in-depth analysis, see for all R. Caranta, *La tutela giurisdizionale (italiana, sotto l'influenza comunitaria)*, p. 1049 ff.

[13]ECJ Judgement of 21 January 1999. Case C-120/97. Upjohn. *European Court reports* 1999 Page I-00223, para. 27 of the grounds.

[14]Para. 37 of the grounds in *Upjohn*. On this point, see for all R. Caranta, *Tutela giurisdizionale effettiva delle situazioni giuridiche soggettive di origine comunitaria ed incisività del sindacato del giudice nazionale* (Kontrolldichte), p. 503 ff.

[15]Judgement of the ECJ of 13 March 2007. Case C-432/05. Unibet. *European Court reports* 2007 Page I-02271.

national provisions are compatible with Art. 49, TEC (now Art. 56 TFEU), if other legal remedies permit the question of compatibility to be determined as a preliminary issue.[16]

Firstly, the ECJ reaffirmed that '*Under the principle of cooperation laid down in Article 10 EC, it is for the Member States to ensure judicial protection of an individual's rights under Community law*'[17] because of the fact that – as we have seen[18] – the procedural competence resides, in principle, with the Member States.[19] It then specified – recalling the jurisprudence that we have examined in the previous chapter – that '*It would be otherwise only if it were apparent from the overall scheme of the national legal system in question that no legal remedy existed which made it possible to ensure, even indirectly, respect for an individual's rights under Community law.*'[20] That is, where the effectiveness of EU law was undermined in its root (and not the right to an effective legal remedy, which is a mere corollary of it).[21] So the problem should be brought back, again and always, to the two *Rewe* criteria, as limits to the procedural autonomy of the Member States,[22] and the national court should assess, in the individual case and on the basis of the instructions provided by the ECJ, respect for the two criteria of equivalence[23] and effectiveness. This is also seen in the reasoning of the ECJ in its recent jurisprudence in the *Impact* case that, in fact, does not reach different results.[24]

---

[16]See para. 36 of the grounds in *Unibet*.

[17]Para. 38 of the grounds in *Unibet*.

[18]See Chap. 2, para. 2.2.

[19]In fact, the ECJ specifies in para. 40 of the grounds in Unibet that '*Although the EC Treaty has made it possible in a number of instances for private persons to bring a direct action, where appropriate, before the Community Court, it was not intended to create new remedies in the national courts to ensure the observance of Community law other than those already laid down by national law.*'

[20]Para. 41 of the grounds in *Unibet*.

[21]As noted in Chap. 2, para. 2.6.

[22]The ECJ, in fact, reaffirms that '*... the principle of effective judicial protection does not require it to be possible, as such, to bring a free-standing action which seeks primarily to dispute the compatibility of national provisions with Community law, provided that the principles of equivalence and effectiveness are observed in the domestic system of judicial remedies.*' (para. 47 of the grounds in Unibet).

[23]The ECJ concludes that '*... the principle of effective judicial protection of an individual's rights under Community law must be interpreted as meaning that it does not require the national legal order of a Member State to provide for a free-standing action for an examination of whether national provisions are compatible with Article 49 EC, provided that other effective legal remedies, which are no less favourable than those governing similar domestic actions, make it possible for such a question of compatibility to be determined as a preliminary issue, which is a matter for the national court to establish.*' (para. 65 of the grounds in Unibet).

[24]ECJ Judgement of 15 April 2008. Case C-268/06. Impact. *European Court reports* 2008 Page I-02483, in particular para.s 49 ff.

4.2 *Continued.* In the Continuous Search of Equilibrium for a Greater 'Unity in Diversity'

In Chapter 2, which concentrated on the importance for our study of the direct effect and primacy as essential features of EU law, an important aspect of this topic was deliberately left out and now it is time to address it. I refer to the fact that, in the opinion of some authors,[25] these two characteristics are a consequence of the requirement of uniform application of EU law, which the ECJ has sometimes defined as '*a fundamental requirement of the Community legal order.*'[26] According to these scholars, from this would emerge the prohibition on the Member States to apply national rules, whichever these might be, that may act as obstacles to the implementation of EU law,[27] with the consequent risk of an irretrievable annihilation of procedural autonomy.

Other authors point out, however – in my opinion, quite persuasively – that the objective of *uniform application* of EU law is actually a purely general one which as such cannot be considered as prevailing over the procedural autonomy of the Member States *tout court*.[28] This can be clearly inferred from the *Milchkontor* jurisprudence, which refers to the need to balance procedural autonomy, on the one hand, and the requirement of uniform application, on the other.[29] In this light,

---

[25]In this sense, for example, D. Simon, *Le système juridique communautaire*, p. 408 ff.

[26]See ECJ Judgement of 21 February 1991. Joined cases C-143/88 and C-92/89. Zückerfabrik, *European Court reports* 1991 Page I-00415, para. 26. In this sense, see also V. Skouris, *L'influence du droit national et de la jurisprudence des juridictions des Etats membres sur l'interprétation du droit communautaire*, p. 241.

[27]See D. Simon, *Le système juridique communautaire*, p. 409, and also C. Blumann, L. Dubouis, *Droit institutionnel de l'Unione européenne*, p. 495.

[28]See W. van Gerven, *Of Rights, Remedies and Procedures*, p. 505, 521 ff.; K. Lenaerts, T. Corthaut, *Towards an Internally Consistent Doctrine of Invoking Norms of EU Law*, p. 495 ff. (500); M. Potacs, *Bestandskraft staatlicher Verwaltungsakte oder Effektivität des Gemeinschaftsrecht?*, p. 596 ff. See also C. Iannone, *Art. 10 TCE*, p. 222 f.; S. Prechal, *Community Law in National Courts: The Lessons From Vam Schijndel*, p. 686 ff.; S. Hegels, *EG-Eigenverwaltungsrecht und Gemeinschaftsverwaltungsrecht. Europäisches Verwaltungsrecht für den direkten und den indirekten Gemeinschaftsrechtsvollzug*, p. 56 ff.

[29]ECJ Judgement of 21 September 1983. Joined cases 205 to 215/82. *Milchkontor*, where it is stated in para. 17 that: '*According to the general principles on which the institutional system of the community is based and which govern the relations between the community and the Member States, it is for the Member States, by virtue of Article 5 of the Treaty, to ensure that community regulations, particularly those concerning the common agricultural policy, are implemented within their territory. In so far as community law, including its general principles, does not include common rules to this effect, the national authorities when implementing community regulations act in accordance with the procedural and substantive rules of their own national law; however, as the Court stated in its Judgement of 6 June 1972 in Case 94/71 (Schluter & Maack v Hauptzollamt Hamburg-Jonas (1972) ECR 307), this rule must be reconciled with the need to apply community law uniformly so as to avoid unequal treatment of producers and traders.*' (Highlighting added). On this point, see also ECJ Judgement of 6 June 1972. Case 94-71. Schlüter & Maack. *European Court reports* 1972 Page 00307, para. 11 of the grounds.

therefore, the interpretation of the famous paragraph of the *Simmenthal* decision of 1978 – where the ECJ declares that the '*direct applicability... means that rules of community law must be fully and uniformly applied in all the Member States*'[30] – as the *requiem* of the ECJ to the procedural autonomy of the Member States is the result of a mistaken reasoning.

If, in fact, the repeatedly recalled criterion of effectiveness of EU substantive law (the famous second limit to the procedural autonomy identified by the *Rewe* jurisprudence) leads to – as mentioned – [31] a real 'obligation of result'[32] on the part of the authorities of the Member States, it is still an obligation of result that can be pursued with the possibility of freely choosing the means.[33] Then, what cannot be done, reinterpreting procedural autonomy in the light of the jurisprudence already cited, is to maintain that the result prescribed by the EU norm of substantive law could not be achieved due to the lack or unsuitability of the 'sanctioning' instruments of domestic law aimed at ensuring the effectiveness of that law.[34] What it is possible for the Member States to do is, instead, to exercise their own procedural autonomy: that is, given the obligation of result prescribed by the EU norm of substantive law, to make – based on the definition of 'procedural autonomy'[35] held here – an 'autonomous' choice of the means aimed at guaranteeing the effectiveness of EU law.

In conclusion, then, with regard to the difficult role played by the ECJ in ensuring the balance in practice between primacy of EU substantive law and procedural autonomy of the Member States, I think it can be said that so far it has performed this task in a careful and very balanced way.[36] The philosophy behind the European Union is, still and always, one which can be summarized in the motto

---

[30]ECJ Judgement of 9 March 1978. Case 106/77. Amministrazione delle Finanze dello Stato v Simmenthal SpA. *European Court reports* 1978 Page 00629, para. 14.

[31]In Chap. 2, para. 2.5.

[32]In this sense, R. Kovar, *Droit communautaire et droit procédural national*, p. 234; O. Dubos, *Les juridictions nationales, juge communautaire*, p. 252 ff.

[33]The *Simmenthal* decision is interpreted in this same sense by S. Prechal, *Community Law in National Courts: The Lessons From Vam Schijndel*, p. 684 f. See on this point, also C. Rodríguez Iglesias, *Sui limiti all'autonomia procedimentale e processuale degli Stati membri nell'applicazione del diritto comunitario*, p. 27 f. See, however, R. Mehdi, *L'autonomie institutionnelle et procédurale et le droit administratif*, p. 718, who affirms that '*La Cour de justice a, dans deux configurations au moins, doublé l'obligation de résultat... par une véritable obligation de moyen.*'

[34]I am obviously referring here to the expression – already recalled – of '*sanction*' as '*... l'ensemble des moyens de contrainte légale qui, dans chaque Etat membre assure le respect du droit en cas de conflit à propos de son application.*' See J. Mertens de Wilmars, *L'efficacité des différentes techniques nationales de protection juridique contre les violations du droit communautaire par les autorités nationales et les particuliers*, p. 390.

[35]See Chap. 2, para. 2.3.

[36]On this point, see the concluding remarks of P. Craig, *EU Administrative Law*, p. 813 ff. and R. Caranta, *La tutela giurisdizionale (italiana, sotto l'influenza comunitaria)*, p. 1062 ff. S. also what recently reported by Th. von Danwitz, *Funktionsbedingungen der Rechtsprechung des Europäischen Gerichten*, p. 771, from the point of view of his experience as judge at ECJ and in Th. Von Danwitz, *Europäisches Veraltungsrecht*, p. 312.

'unity in diversity,'[37] which implies a necessary co-existence – in the sense already explained – of procedural autonomy and primacy, and the continued search for their equilibrium.[38] In fact, the EU system is a system '*that is inclined to be a factor of integration*' and the relationship between legal systems is developed, therefore, not as an alternative or opposition, but in the sense of the '*search for compatibility and osmosis between the legal values of each other.*' This '*original and exciting*' result of '*synthesis between different legal systems*' would not be possible without the fundamental (and I would add, constant) intervention of the ECJ.[39]

4.3 Duty of Sincere Cooperation, Procedural Autonomy of the Member States and Preliminary Ruling: The Role of the National Referring Courts

4.3.1 The Preliminary Ruling, from Its Origins Till Now: A Short Account

The case law that has been examined in Chapter 3 of this work wholly originates, as has been said, from preliminary references. Most of them are references for a preliminary ruling concerning interpretation but, in some important cases, they also concern validity.[40]

The institution of the preliminary ruling is too well known and researched by EU scholars to require a thorough analysis.[41] Therefore, here I will restrict myself to a

[37]On this point, see the reflections of K. Lenaerts, *The Rule of Law and the Coherence of the Judicial System of the European Union*, p. 1625 ff. Regarding the 'respected diversity' see also the comments of D. De Pretis, *La tutela giurisdizionale amministrativa in Europa fra integrazione e diversità*, in particular, p. 16 ff. See lastly Ph. Manin, *La place de la diversité dans le Traité sur l'Union européenne*, p. 395 ff.

[38]See on this point, S. Magiera, *Die Durchsetzung des Gemeinschaftsrechts im europäischen Integrationsprozeß*, p. 173 ff. (183). In this same sense, see also R. Mehdi, *L'autonomie institutionnelle et procédurale et le droit administratif*, p. 725. See also more recently G. Martinico, *L'integrazione silente. La funzione interpretativa della Corte di giustizia e il diritto costituzionale europeo*, p. 73.

[39]So A. Tizzano, in R. Adam, A. Tizzano, *Lineamenti di diritto dell'Unione europea*, p. 212 f. Author's translation. On this point, see also the recent book by G. Martinico, *L'integrazione silente. La funzione interpretativa della Corte di giustizia e il diritto costituzionale europeo, passim.*

[40]On this distinction, see for all A. Barav, *Renvoi préjudiciel*, p. 933 f.

[41]For a historical account of this institution, see particularly P. Pescatore, *Il rinvio pregiudiziale di cui all'art. 177 del Trattato CEE e la cooperazione tra la Corte ed i giudici nazionali*, c. 26 ff. For a more recent analysis see the monographic work by G. Raiti, *La collaborazione giudiziaria nell'esperienza del rinvio pregiudiziale comunitario*, as well as P. Biavati, *Diritto processuale dell'Unione europea*, p. 407 ff.; J. Schwarze, *Artikel 234 (Vorabentscheidung)*, p. 1807 ff. See also the very often quoted paper by T. Tridimas, *Knocking on Heaven's door: Fragmentation,*

brief account aimed at identifying its essential characteristics and features which are specifically relevant for our research topic.

As for the origins of the institution, they are certainly related to the exigency of uniform application of EU law that – as has been said – [42] should be considered as an objective of EU law – at least an objective towards which it is striving.[43] This is so especially when placed in relation to the mechanism, which is often found in international law, that underlies real processes of 'nationalization,' in the sense that, through the interpretation of this law exercised by the individual national courts, international law gradually diversifies in terms of its meaning and scope.[44] Therefore, the main scope and purpose of the preliminary ruling procedure is precisely to avoid the occurrence of this phenomenon and thus to preserve, as far as possible, the EU law from these 'nationalization' drives.

It is in this perspective, I believe, that the whole jurisprudence on the principles and 'institutions' of EU law identified by the ECJ through the method of 'comparative evaluation' should be read.[45] By means of this method, the ECJ – far from simply borrowing from the individual national legal orders – draws from those principles and 'institutions' of the national laws of Member States the raw material, which is then re-elaborated giving life to autonomous, 'EU' principles and institutions. This is the case, for example, of the principles of proportionality[46] and protection of legitimate expectations,[47] as well as the more recent institution of *ex officio* annulment.[48]

Moreover, as is known, the role and the function of the preliminary ruling have been expanded over time far beyond what was originally planned. In particular, the preliminary competence of the ECJ – through what has been defined as an 'alternative use' of the reference for a preliminary ruling – has allowed the submission of questions to the ECJ that are only formally related to a EU principle or institution. Actually, these questions are aimed at challenging a national legal norm or practice in order to test its compatibility with the EU law. Although the ECJ is not competent to

Efficiency and Defiance in the Preliminary Reference Procedure, p. 9 ff. and the quite critical paper of H. Rasmussen, *Remedying the Crumbling EC Judicial System*, p. 1071 ff.

[42]Para. 4.2.

[43]As emphasized by the ECJ in its Information note on references from national courts for a preliminary ruling (*Official Journal of the European Union* of 11 June 2005, 2005/C-143/1), para. 1, '*The preliminary ruling system is a fundamental mechanism of European Union law aimed at enabling national courts to ensure uniform interpretation and application of that law in all the Member States.*'

[44]In this sense, A. Tizzano, in R. Adam, A. Tizzano, *Lineamenti di diritto dell'Unione europea*, p. 303.

[45]In this regard, see V. Skouris, *L'influence du droit national et de la jurisprudence des juridictions des Etats membres sur l'interprétation du droit communautaire*, p. 239 ff. (245 ff.).

[46]As I discovered in my study of 1998. See D.U. Galetta, *Principio di proporzionalità e sindacato giurisdizionale nel diritto amministrativo*, *passim*.

[47]On this point, see D.U. Galetta, *La tutela dell'affidamento nella prospettiva del diritto amministrativo italiano, tedesco e comunitario: un'analisi comparata*, p. 757 ff.

[48]D.U. Galetta, *Autotutela decisoria e diritto comunitario*, p. 39 ff.

directly rule on the compatibility of a national norm with EU law,[49] anyway it has the task of providing the national court with all the elements of interpretation of EU law necessary to enable it to resolve the dispute pending before it.[50]

4.3.2 Continued. *The Distribution of Competences Between the ECJ and the National Referring Court, and the Effect of a Decision on a Preliminary Reference*

The competence for preliminary rulings by the ECJ is a jurisdictional competence of a non-contentious nature,[51] in the sense that when exercising this competence the ECJ does not directly decide on a dispute, but it merely provides the referring court with the necessary elements for its solution.[52]

It is in fact on the national court that the dispute between the parties hinges, develops and ends.[53] And the entire procedure is organized according to the fact that the national court has the responsibility for resolving the dispute.[54]

More generally, the preliminary ruling procedure – which is organized as a 'court-to-court'[55] proceeding, where the parties have a minor role –[56] is based on a clear separation of functions between the ECJ and the national courts. It is for

[49]As it reaffirmed in its Order of 10 July 2008. Case C-156/07. Aiello. *European Court reports* 2008, Page I-00097, para. 42.

[50]On this point, see the recent observations of K. Lenaerts, *The Rule of Law and the Coherence of the Judicial System of the European Union*, p. 1641 ff. See further, also very recently, A. Barone, *Giustizia comunitaria e funzioni interne*, p. 12 ff., and particularly the vast bibliographic references quoted there.

[51]On this point, see ECJ Judgement of 8 May 2008. Case C-491/06. Danske, *European Court reports* 2008 Page I-03339, para. 22 of the grounds and the references to its jurisprudence mentioned there.

[52]I agree with the observations made by Dubos only if interpreted in this sense. See O. Dubos, *Les juridictions nationales, juge communautaire*, p. 665, according to which '*the Court is willing to participate directly in the solution of the pending dispute before the national court which is at the heart of the preliminary reference.*' Author's translation.

[53]In this sense, A. Tizzano, in R. Adam, A. Tizzano, *Lineamenti di diritto dell'Unione europea*, p. 301 f.

[54]The ECJ specifies in the Information note on references from national courts for a preliminary ruling, of 2005, in para. 6, that '*In ruling on the interpretation or validity of Community law, the Court makes every effort to give a reply which will be of assistance in resolving the dispute, but it is for the referring court to draw the appropriate conclusions from that reply...*' On this point, see P. Pescatore, *Il rinvio pregiudiziale di cui all'art. 177 del Trattato CEE e la cooperazione tra la Corte ed i giudici nazionali*, c. 36.

[55]In this sense, P. Pescatore, *Il rinvio pregiudiziale di cui all'art. 177 del Trattato CEE e la cooperazione tra la Corte ed i giudici nazionali*, c. 37.

[56]In this regard, see para.s 10 ff. of the Information note on references from national courts for a preliminary ruling, of 2005. See also A. Barav, *Renvoi préjudiciel*, p. 942; R. Joliet, *L'article 177 du Traité CEE et le renvoi prejudicial*, p. 593 f.

the latter to decide on whether to initiate a preliminary ruling proceeding[57] and to evaluate the need for such ruling, even if the ECJ has already ruled on the matter.[58]

So, even after the elaboration of the so called "acte clair" doctrine, following the well-known jurisprudence in the *Cilfit* case,[59] the established trend of the ECJ still remains applicable. According to this '*As regards the division of jurisdiction between national courts and the Court of Justice under Article 177 of the Treaty the national court, which is alone in having a direct knowledge of the facts of the case and of the arguments put forward by the parties, and which will have to give judgement in the case, is in the best position to appreciate, with full knowledge of the matter before it, the relevance of the questions of law raised by the dispute before it and the necessity for a preliminary ruling so as to enable it to give judgement.*'[60]

However, in the case of questions improperly formulated or which go beyond the scope of the powers conferred on the Court by Art. 267 TFEU (*ex* Art. 234, TEC), the Court has the possibility to rephrase the questions, if necessary,[61] to extract from all the factors provided by the national court '... *and in particular from the statement of grounds contained in the reference, the elements of community law requiring an interpretation – or, as the case may be, an assessment of validity – having regard to the subject-matter of the dispute.*'[62]

The fact however remains that, as explicitly stated by the ECJ, '... *it is for the national court pursuant to the separation of jurisdiction on which Article 177 of the Treaty is based to decide how far the interpretation of community law is necessary for it to give its judgement.*'[63] Thus, as the ECJ has had the opportunity of

---

[57]In this sense, already in ECJ Judgement of 28 June 1978. Case 70/77. Simmenthal SpA v Amministrazione delle finanze. *European Court reports* 1978 Page 01453, para.s 10 s. of the grounds.

[58]On this point, see among many others, ECJ Judgement of 7 July 1988. Case 55/87. Moksel. *European Court reports* 1988 Page 03845, para.s 7 ff.

[59]ECJ Judgement of 6 October 1982. Case 283/81. CILFIT, *European Court reports* 1982 Page 03415. On this decision, see for all, H. Rasmussen, *Remedying the Crumbling EC Judicial System*, p. 1107 ff.

[60]See ECJ Judgement of 29 November 1978. Case 83/78. Pigs Marketing, *European Court reports* 1978 Page 02347, para. 25 of the grounds. In the same vein, see lastly the ECJ Judgement of 16 December 2008. Case C-213/07. Michaniki, *European Court reports* 2008 Page I-09999, para. 32 ff. of the grounds.

[61]On this aspect, see the observations by G. Raiti, *La collaborazione giudiziaria nell'esperienza del rinvio pregiudiziale comunitario*, p. 338 f. See moreover O. Dubos, *Les juridictions nationales, juge communautaire*, p. 666 ff., who provides an overview of the different situations in which the ECJ may have to rephrase the preliminary questions.

[62]Para. 26 of the grounds in *Pigs Marketing*.

[63]ECJ Judgement of 13 March 1979. Case 86/78. SA des grandes distilleries Peureux, *European Court reports* 1979 Page 00897, para. 6 of the grounds.

emphasizing since the *van Gend & Loos* decision, it is not for the ECJ to 'assess' the considerations that could have determined the choice of the questions by the national courts, nor the relevance that those questions may have, according to the referring court, in the proceedings pending before it.[64]

It is thus, in short, a limited competence of the ECJ[65] by virtue of which the knowledge of the facts of the case by the Court is necessary not for themselves but only because (and insofar as) it is necessary to answer the preliminary question.[66]

Neither is it for the ECJ to verify the accuracy of the national normative framework and its correspondence with the facts[67] as this is the responsibility of the national court – either in its fact-finding role[68] or in its responsibility in the assessment of the facts.[69]

Finally, this limited competence of the ECJ has an effect on the fact that it is for the national court to draw the consequences that the answer given by the ECJ to its preliminary questions will have in practice in relation to the disputes pending before it. Therefore, despite what sometimes seems to be believed by certain

---

[64]In this sense, already in ECJ Judgement of 5 February 1963. van Gend & Loos. Case 26-62. *European Court reports* 1963 Page 00001. This is, moreover, a consolidated jurisprudence. See, lastly Judgement of the ECJ of 16 December 2008. Case C-213/07, para. 32 of the grounds. For an in depth analysis on this aspect see for all A. Barav, *Renvoi préjudiciel*, p. 938 f.; A. Tizzano, in R. Adam, A. Tizzano, *Lineamenti di diritto dell'Unione europea*, p. 310 f. As well as R. Lecourt, *L'Europe des juges*, p. 272 f.

[65]See, among others, L. Daniele, *Diritto dell'Unione europea*, p. 301; C. Blumann, L. Dubouis, *Droit institutionnel de l'Unione européenne*, p. 572.

[66]In this sense, see para.s 21 to 24 of the Information note on references from national courts for a preliminary ruling, of 2005. Neither could a different conclusion be drawn from the well-known jurisprudence in the ECJ Judgement of 26 January 1993. Joined cases C-320/90, C-321/90 and C-322/90. Telemarsicabruzzo. *European Court reports* 1993 Page I-00393, para. 5 of the grounds where it is stated that '*the need to provide an interpretation of Community law which will be of use to the national court makes it necessary that the national court define the factual and legislative context of the questions it is asking or, at the very least, explain the factual circumstances on which those questions are based.*' On this aspect see also T. Tridimas, *Knocking on Heaven's door: Fragmentation, Efficiency and Defiance in the Preliminary Reference Procedure*, p. 24 ff.

[67]See already in ECJ Judgement of 16 March 1978. Case 104/77. Oehlschläger. *European Court reports* 1978 Page 00791, para. 4, where it is stated that '*Under Article 177 of the Treaty, which is based on a clear separation of functions between the national courts and the Court of Justice, the latter is empowered only to give rulings on the interpretation or the validity of a community provision on the basis of the facts which the national court puts before it. To verify whether such facts are correct is not within the competence of the Court of Justice, and is a matter for the national court.*'

[68]See P. Pescatore, *Il rinvio pregiudiziale di cui all'art. 177 del Trattato CEE e la cooperazione tra la Corte ed i giudici nazionali*, c. 38.

[69]On this point, see Judgement of the ECJ of 8 May 2008. Case C-491/06, para. 23 and the vast jurisprudential references mentioned there.

authors,[70] it is not possible to identify an automatic link between the answer to the preliminary question and the solution of the concrete case pending before the national court.

The only goal of the answers given by the ECJ to the preliminary questions posed by the national judges is to provide a response that is useful to the national court for the resolution of the dispute pending before it.[71] This may certainly involve the need to take into consideration norms of EU law not expressly mentioned by the national court,[72] but not the consideration of facts other than those identified by the national court or the description of a national legal framework different from that indicated by the national court.[73]

The need for the answer given by the ECJ to be 'useful' lies at the heart of the jurisprudence where the Court has declared that it has no jurisdiction to answer those questions that prove to be fictitious or artificial.[74] But the rejection of preliminary questions by the ECJ has been and still is limited only to extreme cases,[75] given the willingness and the inclination shown by the ECJ

[70]For example, in quite critical tones, E. Bernard, *Entre monologue et dialogue de sourds... Les dérives du «dialogue des juges» dans le cadre de la procédure préjudicielle ?*, p. 21.

[71]See para. 6 of the Information note on references from national courts for a preliminary ruling, of 2005. On this point, see R. Lecourt, *L'Europe des juges*, p. 273, who underlines how the ECJ "*veille à ne pas empiéter dans le domaine de l'application, qui relève du juge national et, à plus fort raison, de l'appréciation du droit interne*". S. also the critical observations of G. Raiti, *La collaborazione giudiziaria nell'esperienza del rinvio pregiudiziale comunitario*, p. 338 f.

[72]See ECJ Judgement of 20 March 1986. Case 35/85. Tissier. *European Court reports* 1986 Page 01207, para. 9 of the grounds where it is stated that '*As far as that point is concerned, it is for the Court, when faced with questions which are not framed in an appropriate manner or which go beyond its functions under Article 177, to extract from all the information provided by the national court, in particular from the grounds of the decision referring the questions, the points of community law which require interpretation or whose validity is at issue, having regard to the subject-matter of the dispute. In order to provide a satisfactory answer to a national court which has referred a question to it, the Court of Justice may deem it necessary to consider provisions of community law to which the national court has not referred in the text of its question. However, it is for the national court to decide whether or not the rule of community law, as interpreted by the Court of Justice pursuant to Article 177, is applicable in the case brought before it.*'

[73]Which – as we will see in para. 4.3.3. – has important consequences in relation to the so-called 'mistaken preliminary rulings.'

[74]I refer here to the well-known ECJ Judgement of 11 March 1980. Case 104/79. Foglia v Novello. *European Court reports* 1980 Page 00745, particularly to para. 10 of the grounds, which exceptionality is addressed, for example, in T. Tridimas, *Knocking on Heaven's door: Fragmentation, Efficiency and Defiance in the Preliminary Reference Procedure*, p. 22 ff. On this aspect see also A. Tizzano, in R. Adam, A. Tizzano, *Lineamenti di diritto dell'Unione europea*, p. 312; O. Dubos, *Les juridictions nationales, juge communautaire*, p. 687 ff.

[75]This has been done – as observed by authoritative doctrine – in order not to discourage national courts from submitting preliminary references. See P. Pescatore, *Il rinvio pregiudiziale di cui all'art. 177 del Trattato CEE e la cooperazione tra la Corte ed i giudici nazionali*, c. 46 s. In this regard, see also the observations of the ECJ in the *Thomasdünger* case, Judgement of the ECJ of 26 September 1985. Case 166/84. *European Court reports* 1985 Page 03001, para. 11 of the grounds, where it is stated that '*In that respect it is sufficient to point out that, except in exceptional cases in which it is clear that the provision of community law which the Court is asked to interpret does not*

to answer anyway, as far as possible, the questions that are submitted by national courts.[76]

Moreover, as established in the Rules of Procedure[77] – and as the ECJ has repeatedly pointed out[78] – the decision on a preliminary ruling is binding.[79] As regards specifically the interpretative preliminary ruling, the respective decision has *erga omnes* effects[80] as well as, in principle, retroactive effects.[81] Only the ECJ has the power to state the non-retroactivity of its own judgements for reasons of legal certainty and after taking into account all the interests at stake in the concrete case.[82] This is because the decision on the interpretation of a EU norm by the ECJ has a merely declaratory value as it expresses what was already established in the norm subject to interpretation.[83]

---

apply to the facts of the dispute in the main proceedings, the Court leaves it to the national court to determine in the light of the facts of each case whether the preliminary ruling is necessary in order to decide the dispute pending before it.'

[76]On this point, see the arguments already developed in Chap. 2, para. 2.9. and the jurisprudence quoted there.

[77]Art. 65 prescribes: '*The judgement shall be binding from the date of its delivery.*' The current version in force of the Rule of Procedure of the ECJ can be accessed at the ECJ's website: http://curia.europa.eu/jcms/jcms/T5_5120/.

[78]In this sense, see Judgement of the ECJ of 24 June 1969. Case 29-68. Eierkontor. *European Court reports* 1969 Page 00165, para. 3 of the grounds.

[79]Pescatore observes that '*it is binding for the national court; then – contrary to what some believe, it is not a simple advice or an opinion.*' See P. Pescatore, *Il rinvio pregiudiziale di cui all'art. 177 del Trattato CEE e la cooperazione tra la Corte ed i giudici nazionali*, c. 40. Author's translation.

[80]See K. Lenaerts, *The Rule of Law and the Coherence of the Judicial System of the European Union*, p. 1642. See however the observations of P. Pescatore, *Il rinvio pregiudiziale di cui all'art. 177 del Trattato CEE e la cooperazione tra la Corte ed i giudici nazionali*, c. 41 s., who notes that we cannot speak about *erga omnes* efficacy in the formal sense of the term. S. also R. Lecourt, *L'Europe des juges*, p. 269 ff. For a recent analysis see the book by G. Martinico, *L'integrazione silente. La funzione interpretativa della Corte di giustizia e il diritto costituzionale europeo*, p. 91 ff., 114 ff., who provides an interesting review of the different positions of the doctrine, so far, on this point.

[81]See K. Lenaerts, *The Rule of Law and the Coherence of the Judicial System of the European Union*, p. 1642.

[82]On this aspect, see ECJ Judgement of 8 April 1976. Case 43-75. Defrenne. *European Court reports* 1976 Page 00455, particularly para.s 71 to 75 of the grounds. See also the *Salumi* decision, Judgement of the ECJ of 27 March 1980. Joined cases 66, 127 and 128/79. *European Court reports* 1980 Page 01237, para. 10 of the grounds where it is stated that '*As the Court recognized... it is only exceptionally that the Court may, in application of the general principle of legal certainty inherent in the community legal order and in taking account of the serious effects which its judgement might have, as regards the past, on legal relationships established in good faith, be moved to restrict for any person concerned the opportunity of relying upon the provision as thus interpreted with a view to calling in question those legal relationships.*'

[83]See further K. Lenaerts, *The Rule of Law and the Coherence of the Judicial System of the European Union*, p. 1642 f. and the jurisprudence quoted there.

4.3.3 'The More Questions the Merrier'? The Role of the National Referring Courts: Too Many Preliminary References and 'Mistaken' Preliminary References

As the statistics published by the ECJ show, over the past twenty years there has been an exponential increase of the requests for a preliminary ruling.[84] This has resulted in an overload for the ECJ and the lengthening of the period for issuing decisions on preliminary rulings.[85]

Thus, the preliminary ruling procedure seems to be a victim of its own success,[86] to the point that some authors have provocatively asked the question, faithfully reported in the title of this paragraph: "The more questions the merrier"?[87]

This is not the place to concentrate on the analysis of the reforms introduced by the Treaty of Nice for reducing, where possible, the length of the EU judicial procedures[88] and of the many proposals for further reform that have been suggested to attempt to solve the numerous problems just mentioned.[89]

Here it is sufficient to point out instead that the 'filtering mechanisms' introduced by the ECJ to avoid artificial or fictitious preliminary references have been used very sparingly.[90] Moreover, they have been used by the ECJ not in order to pursue, through them, a quantitative reduction of cases to be examined,[91] but

[84]That can be traced in the ECJ's website at http://curia.europa.eu/jcms/jcms/j_6/. On this point, see the observations contained in the 1999 discussion paper, 'The Future of the Judicial System of the European Union (Proposals and Reflections),' See also C. Barnard, E. Sharpston, *The Changing Face of Article 177 References*, p. 1113 ff., 1157 ff.

[85]On this point, see G. Raiti, *La collaborazione giudiziaria nell'esperienza del rinvio pregiudiziale comunitario*, p. 426 ff.

[86]In this sense, T. Koopmans, *La procédure préjudicielle – victime de son succès ?*, p. 347 ff.

[87]K. Lenaerts, T. Corthaut, *Towards an Internally Consistent Doctrine of Invoking Norms of EU Law*, p. 500.

[88]On this aspect, see for all, the book edited by B. Nascimbene, *Il processo comunitario dopo Nizza*. S. also, more recently the analysis of Th. von Danwitz, *Funktionsbedingungen der Rechtsprechung des Europäischen Gerichten*, p. 778 ff.

[89]On this point, see in particular the dense discussion paper entitled 'The Future of the Judicial System of the European Union (Proposals and Reflections),' May 1999, that can be accessed from the ECJ's website at http://curia.europa.eu/jcms/jcms/j_6/. For a scholarly analysis of the proposals submitted on this matter see G. Raiti, *La collaborazione giudiziaria nell'esperienza del rinvio pregiudiziale comunitario*, p. 425 ff.; H. Rasmussen, *Remedying the Crumbling EC Judicial System*, p. 1083 ff.; K. Lenaerts, T. Corthaut, *Towards an Internally Consistent Doctrine of Invoking Norms of EU Law*, p. 507 ff.; G. Falcon, *La tutela giurisdizionale*, p. 778 f. and, lastly, M.P. Chiti, *Diritto amministrativo europeo*, p. 685 ff.

[90]On this point, see ECJ Judgement of 16 December 2008. Case C-213/07, para. 34 of the grounds.

[91]T. Tridimas, *Knocking on Heaven's door: Fragmentation, Efficiency and Defiance in the Preliminary Reference Procedure*, p. 21 ff. (23). For a different opinion, see however the observations of C. Barnard, E. Sharpston, *The Changing Face of Article 177 References*, p. 1157.

rather – as mentioned – in order to provide the referring courts with useful answers[92] and, therefore, to concretize the principle of sincere cooperation under old Art. 10, TEC (now Art. 4.3, TEU) that should inspire the action of the ECJ in relation to the courts of the Member States, especially in this specific context.

In addition to the problematic aspect concerning the quantitative element (too many preliminary references), there is also another problem. This is what I will call the 'qualitative' element of the references for a preliminary ruling and which I believe acts – more and better than the quantitative one – as a litmus test with respect to how the national courts relate to the ECJ.

Let me explain this better.

It is certainly true that the quantitative element is important to understand the national courts' approach.[93] As some authors rightly show,[94] the national courts could decide not to refer because they are more prone to resolve their own interpretative doubts[95] by themselves or could decide to 'heavily' use the preliminary reference as a form of protest.[96] In this last sense, they may submit requests for a preliminary ruling on subject-matters that have been already addressed by the ECJ in order to ask for a re-evaluation of the solutions with which they disagree.

As has been rightly noted, '*there are some ways to phrase preliminary questions to facilitate the task of the community Court and... others that make its job more difficult.*'[97] That is to say, compared to the quantitative aspect of the references for a preliminary ruling – which is certainly relevant also in terms of the quality of the ECJ's jurisprudential product,[98] the qualitative one has a much greater impact.

---

[92] As explained in the previous para. 4.3.2. See also works quoted in note 91.

[93] In this sense, in relation to the approach of the Italian administrative courts see the work of M. Gnes, *Giudice amministrativo e diritto comunitario*, p. 331 ff. More generally, see the statistical study of A. Stone Sweet, Th. L. Brunell, *The European Court and the National Courts: A Statistical Analysis of Preliminary References, 1961–95*, p. 1 ff.

[94] T. Tridimas, *Knocking on Heaven's door: Fragmentation, Efficiency and Defiance in the Preliminary Reference Procedure*, p. 37 ff.

[95] This seems to be the approach of the British courts, as noted by T. Tridimas, *Knocking on Heaven's door: Fragmentation, Efficiency and Defiance in the Preliminary Reference Procedure*, p. 38. In this sense, see however the wide and well-documented analysis of D. Chalmers, *The Much Ado about Judicial Politics in the United Kingdom: A Statistical Analysis of Reported Decisions of United Kingdom Courts Invoking EU Law 1973–1998*, p. 1 ff., who calls attention to a constant increase of preliminary references also by the British courts.

[96] Gnes does not seem to take into account this element when he qualifies the quantity of preliminary references as a sign of 'community loyalty.' See M. Gnes, *Giudice amministrativo e diritto comunitario*, p. 335 ff.

[97] P. Pescatore, *Il rinvio pregiudiziale di cui all'art. 177 del Trattato CEE e la cooperazione tra la Corte ed i giudici nazionali*, c. 33. Author's translation.

[98] On this point, see the critical observations of H. Rasmussen, *Remedying the Crumbling EC Judicial System*, p. 1080 ff.

In this perspective, I do not think that the tendency of our national courts[99] – also recently noticed by other scholars[100] – to formulate questions that are constructed in such a way as to request, in fact, an intervention of the ECJ on domestic law issues, is good thing. One also cannot accept the interpretation of 267, TFEU, that, after the *Granital* decision made by the Italian Constitutional Court,[101] equates the preliminary ruling of the ECJ to an incidental judgement ('*giudizio incidentale*') on the conformity of the national law with the EU law, and ultimately identifies it as the '*the main vehicle to assert... the primacy of the community values over the national ones.*'[102]

Interpretations of this kind – probably a result of a genuine 'Euro-enthusiasm'[103] – end up producing negative consequences at least equal, if not greater, than those produced by the Euro-sceptic approach of certain authors. These scholars base their view on similar allegations to attribute to the ECJ an expansionist attitude, which is hardly possible to identify if an objective analysis on its jurisprudence is conducted.[104]

I think it is important to emphasize that the responsible and consistent use of the procedural instruments available, which certain scholars have recently evoked in relation to the so-called sincere cooperation,[105] would imply, in this specific context, the need to restrict the references for a preliminary ruling within the limits of what is really necessary.[106] It implies also the need to avoid posing preliminary questions in such a manner that leaves the ECJ without alternatives. This has happened in the case of the *Lucchini* decision, but also in other equally important cases which are worthy of brief examination in this specific light.

Let me start with the *Lucchini* case which – as has been anticipated[107] – was an unnecessary and 'mistaken' reference for a preliminary ruling. Indeed, from

---

[99]In this regard, it is worth reminding that, as noted by M. Gnes, *Giudice amministrativo e diritto comunitario*, p. 339, the first preliminary reference submitted by an Italian Administrative Tribunal dates back to 1975, while the first reference of the *Consiglio di Stato* only took place in 1991.

[100]See F. Sorrentino, *L'art. 177 del Trattato di Roma nel rapporto tra ordinamento comunitario e ordinamenti interni*, p. 739 ff. (742).

[101]Corte Costituzionale, Judgement 8 June 1984 No. 170 that can be accessed at http://www.giur-cost.it.

[102]In this sense, F. Sorrentino, *L'art. 177 del Trattato di Roma nel rapporto tra ordinamento comunitario e ordinamenti interni*, p. 745 f., 751.

[103]In this perspective the recent book by A. Barone, *Giustizia comunitaria e funzioni interne* should also be analyzed.

[104]S. to this regard the interesting reflections by Th. von Danwitz, *Funktionsbedingungen der Rechtsprechung des Europäischen Gerichten*, p. 771 ff.

[105]See O. Porchia, *I principi dell'ordinamento europeo. La cooperazione pluridirezionale*, p. 248 ff.

[106]On this aspect, see the observations of A. Biondi, *The European Court of Justice and certain national procedural limitations: not such a tough relationship*, p. 1286 f.

[107]In Chap. 3, para. 3.4.

the earlier jurisprudence in the *Alcan*, *Delena Wells* and *Kühne & Heitz* cases[108] it was already possible to infer an obligation on the national administration, in the light of the duty of sincere cooperation under Art. 10, TEC, to review a final administrative decision that was adopted in breach of EU law.[109] In fact, the ECJ had already affirmed in the *Alcan* decision that '*Community law requires the competent authority to revoke a decision granting unlawful aid, in accordance with a final decision of the Commission declaring the aid incompatible with the common market and ordering recovery.*'[110] In the subsequent decision in the *Kühne & Heitz* case, the ECJ already provided all the elements that might enable the national court to draw the necessary consequences in relation to the compulsory character of an administrative action of 'revocation' to be initiated immediately after the decision of the EU Commission became final.[111] There was therefore no need to submit a preliminary reference.

Instead of requesting the ECJ if: '*in view of the generally accepted principle that decisions on the recovery of aid are governed by Community law but the implementation thereof and the associated recovery procedure, in the absence of Community provisions on the matter, is governed by national law*" the recovery procedure is rendered "*legally impossible by virtue of a specific judicial decision that has become res judicata (Article 2909 of the [Italian] Civil Code), thereby being conclusive as between the private individual and the administration, and requires the administration to comply with it,*'[112] the *Consiglio di Stato* should have – in my opinion – simply overturned the decision in the first instance made by the *TAR* of Lazio, that declared unlawful the decree by which the *Ministero dell'Industria, del Commercio e dell'Artigianato* had ordered the recovery of aid (unlawfully paid) as it was actually a case of dutiful *ex officio* annulment.[113] This was the

[108]On this aspect, see Chap. 3, para. 3.3.2. On these three decisions, see also a D.U. Galetta, *Autotutela decisoria e diritto comunitario*, p. 39 ff.

[109]On this point, see also the reflections of M. Potacs, *Bestandskraft staatlicher Verwaltungsakte oder Effektivität des Gemeinschaftsrecht?*, p. 595 ff., 601 ff.

[110]This appears even more clearly in the original version, in German, of the recalled decision, where the exact expression used by the ECJ is: "*die zuständige Behörde ist gemeinschaftsrechtlich verpflichtet*". See Judgement of the ECJ of 20 March 1997. Case C-24/95, para. 38 of the grounds.

[111]On this point, see F. Cortese, *Il riesame di decisioni amministrative definitive tra obbligo di cooperazione e certezza del diritto*, p. 1541 ff.

[112]This is the second preliminary question submitted by the Council of State in the *Lucchini* case.

[113]This situation is well known to Italian administrative law, particularly as a result of the provision in the financial law of 2005 which was a kind of restatement of the consolidated jurisprudential trend on the point. I refer to Law 311/04, whose Art. 1, para. 136, provides that '*In order to save or reduce spending costs for the public administrations, the* ex officio *annulment of unlawful administrative acts can always be ordered, even if their execution is still in progress.*' [Author's translation]. On this point, see D.U. Galetta, *I procedimenti di riesame*, p. 395 ff.

conclusion reached, for example, by the *TAR* of Palermo with a decision of 2007 on a quite similar case.[114]

In the case decided by the *TAR* of Palermo, an appeal had been made against an administrative act of annulment *ex officio*, which the Administration had adopted in order to comply with a decision of the European Commission. The administrative act, which had been annulled *ex officio*, appeared to be, as stated by the *TAR*, '*... aimed at overcoming the effects of a binding decision by the... Commission, as well as obtaining a practical result contrary to the community norm which is directly enforceable.*' Thus, the *TAR* correctly rejected the appeal against the administrative act of annulment *ex officio*, on the grounds that the act of *ex officio* annulment of the administrative act adopted in violation of EU law '*... as it is motivated, seems not only legitimate but, even due, according to the obligation of cooperation which applies to national public administrations under Art. 10 of the EC Treaty.*'

The situation in the *Lucchini* case was, as a matter of fact, very similar, as the national Administration was required to carry out the decision of the Commission 90/555/ECSC, which became final, and there was no margin of appreciation for it in this respect.[115] Therefore, it was a matter of ultimately complying with the obligations under EU law and not continuing to be in the wrong.[116] This is so, since according to the obligations emerging from the duty for sincere cooperation under Art. 10, TEC, the national civil court was already required, before adopting its judgement, to verify whether the obligations deriving from the EU norms on aids were satisfied and if there were decisions of the Commission preventing the payment of the aid.[117]

Against my reasoning, however, it could be argued that in the *Lucchini* case there was in addition the specific problem of *res judicata*. But if the Council of State wanted to submit its preliminary question on *res judicata*, it should have been posed it in a quite different way.[118] The right question (which should obviously be responded to in the negative) was not, in fact, whether the national civil *res judicata* could render the recovery of the aid legally impossible. Rather, the question should have been whether the *res judicata* constituted within the civil procedure between Lucchini and the Italian national administration (based on a decision of the national

[114]See TAR Sicilia, Palermo, II Chamber, Judgement No. 2049/2007 at http://www.giustizia-amministrativa.it. On this decision, see the observations of M.P. Chiti, *Le peculiarità dell'invalidità amministrativa per anticomunitarietà*, p. 497 f.

[115]This point of view is clearly shared by the Italian "Corte di Cassazione" in his recent judgement of 19 may 2008, n. 12641 about the *Lucchini* case.

[116]On this point, see Opinion of Mr Advocate General Geelhoed delivered on 14 September 2006. *European Court reports* 2007 Page I-06199, para.s 65–66.

[117]As noted by Advocate General Geelhoed in his opinion, para.s 62–63.

[118]This is also the opinion of other Italian scholars. See for example F.P. Luiso, *La responsabilità civile del magistrato*, note No. 44.

Court of Appeals adopted in complete disrespect of EU obligations), could be asserted by the Italian state before the European Union.[119]

Given the poor formulation of the preliminary question by the Council of State, there was actually no way out for the ECJ.[120] In fact, despite the arguments posed by the Italian government (which perhaps could have made the real substance of the problem clear, as highlighted earlier),[121] it was impossible for the ECJ to reformulate the question. This is because the procedure to reformulate questions is an exception to the general rule and it is a mean to save the admissibility of a preliminary reference through the inference of the question even when it does not emerge clearly from the wording of the preliminary reference.[122] But it certainly should not be used[123] to turn the question around

---

[119]In this regard, of interest is the reading of ECJ Judgement of 14 December 2000. Case C-344/98. Masterfoods. *European Court reports* 2000 Page I-11369, para. 52, where it is stated that '*It is even more important that when national courts rule on agreements or practices which are already the subject of a Commission decision they cannot take decisions running counter to that of the Commission, even if the latter's decision conflicts with a decision given by a national court of first instance.*' For an in-depth analysis on this point see C. Consolo, *La sentenza Lucchini della Corte di giustizia: quale possibile adattamento degli ordinamenti processuali interni e in specie del nostro?*, p. 234 ff.

[120]The problematic relationship between *res judicata* and effectiveness of EU law was, not surprisingly, already highlighted in a paper written thirty years ago by R. Kovar, *Voies de droit ouvertes aux individus devant les instances nationales en cas de violation des normes et décision du droit communautaire*, p. 282 f.

[121]See Opinion of Advocate General Geelhoed, para.s 22–23, where it is stated that '*According to the Italian Government, the principle of res judicata is not applicable since it presupposes a judgement which has acquired binding force between the same parties, concerns the same subject-matter and has the same legal basis*' and '*It claims that the third of those conditions was not satisfied in view, on the one hand, of the differences between the proceedings in a civil court resulting in the judgement of the Corte d'appello and the administrative court proceedings currently before the referring court and, on the other hand, of the fact that the judgement of the Corte d'appello is neither based on the third aid code nor takes account of Commission Decision 90/555.*'

[122]The ECJ has also made use of this technique especially in the beginning, in order to favour the 'takeoff' of the institution of preliminary ruling. But it seems much less inclined to use it now that this institution is broadly and consistently used and that – as has been said – there is, indeed, the opposite problem of reducing the ever increasing number of preliminary references.

[123]Obviously I'm not ignoring the existence of a different point of view supported by those scholars who are convinced that it should be part of the Court's task to reformulate preliminary questions in order to avoid "difficult situations". Yet in my opinion this would mean, on the one hand, asking too much from the ECJ, and, on the other hand, this would create a sort of hierarchy between the ECJ and national referring courts, which is written nowhere in the Treaties. See on this specific point P. Pescatore, *Il rinvio pregiudiziale di cui all'art. 177 del Trattato CEE e la cooperazione tra la Corte ed i giudici nazionali*, c. 30, who underlines how "*The preliminary ruling ... ... does not create a hierarchy between national courts and the Court of Justice*" (Author's translation). In the same vein R. Lecourt, *L'Europe des juges*, p. 272 f.; R. Joliet, *L'article 177 du Traité CEE et le renvoi prejudicial*, p. 591 ff. (594 f.).

when it is, as in the present case, formulated in a clear and comprehensive, albeit unfortunate, way.[124]

In conclusion, therefore, given the preliminary reference submitted, a different outcome in the *Lucchini* case was almost impossible. The ECJ had no choice but to consider the qualification of *res judicata* (understood as 'intangible rule in the concrete case' within the meaning of Art. 2909 of the Italian Civil Code) as a qualification of national law. As some authors have actually observed,[125] from the perspective of the ECJ, in the case under analysis the *res judicata* was merely an act of the State contrary to the obligation of recovery of the aid that derived from the EU law. A different conclusion would have ended up endorsing repeated acts by the national administrations adopted in clear defiance of EU law.[126] Moreover, here at stake was not only the EU regulation on aid, but also the allocation of competences between Member States and the Commission, with the latter having – as is known – an exclusive competence on this matter.[127]

Another highly relevant case in which, at the end of the day, the preliminary reference was mistaken, is the much earlier jurisprudence in the *Emmott* case.[128] As referred by certain scholars,[129] this decision – the subject of copious academic literature, equally divided between supporters and opponents – originated from an unnecessary preliminary reference. In fact, the relevant norm, contained in the 'Rules of the Superior Courts 1986,'[130] had already been interpreted by the jurisprudence of the Irish Supreme Court in the sense that it was possible to extend the time limit for appeal if the applicant could prove that he had suffered a 'public

[124]On this point, see also the observations of O. Dubos, *Les juridictions nationales, juge communautaire*, p. 670 ff.

[125]In this sense, C. Malinconico, *Il recupero degli aiuti di Stato tra preclusioni processuali nazionali e limiti alla proposizione d'ufficio del ricorso pregiudiziale alla Corte di giustizia*, para. 4.4.

[126]As Tesauro reminds us. See G. Tesauro, *Diritto comunitario*, p. 209. In this sense, also D. Simon, *Autorité de chose jugée de l'arrêt d'une juridiction nationale devenu définitif*, p. 14. See also P. Biavati, *La sentenza Lucchini: il giudicato nazionale cede al diritto comunitario*, p. 1601 ff., who speaks of a real 'community disdain.'

[127]As is rightly pointed out by D. Simon, *Autorité de chose jugée de l'arrêt d'une juridiction nationale devenu définitif*, p. 14.

[128]ECJ Judgement of 25 July 1991. Case C-208/90, in Chap. 3., para. 3.2.3.

[129]In this sense, L. Flynn, *Whatever Happened to Emmott? The Perfecting of Community Rules on National Time-Limits*, p. 66 ff.

[130]As stated in the *Emmott* judgement, para. 13 of the grounds: '*The relevant provision in this regard is Order 84, Rule 21(1)... That provision is worded as follows: "An application for leave to apply for judicial review shall be made promptly and in any event within three months from the date when grounds for the application first arose, or six months where the relief sought is certiorari, unless the Court considers that there is good reason for extending the period within which the application shall be made".*'

wrong' and that the misconduct by the national Administration had had and continued to have a negative impact on his life.[131]

However, instead of referring to this sound precedent, as it could have done, the Irish Supreme Court preferred to submit a preliminary reference in the terms already mentioned.[132] This gave rise to a decision that – also because of the far-reaching (and even distorting) interpretation made by the authors who commented on it[133] – has had a considerable impact,[134] even beyond the relevant national legal order.

Another example of an unnecessary or mistaken preliminary reference is the *Traghetti del Mediterraneo* decision, with the formulation of the second preliminary question being relevant here. Through it, the Court of Genoa requested the ECJ if '*...national legislation on State liability for judicial errors which... precludes liability in relation to the interpretation of provisions of law and assessment of facts and of the evidence adduced in the course of the exercise of judicial functions*'[135] was incompatible with the principles of EU law.

It is obviously not possible here to concentrate on the specificity of this decision which is focused on the problem of the judge's accountability.[136] However, it is necessary to highlight the evident fact that, even in relation to this reference, the question submitted to the ECJ for preliminary ruling was not "the right one".[137] But, given its specific formulation – together with the fact that, as mentioned,[138] the ECJ follows the description of national law made by the referring court – the result could hardly have been different from that obtained.

---

[131]Decision State (Furey) v. Minister for Defence, 1988, in *Irish Law Reports Monthly*, 1989, where Judge McCarthy J. points out that '*Further, I see no logical reason why delay, however long, should of itself disentitle the certiorari applicant for that remedy who can demonstrate that a public wrong has been done to him – that, for instance, a conviction was obtained without jurisdiction, or that, otherwise, the State has wronged him and that that wrong has continued to mar or mark his life.*'

[132]In Chap. 3, para. 3.2.3.

[133]In this regard, see my reconstruction and reinterpretation in Chap. 3, para. 3.2.3.

[134]As correctly observed by L. Flynn, *Whatever Happened to Emmott? The Perfecting of Community Rules on National Time Limits*, p. 67, who speaks of 'dramatic results' for a decision that was not 'really necessary.'

[135]ECJ Judgement of 13 June 2006. Case C-173/03. Traghetti del Mediterraneo. *European Court reports* 2006 Page I-05177, para. 20 of the grounds.

[136]As already explained in Chap. 3, para. 3.4, the topic of State liability is certainly relevant for the argument made here, however it will not be examined.

[137]As rightly noticed by Luiso who analyses the Italian legislation on the matter and observes: '*Are we really sure that the preliminary question has been correctly submitted? In other words, are we sure, in this case, that the judge can be considered as not accountable for the interpretation of legal norms, under the so-called 'safeguard clause'? After what we have seen, this looks unlikely, since what was at stake was not an* error in iudicando, *but an* error in procedendo *by the Corte di Cassazione.*' F.P. Luiso, *La responsabilità civile del magistrato*, para. 6. Author's translation.

[138]In para. 4.3.2.

The last example that I would like to recall here is the *Wienstrom* decision.[139]

This decision is particularly important because, in this case, the Austrian court submitted a preliminary reference that clearly had little to do with the resolution of the dispute before it. Thus, it forced the Court to appeal to the power that it has '*...in exceptional circumstances...* [*to*] *examine the conditions in which the case was referred to it by the national court, in order to assess whether it has jurisdiction.*'[140]

In fact, while the preliminary question was about the provision of Art. 117, 1, 2 of *BVergG* on the irrelevance of the errors in the administrative procedure, those errors related to the tender procedure – which the case under analysis was about – were actually all outside the scope of that provision.[141]

Why, then, once again, a 'mistaken' preliminary reference was submitted to the ECJ?

The answer to this question is, from my point of view, and given what has been hitherto said, quite obvious: it is an attempt to obtain from the ECJ a 'EU law' solution in relation to a matter that is only relevant at the national level. Even more, the national court has the clear objective of forcing in the desired direction the national procedural law, expecting to change, through this trick, a consolidated national jurisprudence with which the national court does not agree or which it considers to be obsolete.[142]

Once again, therefore, the national court uses the preliminary ruling procedure in an instrumental way in order to overcome what it perceives as 'critical elements'[143]

---

[139]That I have already reviewed elsewhere. ECJ Judgement of 4 December 2003. Case C-448/01. EVN AG and Wienstrom GmbH v Republik Österreich, in *Riv. it. dir. pubbl. com.*, 2004/1, with comment by D.U. Galetta, *Vizi procedurali e vizi sostanziali al vaglio della Corte di giustizia (che non si pronuncia sulla questione)*, p. 317 ff.

[140]See para. 75 of the grounds in Wienstrom. In this sense, see in particular, among many, Judgement of the ECJ of 16 December 1981. Case 244/80. Foglia v Novello II. *European Court reports* 1981 Page 03045, para. 21 of the grounds; Judgement of the ECJ of 13 March 2001. Case C-379/98. Preussen-Elektra. *European Court reports* 2001 Page I-02099, para. 39 of the grounds; Judgement of the ECJ of 22 January 2002. Case C-390/99. Canal Satélite Digital SL. *European Court reports* 2002 Page I-00607, para. 19 of the grounds. This is because '*The spirit of cooperation which must prevail in the preliminary-ruling procedure requires the national court to have regard to the function entrusted to the Court of Justice, which is to assist in the administration of justice in the Member States and not to deliver advisory opinions on general or hypothetical questions.*' See, particularly, ECJ Judgement of 16 July 1992. Case C-83/91. Meilicke. *European Court reports* 1992 Page I-04871, para. 25 of the grounds; ECJ Judgement of 10 December 2002. Case C-153/00. der Weduwe. *European Court reports* 2002 Page I-11319, para. 32 of the grounds; ECJ Judgement of 21 January 2003. Case C-318/00. Bacardi-Martini SAS and Cellier des Dauphins. *European Court reports* 2003 Page I-00905, para. 41 of the grounds.

[141]As noted by the ECJ in para. 81 of the grounds in Wienstrom.

[142]Some authors have observed recently that this is a trend especially of the so-called 'lower courts.' See G. Martinico, *L'integrazione silente. La funzione interpretativa della Corte di giustizia e il diritto costituzionale europeo*, p. 70 ff.

[143]This case was about a norm of the Austrian *BVergG* that does not allow the possibility of annulment *in each and every case* of procedural errors within an administrative proceeding, but only when these errors are serious and have an impact on the final administrative act.

of its national procedural law.[144] It does this by means of a preliminary reference that in this specific case was not well constructed and therefore did not pass the ECJ's admissibility scrutiny. But the other cases examined so far have passed this scrutiny producing effects well beyond what it was perhaps possible to predict.

4.3.4 Continued. *The Subsequent Role of the Referring Courts: Binding Force of a Decision on Preliminary Ruling, Margin of Appreciation of the National Court and Obligation of Consistent Interpretation*

Despite the fact that the preliminary ruling procedure often plays the role of an 'action of non-fulfilment submitted by an individual'[145] and that – as already noted – the decision on a preliminary ruling is binding for the national court, the latter is still always left with some margin of appreciation. Hence, the decision on a preliminary ruling only provides the premise for a reasoning which the national court is expected to complete.[146]

Regarding this last point, I must agree with those scholars who rightly observe that the task of the national court is far from mechanical.[147] In fact, it is true[148] that together with the interpretation, the ECJ sometimes also provides the court *a quo* with directions on the application of EU law. Anyway, the procedural autonomy of Member States, as has been defined in the course of this work, is at the bottom end of the mechanism of preliminary ruling and consists of the autonomous choice of means aimed at ensuring the effectiveness of EU law[149]: of those provision of EU law about which the ECJ has given its legally binding interpretation and which is at the source of the reference for a preliminary ruling.

---

[144]In this sense, see also the recent reflections of M.P. Chiti, *Diritto amministrativo europeo*, p. 686.

[145]See P. Pescatore, *Il rinvio pregiudiziale di cui all'art. 177 del Trattato CEE e la cooperazione tra la Corte ed i giudici nazionali*, c. 44, who observes that it is not uncommon for the ECJ to find itself taking up, at the same time, actions of non-fulfilment and preliminary references concerning the same subject.

[146]See P. Pescatore, *Il rinvio pregiudiziale di cui all'art. 177 del Trattato CEE e la cooperazione tra la Corte ed i giudici nazionali*, c. 40 s.

[147]In this sense, P. Pescatore, *Il rinvio pregiudiziale di cui all'art. 177 del Trattato CEE e la cooperazione tra la Corte ed i giudici nazionali*, c. 44. Contrary to what Murgia seems incorrectly to believe. See R. Murgia, *Il rinvio pregiudiziale interpretativo davanti alla Corte di giustizia della C.E.*, p. 441 ff., particularly, para. 4.

[148]As has been observed particularly, by F. Sorrentino, *L'art. 177 del Trattato di Roma nel rapporto tra ordinamento comunitario e ordinamenti interni*, p. 739.

[149]See Chap. 2, para. 2.3.

The inclination of the ECJ not to unnecessarily constrain the procedural autonomy of the Member States is already evident from the well-known *Rheinmühlen* decisions[150] onwards. Equally evident is the possibility for a national court to use the 'margin of manoeuvre' left to it by the ECJ's decision on a preliminary ruling, when the national court is truly willing to use it.

A perfect example in this sense is provided by the decision adopted by the German *Bundesverwaltungsgericht* following the reply given by the ECJ to its preliminary questions in the *i-21 Arcor* case.[151] Taking into account the conclusion according to which '*It is for the national court, in the light of the foregoing, to ascertain whether legislation which is clearly incompatible with Community law, such as that on which the fee assessments at issue in the main proceedings is based, constitutes manifest unlawfulness within the meaning of the national law concerned,*'[152] the Federal Administrative Court with two decisions of 17 January 2007[153] decided with a final verdict on the appeals stating in both cases that, given the circumstances, the applicant was entitled neither to the restitutions of the taxes paid, nor to a new decision.[154] In so doing, it successfully made use of that margin of appreciation which is always left to the national jugde by the decision of the ECJ,[155] even if from the perspective of what was defined here as an obligation of consistent interpretation of national procedural law which can consist ultimately of a duty to 'functionalize' the national procedural law.[156]

This duty of 'functionalization' – which we have already addressed – is part of the broader obligation of sincere cooperation under Art. 4.3, TEU (*ex* Art. 10, TEC). Therefore, it not only preserves the margin of appreciation reserved for the national court when delivering a final decision on the proceeding subject to preliminary ruling. But it also – and it is worth expressing it clearly – requires a particular way of exercising this discretion. This means, in my view, that the national court that uses the EU law as an excuse to 'force' the national procedural

[150]See Chap. 3, para. 3.5. On this same point, see in particular G. Raiti, *La collaborazione giudiziaria nell'esperienza del rinvio pregiudiziale comunitario*, p. 282 ff.

[151]ECJ Judgement of 19 September 2006. Joined cases C-392/04 and C-422/04, in Chap. II, para. 2.2.2.

[152]See para. 71 of the grounds in *i-21 Arcor*.

[153]*BVerwG*, decisions of 17 January 2007 – 6 C 32/06 and 6 C 33/06, respectively in *BeckRS*, 2007, No. 2207 and in *BeckRS*, 2007, No. 22258.

[154]In fact, it is stated in both decisions (respectively para.s 7 and 6) that '*Der Rechtsstreit ist fortzusetzen, nachdem der EuGH über die Vorlage des Senats entschieden hat. Die Revision ist unbegründet, so daß sie zurückzuweisen ist (§ 144 II VwGO). Das Oberverwaltungsgericht hat die Klage zu Recht abgewiesen. Die Kl. hat weder einen Anspruch auf Erstattung der Gebühren (1.) noch auf erneute Bescheidung.*'

[155]Of the same opinion, M. Taborowski, *Joined cases C-329/04 e C-422/04, Arcor e.a.*, p. 1476 ff. (1477).

[156]See Chap. 3, para. 3.3.

law beyond what is legally allowed it, also acts in violation of the duty for sincere cooperation prescribed by the EC Treaty.

The importance of these recent decisions of the German *Bundesverwaltungsgericht* in terms of a correct interpretation, in this specific context, of the duty of sincere cooperation is in my opinion even greater if we consider that – as we have seen – the ECJ had already intervened on this problem over the duty of potential 'functionalization' of § 48 *VwVfG*. It did so, particularly, with its decision in *Alcan* of 1997[157] that originated from a reference for a preliminary ruling of the *Bundesverwaltungsgericht* as well.

This decision – which has had a rather modest echo among Italian and other foreign scholars – was the culmination, and also the turning point, of a conflict long existing between the European Commission and the German national administrations.[158] The solution consisted in a reinterpretation by the German courts of the principle of protection of the legitimate expectation – of which § 48 *VwVfG* is its maximum expression – that is compatible with EU law, particularly in the case of the implementation of decisions on the recovery of aid adopted by the Commission.[159] Therefore, again, taking into consideration the obligation of sincere cooperation – and after more than thirty years of worthless antagonism[160], the German courts have finally 'functionalized' § 48 *VwVfG* in order to ensure the effectiveness of EU law on matters of aid. This, however, has not prevented the *Bundesverwaltungsgericht* from ruling in a different way in a case related to the recovery of sums levied in breach of the EU law, which differs in several aspects from that related to the recovery of aid unlawfully paid.

I believe that the recent approach of the German courts in this context, which emerges from the decisions already examined, coincides with a correct interpretation of the 'procedural competence' of the Member States, as defined in Chapter 2. In fact, while meeting the exigency of effectiveness of EU substantive law, this approach preserves the discretion on the choice of means that characterize – as has been said – the concept of 'procedural autonomy.' In this sense, it is entirely consistent with the obligation of sincere cooperation under Art. 4.3, TEU.

---

[157]ECJ Judgement of 20 March 1997. Case C-24/95, in Chap. 3, para. 3.3.2.

[158]Suffice it to say that, as Hatje reports, between 1958 and 1993 only about 10% of the decisions on the recovery of aid declared unlawful have been enforced by the German administration. This is because the Administration has considered that in 90% of the cases there was a legitimate expectation by the recipient of the aid in the sense of § 48 *VwVfG*. See A. Hatje, *Rechtssicherheit und Vertrauensschutz – Wechselseitige Einwirkumgen zwischen Europäischem Gemeinschaftsrecht und deutschem Verfassungs- und Verwaltungsrecht*, p. 234.

[159]On this point, see D.U. Galetta, *La tutela dell'affidamento nella prospettiva del diritto amministrativo italiano, tedesco e comunitario: un'analisi comparata*, p. 785 ff.

[160]It was an unnecessary and counterproductive conflict that could, however, be repeated in relation to the issue of public contracts awarded by German administrations in violation of the provisions of the EU directives on the subject, as we will see in para. 4.5.

4.3.5 The Relationship Between Obligation of Sincere Cooperation Under Art. 4, Third Paragraph, TEU (ex Art. 10 TEC) and Preliminary Ruling: Concluding Remarks

Art. 4, third paragraph, TEU, is a true hymn to cooperation. It states, in fact, that "*Pursuant to the principle of sincere cooperation, the Union and the Member States shall, in full mutual respect, assist each other in carrying out tasks which flow from the Treaties*" and that "*The Member States shall take any appropriate measure, general or particular, to ensure fulfilment of the obligations arising out of the Treaties or resulting from the acts of the institutions of the Union*". Also, that "*The Member States shall facilitate the achievement of the Union's tasks and refrain from any measure which could jeopardise the attainment of the Union's objectives*". According to the unanimous interpretation of doctrine and jurisprudence, it is a mutual duty of cooperation between EU institutions and Member States.[161]

At this point of the analysis, I think the crucial role that the instrument of preliminary ruling plays in the context of this mutual duty of cooperation between Member States and EU institutions is evident. In this respect, Pescatore observed more than twenty years ago that '*The preliminary ruling is based on a distribution of the functions between national court and community court, on the association between the two to achieve a common goal, constituted by the correct application of the community law within the Community. It does not create a hierarchy between national courts and the Court of Justice.*'[162] In his opinion it is rather a dialogue that has started and must continue '*in the spirit of a cooperation that can only work if it is mutual.*'[163] In this sense – and to conclude with this point, it seems to me that, based on the analysis made so far, there is instead an attitude in certain national courts (often supported by some apparently unconscious academics) that seems symptomatic of what the above mentioned author described as a '*rejection of dialogue*' and even sometimes identified as '*refusal to accept the consequences of the creation of the European Community.*'[164]

---

[161]On this point, see for all O. Porchia, *I principi dell'ordinamento europeo. La cooperazione pluridirezionale*, p. 7 f., particularly note No. 26.

[162]See P. Pescatore, *Il rinvio pregiudiziale di cui all'art. 177 del Trattato CEE e la cooperazione tra la Corte ed i giudici nazionali*, c. 30 s. and (in exactly the same sense) R. Lecourt, *L'Europe des juges*, p. 272 f.; R. Joliet, *L'article 177 du Traité CEE et le renvoi prejudiciel*, p. 595. On this point, see however, more recently, the observations of G. Falcon, *Separazione e coordinamento tra giurisdizioni europee e giurisdizioni nazionali nella tutela avverso gli atti lesivi di situazioni soggettive europee*, p. 1153 ff.; O. Dubos, *Les juridictions nationales, juge communautaire*, p. 705.

[163]See P. Pescatore, note above. Author's translation. See also R. Lecourt, *L'Europe des juges*, p. 272 f.

[164]See P. Pescatore, *Il rinvio pregiudiziale di cui all'art. 177 del Trattato CEE e la cooperazione tra la Corte ed i giudici nazionali*, c. 45. Author's translation.

However, if it is true – as I believe – that the history of European integration is also and above all the history of the integration between the courts,[165] then we must believe in the value of the prophecy about the fate of progressive isolation to which the national courts are predestined if they refuse to cooperate.[166] They – it has been stated – will inevitably be forced to fight in their defence and be beaten by the unstoppable progress of legal integration.[167] This seems to be confirmed by the 'EU compatible' outcome that has distinguished most of the important jurisprudential developments analyzed in the third Chapter.

There remains to be assessed, however, the other aspect of the matter discussed earlier in relation to the so called unnecessary or 'mistaken' preliminary references. To conclude, I will identify this aspect more clearly as a duty on the national courts, in consideration of the obligation of sincere cooperation under Art. 4.3, TEU (*ex* Art. 10 TEC), not to submit preliminary references to the ECJ that do not have the purpose of obtaining the interpretation of EU law that is necessary and instrumental to the solution to the dispute pending before them. In fact, preliminary references are instead often used to essentially asking the ECJ for directions to implement in its national law a provision of EU law already clear in itself, but whose observance is hindered by procedural domestic norms[168] that do not allow the swift and lineal fulfilment of the effectiveness of EU substantive law. But this is an objective which, considering the duty of sincere cooperation, the national courts as decentralized EU courts[169] must pursue as much as possible 'on their own.' Thus, they should face the risks and difficulties that this task entails[170] and without necessarily involving the

---

[165]R. Joliet, *L'article 177 du Traité CEE et le renvoi prejudicial*, p. 616 points out that "*Tout le monde s'accorde à dire que la coopération entre la Cour de justice et les juridictions nationales instituée par l'art. 177 du Traité de Rome set l'un des plus grand succès dont puisse s'enorgueillir la construction communautaire*". This has been pointed out again by some authors recently. See G. Martinico, *L'integrazione silente. La funzione interpretativa della Corte di giustizia e il diritto costituzionale europeo*, p. 138 ff. On this point, see also the study of R. Caranta, *Giustizia amministrativa e diritto comunitario, passim.*

[166]For a recent analysis on the methods of non-cooperation see further N. Gross, *Le renvoi préjudiciel devant la Cour de Justice des Communautés Européennes – Contraintes, Hésitation et Refus*, 331 ff.

[167]In this sense, P. Pescatore, *Il rinvio pregiudiziale di cui all'art. 177 del Trattato CEE e la cooperazione tra la Corte ed i giudici nazionali*, c. 46.

[168]On this point, see the reflections of C. Schepisi, *Sull'applicabilità d'ufficio delle norme comunitarie da parte dei giudici nazionali*, para. 6.

[169]See A. Tizzano, in R. Adam, A. Tizzano, *Lineamenti di diritto dell'Unione europea*, p. 304. In this regard, see also J. Ziller, J. Lotarski, *Institutions et organes judiciaires*, p. 70, who proposed to introduce in the EC Treaty a specification about the role of the national courts stating that they '*sont associées à la mission de la Cour de justice.*'

[170]See the recent reflections of O. Porchia, *I principi dell'ordinamento europeo. La cooperazione pluridirezionale*, p. 240 ff., regarding the need for the national authorities (including judges) to '*assume their own responsibility*' (p. 252). Author's translation.

ECJ, through the use of preliminary references as pretexts to 'shift' the (political and moral) responsibility of the final decision to the ECJ.[171]

4.4 The Directives on Public Procurement Procedures and the Procedural Competence of the Member States: Brief Remarks to Better Understand the Distinction Between the Lack of Procedural Competence and Functionalized Procedural Competence of the Member States

When it comes to the procedural autonomy of the Member States we need to distinguish clearly between two types of cases. On the one hand, those cases in which this autonomy exists, but suffers from serious limitations as a result of the indications emerging from the ECJ's jurisprudence. In these cases, procedural autonomy should be more properly qualified as 'functionalized procedural competence.' On the other hand, in other cases this autonomy disappears altogether,[172] because there are specific EU provisions on procedural matters (where 'procedural matters' should always be understood in the broader sense, as explained in Chapter 1)[173] and, as a consequence, there is no residual competence of the Member States in these matters, not even in the 'functionalized' form.

We have dealt with the first aspect of the problem in the previous chapters.

At this point, then, it is worth rapidly examining the second aspect in order to better clarify the boundaries of the concept of 'procedural autonomy' and clear away from the field possible misunderstandings regarding its actual framing.

---

[171]In addition to those thus far examined a further example of this approach is the preliminary reference of the TAR di Milano in the *Santex* case of 2003 (ECJ Judgement of 27 February 2003. Case C-327/00. Santex. *European Court reports* 2003 Page I-01877) where the ECJ was requested once again to give its opinion on the question of compatibility of the time limits prescribed in national law with the EU law – in this case, in the particular context of public contracts. The question – as seen in Chap. 3 – has been posed in other cases before the ECJ, which had already decided on the matter in its *Rewe* jurisprudence. The ECJ had always consistently maintained the compatibility of such time limits with EU law provided that they respect the principles of equivalence and effectiveness. Also in this case the ECJ reaffirms its consolidated case law on the point, stating in perfect harmony with its *Emmott* jurisprudence of 1991 that '*In the circumstances of the case in the main proceedings, the changing conduct of the contracting authority may be considered, in view of a limitation period, to have rendered excessively difficult the exercise by the harmed tenderer of the rights conferred on him by Community law.*'(para. 61). Though, it was clear that the TAR's reference was aimed at 'shifting' to the ECJ the responsibility over an outcome that it could have well found by itself in the national procedural law by appealing to the institution of the so called 'excusable error' ('*errore scusabile*'). On this point, see in particular G. Biagioni, *Norme processuali e principio di effettività: ulteriori sviluppi nella giurisprudenza comunitaria*, p. 211 ff.

[172]As will be explained below, it only remains the competence of '*national authorities* [*on*] *the choice of form and methods*' laid down in Art. 288, para. 3, TFEU (*ex* Art. 249.3, TEC), given the fact that the legislation in question has been adopted using directives and not regulations.

[173]In para. 1.1.

Given this specific objective, the directives that are particularly relevant are the so-called directives on public procurement procedures (directives 89/665/EEC and 92/13/EEC[174], recently modified by Directive 2007/66/EC), many times mentioned throughout this study.

Although they are not, in fact, the only example of EU legislation that includes detailed rules on procedure,[175] they are however the only example of EU norms containing common procedural rules whose exclusive legal basis is Art. 95, TEC (now Art. 114, TFEU). Then, these norms fall into this specific scenario of the 'exceptional' EU competence on procedural matters already mentioned (which is, thus, an exception to the rule of the procedural competence of the Member States, identified in Chapter 2)[176] and which has been recognised by the ECJ since the *Rewe* decision. In this important precedent the ECJ in fact emphasized that '... *Articles 100 to 102*[177] *and 235 of the Treaty enable appropriate measures to be taken to remedy differences between the provisions laid down by law, regulation or administrative action in Member States if they are likely to distort or harm the functioning of the common market.*'[178]

In fact, as is apparent from the reading of the first recital of both directives, the problem that underlies their adoption was precisely the need to ensure the effectiveness of EU directives that coordinate the procedures for the award of public contracts in various sectors. As the second recital of Directive 89/665/EEC states,

---

[174]These are the Council Directive 89/665/EEC, of 21 December 1989 on the coordination of the laws, regulations and administrative provisions relating to the application of review procedures to the award of public supply and public works contracts, *Official Journal of the European Communities* L 395, 30.12.1989, p. 33, and the Council Directive 92/13/EEC, of 25 February 1992 coordinating the laws, regulations and administrative provisions relating to the application of Community rules on the procurement procedures of entities operating in the water, energy, transport and telecommunications sectors, *Official Journal of the European Communities* L 76, 23.3.1992, p. 14.

[175]As noted by E. Picozza, *L'effettività della tutela giurisdizionale nel processo amministrativo, rispetto al diritto comunitario*, p. 1 ff. On this matter, we can mention here in particular a number of directives on consumer protection. Particularly, Directive 98/27/EC of the European Parliament and of the Council of 19 May 1998 on injunctions for the protection of consumer interests, *Official Journal of the European Communities* L 166, 11. 6. 98, p. 51; in a less detailed way also Council Directive 93/13/EEC of 5 April 1993 on unfair terms in consumer contracts, *Official Journal of the European Communities* L 95, 21.4.1993, p. 29; as well as Directive 2002/65/EC of the European Parliament and of the Council of 23 September 2002 concerning the distance marketing of consumer financial services and amending Council Directive 90/619/EEC and Directives 97/7/EC and 98/27/EC, *Official Journal of the European Communities* L 271, 9.10.2002, p. 16. On this topic, see also G. Morbidelli, *La tutela giurisdizionale dei diritti nell'ordinamento comunitario*, p. 35 ff.

[176]See Chap. 2, para. 2.2.

[177]I am not ignoring the implications that may arise from the decision to use Art. 114, TFEU (*ex* Art. 95, TEC), as legal basis, instead of Art. 115, TFEU (*ex* Art. 94, TEC – former A\rt. 100, EEC). But this is not the place for a thorough analysis of this point. To that end, see among others F. Caruso, *Art. 94 TCE*; Id., *Art. 95 TCE*.

[178]ECJ Judgement of 16 December 1976. Case 33-76. Rewe. *European Court reports* 1976 Page 01989, para. 5.

'*...the existing arrangements at both national and Community levels for ensuring their application are not always adequate to ensure compliance with the relevant Community provisions particularly at a stage when infringements can be corrected.*'[179]

Without the need to enter into details of the individual provisions of the two directives mentioned here – which have been extensively examined by many scholars[180] – suffice it to say that in order to adapt them to the current conditions, these directives have been recently modified by Directive 2007/66/EC.[181] The process of approval of this directive demonstrates the significant effort made by the EU institutions to achieve a high degree of uniformity in the field of public procurement also with regard to procedural matters. In fact, the third recital states that '*Consultations of the interested parties and the case law of the Court of Justice have revealed a certain number of weaknesses in the review mechanisms in the Member States*' and that '*As a result of these weaknesses, the mechanisms established by Directives 89/665/EEC and 92/13/EEC do not always make it possible to ensure compliance with Community law, especially at a time when infringements can still be corrected.*' This fact clearly emerges from an analysis of the jurisprudence of the ECJ on this issue, where there are a considerable number of actions of non-fulfilment submitted by the Commission against the Member States according to Art. 226, TEC (now Art. 258, TFEU).

If the ultimate goal of the new directive is, therefore, to allow for greater effectiveness of EU norms on public procurements, the instrument used – according to the scheme already analyzed in Chapter 2[182] – is to provide uniform procedural norms that ensure the effectiveness of the judicial protection of the private parties concerned.

In this regard and particularly in relation to the stage prior to the conclusion of the contract, given the fact that '... *the absence of a period allowing an effective*

---

[179] And in an almost similar sense the second recital of Directive 92/13/EEC.

[180] For an in depth analysis of the specific content of these directives, whose study exceeds the scope of the present work, see in particular M. Protto, *L'effettività della tutela giurisdizionale nelle procedure di aggiudicazione di pubblici appalti*, p. 112 ff. and, more recently, S. Tarullo, *Il giusto processo amministrativo*, p. 89 ff. See moreover, among others, O.M. Papadopoulou, *Vers une protection juridictionnelle commune en Europe: la directive « Recours » 89/665/CEE*, p. 947 ff. and, finally, M. A. Sandulli, *Diritto europeo e processo amministrativo*, p. 41 ff.

[181] Directive 2007/66/EC of the European Parliament and of the Council of 11 December 2007 amending Council Directives 89/665/EEC and 92/13/EEC with regard to improving the effectiveness of review procedures concerning the award of public contracts, in http://europa.eu/index_en.htm. For a comment on this directive see, in particular, A. Bartolini, S. Fantini, *La nuova direttiva ricorsi*, p. 1093 ff.; G. Greco, *La direttiva 2007/66/CE: illegittimità comunitaria, sorte del contratto ed effetti collaterali indotti*, p. 1029 ff.; G. Kalflèche, *La modification des directives « recours » en matière de marchés publics. Une boule de cristal pour le contentieux des contracts publics*, p. 4 ff.; M. Lipari, *Annullamento dell'aggiudicazione ed effetti del contratto: la parola al diritto comunitario*, p. 1 ff.; F. Satta, *Annullamento dell'aggiudicazione: la fine di un problema*, p. 1 ff. See as well M.A. Sandulli, *Il processo amministrativo superaccelerato e i nuovi contratti ricorso-resistenti*, p. 1 ff.

[182] See in particular Chap. 2, para. 2.6.

review between the decision to award a contract and the conclusion of the contract in question... sometimes results in contracting authorities and contracting entities who wish to make irreversible the consequences of the disputed award decision proceeding very quickly to the signature of the contract,'[183] the new directive introduces the obligation to provide for a standstill period.[184]

Regarding the effectiveness of the instruments that should be made available once the contract has been concluded – and in addition to the new provisions concerning precautionary protection and punitive damages[185] – the norms of the new directive imposing the obligation to render ineffective a contract already concluded in case of the most serious violations – when explicitly stated – are particularly relevant.[186] This is particularly true in the case of the unlawful direct award of contracts.

As is stated in the fourteenth recital, '*Ineffectiveness is the most effective way to restore competition and to create new business opportunities for those economic operators which have been deprived illegally of their opportunity to compete*' with the specification that '*Direct awards within the meaning of this Directive should include all contract awards made without prior publication of a contract notice.*'[187] This is in order to guarantee the effectiveness of the EU substantive law on public procurements, through the provision of '*effective, proportionate and dissuasive sanctions.*'[188] In fact, as has correctly been noted, the directive links the deprivation of the effects of a contract to a strong punitive element to the disadvantage of the administration that was wrong, and not to a restorative function of the legal position of the person injured by the violation.[189]

In conclusion, therefore, it can be said that the new directive intervenes in a more incisive way in comparison with the two previous ones by reducing even more the sphere of the procedural competence of the Member States in the specific field of public procurements. In this particular area – as we have already advanced – the Union has exercised a normative competence in procedural matters that it has drawn from the norm of Art. 95, TEC (now Art. 114, TFEU). Then, regarding the legal provisions included in the Directive in question, the procedural competence of the Member States entirely disappears and, as a consequence (as already put forward in point B of the Introduction), we can no longer speak of the procedural autonomy of the Member States.

In this specific context, therefore, the Member States are only left with the competence of '*national authorities* [*on*] *the choice of form and methods*' laid

---

[183]See recital 4 of Directive 2007/66/EC.

[184]Since, as recital 4 continues, this absence '*... is a serious obstacle to effective judicial protection for the tenderers concerned, namely those tenderers who have not yet been definitively excluded.*'

[185]On this, see particularly M. Lipari, *Annullamento dell'aggiudicazione ed effetti del contratto: la parola al diritto comunitario*, para. 6 and 16 ff.

[186]See new Article 2d, introduced by Directive 66/2007.

[187]See recital 14 of Directive 2007/66/EC.

[188]Requirement reaffirmed in recital 13 of the Directive 2007/66/EC.

[189]In this sense, M. Lipari, *Annullamento dell'aggiudicazione ed effetti del contratto: la parola al diritto comunitario*, para. 8.

down in Art. 288, paragraph 3, TFEU (*ex* Art. 249.3, TEC), because of the fact that the legislation in question has been adopted using the instrument of the directive and not by adopting a regulation.[190] And if – as we have seen[191] – there is certainly a fundamental affinity between the idea of procedural autonomy and the mechanism that underlies the use of the directive, they are, however, two quite different situations. In fact, from the perspective of the judicial supervisory role of the ECJ, the disappearance of the procedural competence that has been outlined here is quite a different matter from the limitation of procedural autonomy in the light of the 'functionalized procedural competence.'

Regarding the ambit specifically regulated by the directives, the principles of direct effect and primacy of EU procedural law over the national procedural law that is in conflict with the provisions of these directives, apply.

As to the consequences that may be drawn from them to date for the Italian national legal order, the answer should necessarily be broken down.

If we take into account the legal framework outlined by the Italian Code of Public Contracts,[192] the new Directive introduced very few new substantial elements as its content had been largely anticipated by the Code itself.[193] So regarding this specific normative context, the only major innovation introduced by the new Directive is the obligation to state the possibility that the decision on the ineffectiveness of a contract awarded in contrast to EU law be ordered by '*a review body independent of the contracting authority*' or that '*is the result of a decision of such a review body.*'[194] But apart from this specific obligation imposed by the new Directive – and which applies only to cases of serious breach of substantive law, specifically listed in the new Article 2d, for all other cases, the EU legislator deliberately does not address the question of the relationship between the annulment of awards that are in conflict with EU law and the consequences for the contract,[195] leaving the national legislators with a broad margin for manoeuvre on the issue.

[190]That, according to 288.3, TFEU is binding on the Member State to which it is addressed with regard to the result to be achieved, but shall leave to the national authorities the choice of form and methods.

[191]In Chap. 2, para. 2.5.

[192]I refer to the Legislative Decree of 12 April 2006, No. 163 'Codice dei contratti pubblici relativi a lavori, servizi e forniture in attuazione delle direttive 2004/17/CE e 2004/18/CE,' in *GU* n. 100 of 2 May 2006, s.o. n. 107.

[193]See M.A Sandulli *Il processo amministrativo superaccelerato e i nuovi contratti ricorso-resistenti, passim.*

[194]See Art. 2, d. And to this end, it would be appropriate to provide, in the transposed national legislation, a broader *ius standi* that includes the contract between the legitimate parties in the procedure to deprive the contract of its effects. On this point, see M. Lipari, *Annullamento dell'aggiudicazione ed effetti del contratto: la parola al diritto comunitario*, para. 14.

[195]As observed by M. Lipari, *Annullamento dell'aggiudicazione ed effetti del contratto: la parola al diritto comunitario*, para. 8, '*In this regard, the "neutrality" of the community directive is the greatest. There is neither a particular advantage, nor a particular disadvantage in the provision on the deprivation of effects of the contract.*' Author's translation.

This national legal framework, which is substantially compatible with the provisions of Directive 66/2007, however, has been drastically altered by the recent Law of 28 January 2009, No. 2[196] and, in particular, by the provision in its Art. 20 that states: '*Extraordinary rules for speeding up the enforcement proceedings of projects which form part of the national strategic framework and the symmetrical reform of its respective administrative regime.*' As has rightly been stated,[197] the norm in question – whose ambit of application is actually very broad and not limited solely to 'strategic infrastructure'[198] – contains provisions to 'accelerate' the process,[199] which clearly are in the opposite direction to the regulation of the new Directive

[196] Law of 28 January 2009, No. 2 'Conversione in legge, con modificazioni, del decreto-legge 29 novembre 2008, n. 185, recante misure urgenti per il sostegno a famiglie, lavoro, occupazione e impresa e per ridisegnare in funzione anti-crisi il quadro strategico nazionale,' in *GU* n. 22 of 28 January 2009, s.o. n. 14.

[197] By M.A. Sandulli, *Il processo amministrativo superaccelerato e i nuovi contratti ricorso-resistenti*, p. 1 ff.

[198] See Author op.cit., note above, p. 7.

[199] In particular, para.s 8 and 8 bis of Art. 20 Para. 8 stipulates that: '*I provvedimenti adottati ai sensi del presente articolo sono comunicati agli interessati a mezzo fax o posta elettronica all'indirizzo da essi indicato. L'accesso agli atti del procedimento è consentito entro dieci giorni dall'invio della comunicazione del provvedimento. Il termine per la notificazione del ricorso al competente Tribunale amministrativo regionale avverso i provvedimenti emanati ai sensi del presente articolo è di trenta giorni dalla comunicazione o dall'avvenuta conoscenza, comunque acquisita. Il ricorso principale va depositato presso il T.a.r. entro cinque giorni dalla scadenza del termine di notificazione del ricorso; in luogo della prova della notifica può essere depositata attestazione dell'ufficiale giudiziario che il ricorso è stato consegnato per le notifiche; la prova delle eseguite notifiche va depositata entro cinque giorni da quando è disponibile. Le altre parti si costituiscono entro dieci giorni dalla notificazione del ricorso principale e entro lo stesso termine possono proporre ricorso incidentale; il ricorso incidentale va depositato con le modalità e termini previsti per il ricorso principale. I motivi aggiunti possono essere proposti entro dieci giorni dall'accesso agli atti e vanno notificati e depositati con le modalità previste per il ricorso principale. Il processo viene definito ad una udienza da fissarsi entro 15 giorni dalla scadenza del termine per la costituzione delle parti diverse dal ricorrente; il dispositivo della sentenza è pubblicato in udienza; la sentenza è redatta in forma semplificata, con i criteri di cui all'articolo 26, quarto comma, della legge 6 dicembre 1971 n. 1034. Le misure cautelari e l'annullamento dei provvedimenti impugnati non possono comportare, in alcun caso, la sospensione o la caducazione degli effetti del contratto già stipulato, e, in caso di annullamento degli atti della procedura, il giudice può esclusivamente disporre il risarcimento degli eventuali danni, ove comprovati, solo per equivalente. Il risarcimento per equivalente del danno comprovato non può comunque eccedere la misura del decimo dell'importo delle opere che sarebbero state eseguite se il ricorrente fosse risultato aggiudicatario, in base all'offerta economica presentata in gara. Se la parte soccombente ha agito o resistito in giudizio con mala fede o colpa grave si applicano le disposizioni di cui all'articolo 96 del codice di procedura civile. Per quanto non espressamente disposto dal presente articolo, si applica l'articolo 23-bis della legge 6 dicembre 1971 n. 1034 e l'articolo 246 del decreto legislativo 12 aprile 2006, n. 163 e successive modificazioni. Dall'attuazione del presente comma non devono derivare nuovi o maggiori oneri a carico della finanza pubblicai.*' While para. 8 bis specifies that '*Per la stipulazione dei contratti ai sensi del presente articolo non si applica il termine di trenta giorni previsto dall'articolo 11, comma 10, del codice dei contratti pubblici relativi a lavori, servizi e forniture, di cui al decreto legislativo 12 aprile 2006, n. 163.*'

66/2007. In fact, those provisions are essentially aimed to discourage any form of judicial action in order to enable the prompt execution of the works.[200] And even though the deadline for transposing the Directive expired on 20 December 2009, according to the jurisprudence of the ECJ on the so called standstill obligation, if Member States are not required to fulfil their obligations of transposition prior to the expiration of the deadline, they still must refrain, in the meantime, from adopting measures which may seriously jeopardize the result prescribed by the directive.[201]

As for the consequences arising from this obvious contrast between Art. 20 (Law 2009/2) and the new Directive, in addition to the risk of a decision against Italy under Art. 258 TFEU (for non-compliance with the obligations of the Member States under the EU Treaty), it is clear that – since we are dealing here with a case of advocation of the competence on procedural matters to the Union – the possible conflict between EU procedural norms and national procedural norms arises in relation to the principle of primacy. Then, now that the deadline for transposing the Directive has expired, the national provisions in conflict with those contained in the Directive should (by virtue of the principle of primacy) be disapplied by the national courts and eventually replaced by the norms of Directive 66/2007, which have the necessary requirements to be considered of direct effect.[202]

4.5 *Continued.* Procedural Autonomy of the Member States in the Areas Not Explicitly Regulated by the Directives on Public Procurement Procedures: Concluding Remarks on 'Functionalized Procedural Competence' in the Field of Public Procurements in View of the ECJ's Recent Jurisprudence

The disappearance of procedural competence and, therefore, of the procedural autonomy of the Member States – with the consequences already mentioned – is

[200]See M.A. Sandulli, *Il processo amministrativo superaccelerato e i nuovi contratti ricorso-resistenti*, p. 2.

[201]See particularly ECJ Judgement of 18 December 1997. Case C-129/96. Inter-Environnement Wallonie. *European Court reports* 1997 Page I-07411, para. 45. In this regard, Sandulli correctly points out that this is the situation in the present case. She speaks of norms that are '*aimed at discouraging from the beginning any action, both abrogative and restorative ones.*' (p. 21). M.A. Sandulli, *Il processo amministrativo superaccelerato e i nuovi contratti ricorso-resistenti*, p. 1 ff. Author's translation.

[202]However, in the meantime the Italian Parliament has delegated the Government to adopt a law reforming the whole of the Italian administrative process with art. Art. 44 *(Delega al Governo per il riassetto della disciplina del processo amministrativo)* of the Law of 18 June 2009, n. 69 "Disposizioni per lo sviluppo economico, la semplificazione, la competitività nonché in materia di processo civile", in *Gazzetta Ufficiale* n. 140 of 19 June 2009. In the mean time, while the book was already being printed, the Directive 66/2007 has been transposed with legislative decree of 20 March 2010, No 53, in *GU* n.84 of 12 April 2010.

true only for specific areas in which the EU legislator has provided for norms on procedural matters. In this sense, he substitutes the *autonomous choice of sanction*,[203] which as stated should constitute the procedural autonomy,[204] with the adoption of the same legal tools for everyone (the Member States). But in the remaining procedural areas not covered by the directives on public procurement procedures, the concept of procedural autonomy obviously comes back into play.

Regarding public contracts there is, then, a procedural area covered by the provisions of the directives in this field – and removed, thus, from the procedural competence of the Member States – which is now broader, as a result of the new Directive 2007/66/EC. However, for all matters not expressly regulated by this directive, it remains an area of competence of the Member States and, consequently, of procedural autonomy.

This does not exclude, however, the restriction of the procedural autonomy by the ECJ according to the criteria examined in the previous chapter: the two *Rewe* criteria of equal treatment and effectiveness, together with the obligation of consistent interpretation of national procedural law with the requirements imposed by the EU substantive law. As a result, this is therefore defined in terms of 'functionalized procedural competence' with respect to the objective of ensuring the effectiveness of the EU substantive law on public procurements.

To better understand this reasoning, it is possible to provide a concrete example of what we have just described, drawn from the recent case law of the ECJ. This is the judgement of 10 April 2003 in joined cases C-20 and C-28/01,[205] and the subsequent judgement of 18 July 2007 (which decides over the lack of compliance with the previous decision) in case C-503/04,[206] which form a very interesting whole. For the first time the ECJ – as a result of the comments submitted by the German government and supported by the United Kingdom government[207] – has

---

[203]Understood, as mentioned above, in the sense indicated by *Mertens de Wilmars*, that is, as instruments of legal coercion aimed at ensuring the effectiveness of the EU substantive law. J. Mertens de Wilmars, *L'efficacité des différentes techniques nationales de protection juridique contre les violations du droit communautaire par les autorités nationales et les particuliers*, p. 390.

[204]In Chap. 2, para. 2.3.

[205]ECJ Judgement of 10 April 2003. Joined cases C-20/01 and C-28/01. Commission of the European Communities v Federal Republic of Germany. *European Court reports* 2003 Page I-03609.

[206]ECJ Judgement of 18 July 2007. Case C-503/04. Commission of the European Communities v Federal Republic of Germany. *European Court reports* 2007 Page I-06153.

[207]As is stated in para. 31 of the Opinion of Mr Advocate General Geelhoed delivered on 28 November 2002 '*The United Kingdom Government points out in its statement in intervention that it calls into question not the admissibility of the actions but — in part — their merits. In the light also of Directive 89/665, it submits that the question whether it is possible to terminate a contract for which, wrongfully, no invitation to tender was issued, in breach of Community law, is always a matter which falls within the competence of the Member State concerned.*' It is for this reason that the ECJ explicitly decides on an aspect that – as we shall see – does not seem to be central for the settlement of the dispute.

looked specifically at the issue concerning the fate of the contract concluded as a result of an award procedure in breach of EU law. Even if – as we have seen – the new Directive introduces slight changes on this point, the considerations of the ECJ in these important decisions are still in any case of great relevance because they will be valid in the future for all those cases in which the new Directive leaves Member States free to decide on the fate of the contracts.

Turning to the dispute under examination by the referred decisions, as said, the previous directives left Member States entirely free to decide over the fate of the contract. They both explicitly provided that '*The effects of the exercise of the powers referred to in paragraph 1 on a contract concluded subsequent to its award shall be determined by national law.*'[208]

The provision quoted above has to be framed in the context of directives whose specific objective – as is apparent from the recitals of the directives in question – is to ensure that Member States provide for 'effective remedies,' so that the opening of public procurements to EU competition is effective and businesses are encouraged to participate in procedures for the award of public contracts in the various Member States. Thus, it implies the possibility for Member States to decide freely, but according to the principle of effective judicial protection of the applicants, what the specific effects on the already concluded contract will be of review mechanisms that should anyway involve the possibility of obtaining precautionary protection, the annulment of the award and the reparation of the damages.[209] This means that in this particular context – according to our observations in the previous paragraph – we are not dealing with a problem of procedural autonomy of the Member States, but rather with one of correct or incorrect transposition of the directive regarding the specific outcome of effective judicial protection that it pursues.

This means though that – apart from this specific area covered by the directives and which concerns, I repeat, only the protection of the applicant affected by the unlawful award – moreover the action of the Member States aimed at ensuring the effectiveness of EU substantive law on public contract[210] is subject to the limitations to which, more generally, the procedural autonomy of Member States is subjected. As we shall see, this is why in its decision in Case C-503/04 and completely in line with the criteria defining the concept of procedural autonomy, the ECJ concluded that, since there had been no rescission of the contract concluded as a result of an award procedure in breach of EU law, Germany had not adopted '... *at the date on which the period laid down in the reasoned opinion issued by the Commission pursuant to Article 228 EC, ... all the necessary measures to comply with the judgement in Joined Cases C-20/01 and C-28/01 Commission v Germany*

[208]See Art. 2, No. 6, of both directives.

[209]See Art. 2, No. 1, of both directives.

[210]Because, certainly, the directives on public procurement procedures are also ultimately aimed at this goal of ensuring the effectiveness of the EU substantive law on public procurement. But this does change the fact that their specific objective is only the provision of effective legal remedies for persons affected by an award that contravenes EU law.

regarding the conclusion of a contract for waste disposal by the City of Brunswick' and it therefore '... *has failed to fulfil its obligations under that article.*'[211]

But let's proceed step by step.

In order to understand the decision in Case C-503/04 it is necessary therefore to know what had happened before: that is, what was the decision issued by the ECJ on 10 April 2003 against Germany about?[212]

In essence, it was a decision that, by bringing together two applications of the Commission under Art. 226, TEC (now Art. 258, TFEU) condemned Germany for the violation, committed by two German municipalities, of Directive 92/50/EEC on the procedures for the award of public service contracts.[213] Both contracts were awarded without inviting tenders, contrary to the requirements of the said Directive.

In both cases, the German government argued in its defence among other things that the national legislation did not offer possibilities for bringing to an end the violation of the directive after the conclusion of the contracts, because under German law the concluded contracts, although unlawful under EU law, could only have been terminated through the payment of very high indemnity and this consequence was disproportionate to the aim pursued by the Commission.[214] Again in this regard, the German government referred to the provision of Art. 2 No. 6 of Directive 89/665/EEC, already recalled, as a suitable element to adapt its own decision to maintain contracts concluded as a result of awards unlawful according to EU norms, and despite the reasoned opinion issued by the Commission under Art. 226 paragraph 1, TEC. But the defence that consisted on arguing the margin of discretion left to the national legislator by the Directive on public procurement procedures, as an excuse for a violation that, instead, is related to EU substantive law on public procurements (and which had been challenged by the Commission in its motivated opinion) was obviously doomed to be unsuccessful. This is because – as explained earlier – the provision of the Directive 89/665/EEC was related to the procedural instruments that should be adopted to guarantee the effective protection of the applicants affected by the unlawful award. However, it did not concern the obligations of the Member States – and, therefore, of all the national administrations – regarding the compliance with EU substantive law on public procurements.

In rejecting the arguments of the German government, the ECJ merely pointed out – assuming the line of reasoning outlined above – that the norm of the Directive on public procurement procedures which aims at protecting the legitimate expectations of the parties '... *cannot be, unless the scope of the Treaty provisions establishing the internal market is to be reduced, that the contracting authority's conduct vis-à-vis third parties is to be regarded as in conformity with Community law following conclusion of such contracts*' and that '*Since the finding of failure by a*

[211]Para. 42 in Case C-503/04.

[212]ECJ Judgement of 10 April 2003. Joined cases C-20/01 and C-28/01.

[213]Council Directive 92/50/EEC of 18 June 1992, *Official Journal of the European Communities* L 209, 24/07/1992 P. 0001 - 0024.

[214]See para.s 11 and 18 of decision in Joined cases C-20/01 and C-28/01.

Member State to fulfil its obligations is not bound up with a finding as to the damage flowing therefrom..., the Federal Republic of Germany may not rely on the fact that no third party has suffered damage in the case of the contracts concluded by the Municipality of Bockhorn and the City of Brunswick.'[215] This makes sense given that the specific aim of the Directives on public procurements is the establishment of the common market in this area and not the mere provision of effective legal remedies to protect third parties affected by awards that are in breach of EU law. In fact, this is only one of the means directed to ensure the greatest effectiveness of the EU substantive law,[216] and it certainly does not exhaust the coercive means that may be used by the Union to enforce the EU substantive law on public procurements upon Member States. This is clearly demonstrated in the decision in Case C-503/04, enacted as a result of the action for non-fulfilment of the judgement of 10 April 2003, submitted by the Commission under Art. 228, TEC (now Art. 260, TFEU).[217]

In this regard, after referring to the above mentioned paragraph 39 of the judgement of 10 April 2003, the ECJ specifies that Art. 2, No. 6 of the Directive 89/665 '*... relates, as is apparent from its wording, to the compensation which a person harmed by an infringement committed by a contracting authority may obtain from it. That provision, because of its specific nature, cannot be regarded also as regulating the relations between a Member State and the Community in the context of Articles 226 EC and 228 EC.*'[218] The ECJ concludes, thus that, with regard to the fact that , '*... the principles of legal certainty and of the protection of legitimate expectations, the principle* pacta sunt servanda *and the right to property could be used against the contracting authority by the other party to the contract in the event of rescission, Member States cannot rely thereon to justify the non-implementation of a judgement establishing a failure to fulfil obligations under Article 226 EC and thereby evade their own liability under Community law.*'[219]

Therefore, even if the decision of the German national Administration not to bring to an end the effects of a contract concluded as a result of an award that violated EU law is not in contrast to the provisions of the directives on public procurement procedures (that explicitly recognize this right), this does not mean, that this '*right is sufficient to exclude the smallest contrast with secondary community law.*'[220] This is so because the exercise of this right is legitimate only in relation

[215]See para.s 39 and 42 of the decision in joined cases C-20/01 and 28/01.

[216]As clearly emerges from the recitals of the directives.

[217]In particular, while one of the two contracts covered by the decision of 10 April 2003 had been annulled during the procedure laid down in Art. 228, TEC (now Art. 260, TFEU), the other had been annulled once the deadline set by the decision expired. It is therefore to this last one that the ECJ's judgement is related.

[218]See para. 35 of the decision in Case C-503/04.

[219]See para. 36 of the decision in Case C-503/04.

[220]This is instead the opinion of G. Greco, *Superprimato del diritto europeo: le direttive sui mezzi di ricorso vincolano tutti, ma non la Commissione e la Corte di Giustizia*, p. 435. Author's translation.

to the exigency of effective judicial protection of the applicant (third party affected), as established in the directives. However, this cannot be brought into play as a defence in relation to a violation – which is moreover a 'continuing' one[221] – of the secondary EU law that is represented, instead, by the directives of substantive law on public procurements. It is precisely this kind of violation that was at stake in the present case. Not to mention, of course, the violations of those norms of the Treaty – and, therefore, primary legislation – on competition and internal market which are certainly endowed with direct effect and act here as 'main premise.'[222]

To sum up, therefore, the conclusion that can be drawn, also for the future, from the judgements examined above is that Member States are obliged to bring to an end (obviously also in relation to illegitimate recipients) the effects of contracts concluded as a result of an award in breach of EU law in order to cease the 'continuing' violation of EU substantive law on public procurements. This is so despite the fact that, according to the directives on the coordination of review procedures to the award of public contracts, Member States may not be obliged to prescribe that the competent body to decide disputes on this matter should rule against the validity of the effects of those contracts as a remedy for the affected applicant. From this perspective, then, Member States have a procedural autonomy that is 'functionalized procedural competence' with regard to the duty of ensuring the effectiveness of EU substantive law on public procurements. In turn, this duty is a consequence of the principles and criteria governing the relationships between domestic law and EU law, as was explained in Chapter 2 of this book.

In any case Germany, then, could not keep alive a thirty-year contract awarded in breach of EU norms. But it could have freely chosen the means to achieve the result of bringing to an end the effects of the contract[223] and, consequently, the 'continuing' violation of EU substantive law on public procurements.[224] In fact, in this respect, Germany was not subject to the specific constraints of its 'procedural competence' arising from the secondary EU legislation.

As for the possibility of 'functionalizing' the national 'procedural' law, from the perspective of the two *Rewe* criteria reinterpreted in the light of the duty of consistent interpretation, I tend to believe that in fact there was such a possibility. When reading paragraph 25 of the judgement of 10 April 2003, it is evident that

[221]In fact, we are talking here of a contract that violated EU law continuously, as it was meant to persist for a period of 30 years!

[222]On this point, see the reflections in para. 4.6 and the literature quoted there.

[223]In this regard, see the recent Opinion of Advocate General Trstenjak, of 11 September 2008, Case C-351/07, particularly para. 63 ff., for which we are still awaiting the decision of the Court of Justice.

[224]As has been said many times, the procedural competence of the Member States must be understood as 'autonomous' choice of the 'procedural' means aimed at ensuring the effectiveness of the EU substantive law. Where, of course, the concepts of procedural and substantive law are EU law concepts that do not necessarily coincide with those in national law. On this point see Chap. 1 and Chap. 2.

according to the German legislation, '... *a contract entered into by a contracting authority in breach of the provisions on public procurement may be terminated ... for a serious reason.*' In this specific respect, from the jurisprudence of the ECJ on 'functionalized procedural competence' comes out clearly that it is not relevant at all the fact that, according to the 'domestic' interpretation of the concept of 'serious reason,' this '*does not include the circumstances leading up to conclusion of the contract*'.[225]

The 'procedural' solution to the problem promises to be much easier in the Italian national legal order, where – given the particular configuration as 'open to tenders' ('*ad evidenza pubblica*') of those contracts that are instead considered by German law in all cases as private law ones – there is always the possibility for the administration to bring to an end the effect of the contract by appealing to its powers to revoke the contract ('*autotutela*').[226] In this respect, it seems clear that the Italian legal version of the public contracts is certainly more 'Euro-compatible' than the German one.[227]

4.6 Procedural Autonomy of the Member States, Between Judges and Legislators, from the Perspective of a Necessarily Compound Normative System: *Paradise Lost*?

In the case of the directives on public procurement procedures, which we have just analyzed, we certainly face a problem of 'procedural primacy' of EU law,[228] which involves a direct invasion of the EU legislator in the sphere of the procedural competence of the Member States and which, according to some scholars, would recognize no limits.[229]

We have seen in Chapter 2, however, that a broad interpretation of EU competences in this area is actually not compatible with the provisions of the Treaties. In fact, given the lack of a specific legal basis in this regard, the Union may only exceptionally legislate on procedural matters whenever, as explained, an intervention by the EU is necessary '...*to remedy differences between the provisions laid down by law, regulation or administrative action in Member States if they are likely*

[225] Para. 25 of the decision in joined cases C-20/01 and 28/01.

[226] On this point, see moreover the recent decision of the Italian Council of State of 8 September 2008, No. 4236, at http://www.lexitalia.it, fasc. 9/2008.

[227] The number of applications submitted by the Commission against Germany on non-fulfilment of EU law rules on public procurement is clear evidence of it.

[228] On this point, see for all, M. Accetto, S. Zleptnig, *The Principle of Effectiveness: Rethinking Its Role in Community Law*, p. 395 ff.

[229] I refer in particular to the well-known paper by C.N. Kakouris, *Do the Member States possess Judicial Procedural "Autonomy"?*, p. 1389 ff.

to distort or harm the functioning of the common market.'[230] And in this respect nothing will change even after the entry into force of the Lisbon Treaty, as it does not introduce any (positive) innovation in this regard.[231]

So, when national legislators introduce changes on procedural matters, appealing as justification to the 'requirements imposed' by the EU law, if they do not entirely lie, they at least tell half of the truth: namely, that the influence of the EU towards a partial harmonization of the national procedural systems is undeniable.[232] But its actual dimension is exaggerated and exploited in the domestic debate, in order to shift to Europe a responsibility that seems 'politically' inconvenient. Or, even more, in order to carry reforms that face resistance within the national legal system.[233]

Whereas the role of EU jurisprudence in this contest is concerned, even to this regard, rather than 'crying shame', we should stop and think – as I have tried to do here – on the role of the national referring courts. While, on the one hand, they must refer cases when really necessary, on the other hand, they should not abuse – as they have often consciously done – the instrument of preliminary ruling.

An unnecessary preliminary reference is never without consequences. This is so because the policy of the ECJ, at least until now, has been clearly directed to admit as many preliminary references as possible, in a spirit of active cooperation with the national courts. These have been rejected only in the extreme case of a fictitious or artificial dispute, identified from the jurisprudence of *Foglia v. Novello*[234] onwards. In all other cases, the ECJ has always endeavoured to provide a useful answer to the referring court. In doing so, though, it has been forced to put under the spotlight problematic issues full of implications, such as those related to the value of the *res judicata* which clearly emerged as a result of the preliminary reference in the *Lucchini* case.[235]

While they are supposed to seek to circumvent and overcome the cases of potential conflict between EU (substantive) law and national (procedural) law, the national courts accentuate this conflict, through unnecessary preliminary references or 'tailor-made' questions. They forget, in fact, that the duty of cooperation

[230] ECJ Judgement of 16 December 1976. Case 33-76. Rewe. *European Court reports* 1976 Page 01989, para. 5.

[231] With regard to the situation after the entry into force of the Lisbon Treaty see the remarks already made in Chap. 2, par. 2.2., note 9.

[232] In this sense, for example, A. Tizzano, *La tutela dei privati nei confronti degli Stati membri dell'Unione europea*, c. 24, who observed some time ago that '*...what can be characterized as an authentic "European standard of judicial protection"*' is being progressively delineated. On this point, see moreover in particular M. Fromont, *Die Annäherung der Verwaltungsgerichtsbarkeiten in Europa*, p. 93 ff.

[233] Both of these cases occurred during the reform in the early 2000s of the Italian rules on administrative procedure concerning in particular those aspects related to precautionary protection.

[234] The already quoted ECJ Judgement of 11 March 1980. Case 104/79.

[235] ECJ Judgement of 18 July 2007. Case C-119/05.

mentioned by Art. 4.3 TEU – of which the national judges are the primary recipients as 'decentralized EU judges'[236] – refers to a duty of 'sincere' cooperation.

The concept of "sincere cooperation" entails – in my opinion – a duty of 'circular cooperation,'[237] which appears to be contrary to the habit of some national judges to involve the ECJ, through preliminary references that are unnecessary and/or used as pretexts, within disputes that could have well been resolved by the national courts themselves. In fact, these cases should be resolved by applying the principles of equal treatment and effectiveness of the EU substantive law, and the duty of consistent interpretation of national procedural law that – as we have seen – are the necessary corollaries of the direct effect and primacy of EU substantive law, and contribute therefore to identifying what is the main premise of the reasoning of the national court. This is a main premise that – as has been recently correctly observed – '*... is nowadays a compound premise*'[238] always and everywhere: that is, besides and despite of the specific problems posed by the so called multilevel, EU legal order.[239]

So, from this perspective, the criticisms of certain scholars heavily attacking the ECJ, insinuating that with its jurisprudence the ECJ undermines the integrity of the national legal system, seems to me somewhat out of place.[240] In fact, the national legal system is nowadays necessarily 'broken down' in a complex and strongly articulated system of sources.[241]

Then, there is no 'Paradise lost.' In this sense, if we really want to contribute to the simplification of this framework, it would be appropriate – as I have already argued elsewhere[242] – that the doctrine definitively abandons the dualist representation of the national and EU legal orders, to which the Italian constitutional judges continue to adhere,[243] and finally accept the idea that the relationship between legal

---

[236]According to the fortunate expression, to which I have already referred many times, by A. Tizzano, *La tutela dei privati nei confronti degli Stati membri dell'Unione europea*, c. 17.

[237]This expression is used by A. Tizzano, note above, c. 22.

[238]In this sense, V. Italia, *Il ragionamento giuridico*, p. 115, and see also *passim*, in particular p. 35 ff.

[239]In this regard see the interesting comments of M.P. Chiti, *Diritto amministrativo europeo*, p. 39 ff.

[240]See, for example, in this sense C. Harlow, *A Common European Law of Remedies*, p. 82. Id., *Voices of Difference in a Plural Community*, p. 1 ff. And also among many others, P.J. Wattel, *Köbler, Cilfit and Welthgrove: we can't go on meeting like this*, p. 184 ff., 190; Id., *National Procedural Autonomy and Effectiveness of EC Law: Challenge the Charge, File for Restitution, Sue for Damages*, p. 109 ff.

[241]In this regard, see the observations of H. Rasmussen, *Remedying the Crumbling EC Judicial System*, p. 1103, stressing out how common it is for a legal scholar to deal with such a complex system.

[242]D.U. Galetta, *La previsione di cui all'articolo 3, comma 1, cpv. 1, della legge di revisione del titolo V della Costituzione come definitivo superamento della teoria dualista degli ordinamenti*, p. 293 ff.

[243]It cannot be said that the decisions of the Italian Constitutional Court of 22 October 2007, No. 348, and 24 October, No. 349, in addition to providing important clarifications on the

systems[244] is subject to the 'invisible' rule of the hierarchy between EU law and national law. It is this rule that should enable the judge to correctly identify the general premise of his syllogism, through the reconstruction of the segments of rules that contribute to its formation.[245]

4.7 *'The Unsafe Haven of National Procedural Autonomy:'*[246] EU Normative Competences, Primacy of Substantive EU Law and Functionalized Procedural Competence of the Member States. Concluding Remarks

At the end of the day, more than an aggregate of values, arguments and methods of reasoning closely anchored to national cultural roots[247] – which could be integrated into the idea of 'perfection' that is implicit in the Paradise Lost metaphor, I think that the procedural autonomy of the Member States can rather be compared, sticking to the metaphor, to an unsafe harbour. This image seems in fact to better match the nature of the phenomenon under analysis, if we identify the procedural autonomy as the harbour and the EU legislator, on the one hand, and the ECJ, on the other, as potential attackers of the security of this harbour.

On the one hand, it has been explained that the concept of procedural autonomy disappears when the EU decides to legislate on the subject of procedure, thus advoking to itself the competence on procedural matters. Though, in the absence of a specific legal basis, this is necessarily an exceptional case. Things, however, may change if Member States decide by mutual agreement to establish one by amending the Treaties in force.[248]

---

relationships between domestic law, EU law and The European Convention on Human Rights, are clear signs of the intention of the Italian Constitutional Court to abandon the theory of the separation between legal orders in favour of a more integrationist approach. For a thorough analysis of these decisions and of their possible implications see moreover the many comments published on the site: //www.giurcost.org, where it is also possible to find the text of the decisions.

[244] On the implications for our topic of analysis of the different theoretical approaches about the relationship between legal orders see the reflections of E. Cannizzaro, *Sui rapporti fra sistemi processuali nazionali e diritto dell'Unione europea*, p. 447 ff.

[245] On this point, see further V. Italia, *Il ragionamento giuridico*, in particular p. 7 ff., 16 ff., 65 ff. In this regard, it is very useful to read the work by R. Kovar, *Le droit national d'exécution du droit communautaire: essai d'une théorie de l' « écran communautaire »*, p. 341 ff.

[246] This fortunate expression has been already used by C. Kilpatrick, in his article *Turning Remedies Around: A Sectoral Analysis of the Court of Justice*, p. 165.

[247] On this, see in particular C. Harlow, *Voices of Difference in a Plural Community*, p. 1 ff.

[248] In any case, with the Lisbon Treaty the Lords of the Treaties have apparently made the opposite choice in that Art. 291.1 TFEU states that: "*Member States shall adopt all measures of national law necessary to implement legally binding Union acts*" and Art. 292.2 points out that only "*Where uniform conditions for implementing legally binding Union acts are needed, those acts shall confer implementing powers on the Commission, or, in duly justified specific cases and in the cases*

On the other hand, the procedural autonomy of the Member States is subject to continuous interventions by the ECJ that, with its jurisprudence, has progressively outlined the limits of what has been identified here as a 'functionalized procedural competence' of the Member States. This competence is constrained by the limits that emerge from the two *Rewe* criteria of equal treatment and effectiveness, re-read in the light of the duty of consistent interpretation.

To summarize what has been explained so far, in order to ensure the desired objective of uniform application of EU law, which guarantees equal treatment throughout the territory of the Union and regarding which the doctrine of primacy and direct effect are the main instruments, there are three courses of intervention over the procedural autonomy of Member States drawn from the EU jurisprudence that has been analyzed.

First, from the EU jurisprudence on the matter the need clearly emerges for national courts to always interpret the national procedural laws 'consistently' with the objective of effectiveness of EU substantive law that they, as decentralized EU courts, should contribute to pursuing.

This obligation of consistent interpretation may imply, secondly, what some scholars refer to as the '*exploitation intensive des virtualités procédurales du droit national.*'[249] As has been said, this is nothing else but the search for the best road to 'functionalize' institutions of the national procedural legislation (in the European Union sense of the term), so as to enable the achievement of the objectives identified by the norms of EU substantive law with greater effectiveness. This is the consequence – as stated – of the raising of the 'standards of effectiveness' of the EU law asked of the Member States after the Maastricht Treaty of 1992.[250]

In this second hypothesis, the preliminary reference is often unnecessary and superfluous because, in accordance with its role, the ECJ in its response merely identifies the requirements of EU law that ought to be met.[251] However, it is not for the ECJ to indicate to the national court the solution under domestic law that is instrumental to that end.[252] When it does so, though, it is actually through mere *obiter dicta*, which should be read in the light of the duty of cooperation stipulated

---

provided for in Articles 24 and 26 of the Treaty on European Union, on the Council.". Which means – in my opinion – that the EU will regulate in procedural matters only in the exceptional situations expressly mentioned. This point of view is shared by Th. Von Danwitz, *Europäisches Veraltungsrecht*, p. 303 f. With regard to the situation after the entry into force of the Lisbon Treaty see also the remarks already made in Chap. 2, par. 2.2.

[249]See D. Simon, *Lex exigences de la primauté du droit communautaire; continuité ou métamorphoses ?*, p. 485. For such an approach see moreover the work by the then President of the TAR Milan E.M. Barbieri, *Poteri del giudice amministrativo e diritto comunitario*, in particular p. 696 ff.

[250]On this point, see what has been explained in Chap. 3, para. 3.2.

[251]See F. Grévisse, J.C. Bonichot, *Les incidences du droit communautaire sur l'organisation et l'exercice de la fonction juridictionnelle dans les Etat membres*, p. 309.

[252]In this sense, very clearly, for example, W. van Gerven, *Of Rights, Remedies and Procedures*, p. 509, as well as, more recently K. Lenaerts, *The Rule of Law and the Coherence of the Judicial System of the European Union*, p. 1645 f.

in Art. 4.3, TEU, which, as mentioned above, also applies to the EU institutions in respect of the Member States, and not only vice versa.[253]

We may lastly verify a third hypothesis. This is the case in which the national court cannot meet the requirements of effectiveness prescribed by EU substantive law, not even by 'functionalizing' the national procedural law by means of its consistent interpretation.

In this last case, the national court will be required to "disapply"'[254] those national 'procedural' norms that are entirely inadequate (or, moreover, opposed) to the pursuit of the result prescribed by the EU substantive law.[255] As specified by the ECJ in its Informative note of 2005 on preliminary rulings, '*In ruling on the interpretation or validity of Community law, the Court makes every effort to give a reply which will be of assistance in resolving the dispute, but it is for the referring court to draw the appropriate conclusions from that reply, if necessary by disapplying the rule of national law in question.*'[256]

Since in this case there is, however, no conflict between a norm of EU procedural law (which does not exist) and the provision of national procedural law, this is actually a case where there is a duty to "disapply" the national procedural norms in the absence of primacy (as mentioned in para. 3.5). But this is the logical consequence of what has been defined in Chapter 2 as the '*effet utile* of the direct effect' of the EU substantive law. Therefore, it is the result of those principles that govern, more generally, the relationship between national law and EU law,[257] and that make EU law peculiar in relation to the 'classic' international law.[258]

---

[253]In this sense should be read the statement in, for example, Judgement of the ECJ of 13 July 2006. Joined cases C-295/04 to C-298/04. Manfredi. *European Court reports* 2006 Page I-06619, para. 48, according to which '...*the Court may, where appropriate, provide clarification designed to give the national court guidance in its interpretation.*' In the same vein, see also Judgement of the ECJ of 17 October 2002. Case C-79/01. Payroll. *European Court reports* 2002 Page I-08923, para. 29.

[254]It is worth noting in this regard that, while the ECJ often uses the term 'disapply' when referring to the mechanism that governs the relationship between a EU norm with direct effect and a national norm that is in conflict with it, the Italian Constitutional Court uses the term 'disapply' incidentally, only in its decision No. 389/1989. However, later, in the *Giampaoli* decision of 18 April 1991, No. 168, it quickly makes clear that instead of 'disapplying,' we should speak of 'not applying' the national norm because 'disapplying' '*refers to defects of the norm that does not actually subsist precisely because of the autonomy of the two legal orders.*' Author's translation.

[255]On this point, see M.P. Chiti, *Le peculiarità dell'invalidità amministrativa per anticomunitarietà*, p. 501. See moreover the observations of S. Amadeo, *Norme comunitarie, posizioni giuridiche soggettive e giudizi interni*, p. 179 ff., 212 ff.

[256]ECJ, Information note on references from national courts for a preliminary ruling, cit., para. 6. On this matter, see N. Gross, *Le renvoi préjudiciel devant la Cour de Justice des Communautés Européennes – Contraintes, Hésitation et Refus*, p. 333, 338 ff.

[257]These principles are, therefore, for the national court the 'main premise' (understood in the terms indicated in the already mentioned study by V. Italia, *Il ragionamento giuridico, passim*) of any discourse on procedural autonomy of the Member States.

[258]In this respect, there is in fact a peculiarity of the EU law. See on this point, D. Simon, *L'autonomisation du contrôle d'euro-compatibilité: une rupture épistémologique dans les rapports de systèmes ?*, p. 497 ff.

Lastly, regarding the role of the national legislator in this particular context, it should be noted that, while the national judge is obliged (in the absence of primacy over the matter) to 'disapply' the national procedural norms preventing the effectiveness of EU substantive law, the national legislature has of course the duty to remove from its legal order every legal provision that is incompatible with EU law.[259] Then (and to answer the question that we posed at the end of para. 2.5) in this third and last hypothesis – and, therefore, as a last resort[260] – when not even the 'functionalization' through consistent interpretation of the national courts can help,[261] the duty to eventually establish new procedural instruments may come into play here.[262] This is because – as has been mentioned at the end of Chapter 2 – the national legislature is also responsible for constantly verifying the suitability of the '*arsenal of national judicial protection*'[263] in relation to the main goal of ensuring compliance with EU law.

Here, though, there is no specificity of the EU law since -and it is well to repeat it- this is an obligation on the legislator that applies in general to any obligation from international law that is binding for the Italian State by virtue of signing a treaty (or international agreement) and that directly derives from the principle of international law '*pacta sunt servanda.*'[264] In this sense, '*Italy agrees, on conditions of equality with other States, to the limitations of sovereignty that may be necessary to a world order ensuring peace and justice among the Nations*'[265] as stated in Art. 11 of the Italian Constitution: that refers also to the limitations of sovereignty that derive from EU treaties.

---

[259]See. A. Barav, *La plénitude des compétences du juge national en sa qualité de juge communautaire*, p. 5 f.

[260]In this sense, see A. Barav, *La plénitude des compétences du juge national en sa qualité de juge communautaire*, p. 6 ff. See also S. Hegels, *EG-Eigenverwaltungsrecht und Gemeinschaftsverwaltungsrecht. Europäisches Verwaltungsrecht für den direkten und den indirekten Gemeinschaftsrechtsvollzug*, p. 70 ff. Of a different opinion, Caranta, *L'ampliamento degli strumenti di tutela cautelare e la progressiva "comunitarizzazione" delle regole processuali nazionali*, p. 2556 ff.

[261]In this sense, see the very recent remarks of R. Kovar, *L'interprétation des droits nationaux en conformité avec le droit communautaire*, p. 391, in relation to what he calls «*La fonction supplétive de l'interprétation conforme*».

[262]K. Lenaerts, *The Rule of Law and the Coherence of the Judicial System of the European Union*, p. 1625 ff, actually points out that in principle the ECJ only requests the national court '*to make best endeavours*' (p. 1628).

[263]The expression – already quoted – is from J. Mertens de Wilmars, *L'efficacité des différentes techniques nationales de protection juridique contre les violations du droit communautaire par les autorités nationales et les particuliers*, p. 392.

[264]On this point, see the reflections of K-H. Ladeur, *Supra und transnationale Tendenzen in der Europäisierung des Verwaltungsrechtes – Eine Skizze*, in particular p. 236 ff.

[265]Official translation. See in http://legxven.camera.it/cost_reg_funz/345/346/listaarticoli.asp

Conclusions

They, looking back, all the eastern side beheld
Of Paradise, so late their happy seat,
Waved over by that flaming brand; the gate
With dreadful faces thronged, and fiery arms:
Some natural tears they dropped, but wiped them soon; [645]
The world was all before them, where to choose
Their place of rest, and Providence their guide:
They, hand in hand, with wandering steps and slow,
Through Eden took their solitary way.

(John Milton, Paradise Lost, Book XII)

The analysis developed so far on the procedural autonomy of the Member States has had the goal (already stated in the Introduction) of identifying the rationale that lies behind the many interventions of the ECJ in this field, in order to demonstrate specifically (based on the author's point of departure) that there is a clear logic behind the ECJ's approach.

As we have seen, these are not extemporaneous interventions aimed solely at solving the individual case. Rather, they relate to a question of applying to this specific context all those lines of reasoning that the ECJ has developed in its jurisprudence since its decisions in the cases of *van Gend & Loos* and *Costa v. Enel* to answer fundamental questions about the relationship between EU law and national law.

Only when interpreted in this specific perspective, do the ECJ's decisions on procedural autonomy of Member States reveal their inner rationale and their consistency with the broader framework of relationships between legal orders that has been set down until now. This is a framework of relationships that is characterized by being still in a transitional phase[1] where -as has been said- although there is no EU competence in procedural matters (due to the lack of a specific legal basis on this regard, even in a *post* Lisbon scenario), there is though an implicit

[1]On this point see the reflections, still very topical, of B. Nascimbene, *Il diritto comunitario nel futuro*, p. 857 ff.

EU competence in its attenuated form, identified by the so called '*effet utile*.' As already said,[2] this is the so called '*effet utile* of the direct effect' (of the EU substantive law) in relation to which the issue of consistent interpretation, with all its implications in terms of 'functionalization' of the national procedural law, plays a fundamental role.

The objections raised by some authors in relation to the reasoning of the ECJ are many and the most common concern the unpredictability of its decisions, which are thought to be characterized by a continuously evolving approach.

Even if it is true that the ECJ's jurisprudence in this context seems to be constantly evolving, it is not correct to affirm that its developments are entirely unpredictable. The evolutionary component of the ECJ's jurisprudence[3] is, in fact, a perfectly natural characteristic of a system (such as the EU one) that is in a perpetually transitory phase. This phase still seems perfectly described by the words of Robert Schumann in his famous statement of 9 May 1950: '*L'Europe ne se fera pas d'un coup, ni dans une construction d'ensemble: elle se fera par des réalisations concrètes créant d'abord une solidarité de fait*.'[4]

In other words, European integration is not a fact but a process.[5] And while in this specific context of 'perpetual process,' the ECJ's jurisprudence certainly passes through phases (as has been highlighted during the analysis above),[6] these phases are not unpredictable. In fact, they are part of the many evolutionary phases of the law interpreted and applied by the ECJ. We cannot ask the ECJ to establish the general lines of this development,[7] since this task is expected first of all of the so-called '*Herren der Verträge*'[8] -and, in the second place, from the EU legislature.

Finally, it is worth noting that an analysis of historical cases of 'transition' already experienced perhaps may be useful to understand the peculiar problems of the EU law. For example -and in order to limit ourselves to the Italian national context- a comparison with the experience of the different national procedural systems that existed during the transition from the different nation states to the

---

[2]In Chap. 2, para. 2.5.

[3]That transpires from, for example, the thick 'Case book' of 2007 by B. Nascimbene, M. Condinanzi, *Giurisprudenza di diritto comunitario*.

[4]Europe will not be made all at once, or according to a single plan. It will be built through concrete achievements which first create a de facto solidarity.

[5]At present even a reversible one, in as far as the new Art. 50.1 TEU contains a provision according to which "*Any Member State may decide to withdraw from the Union in accordance with its own constitutional requirements*". From this point of view the "irréversibilité" referred to by R. Lecourt, *L'Europe des juges*, p. 299 ff. (especially p. 304) no longer exists.

[6]Particularly, in Chap. 3.

[7]In this perspective, it is interesting to read the considerations expressed by the German judge of the ECJ Th. von Danwitz, *Funktionsbedingungen der Rechtsprechung des Europäischen Gerichten*, p. 775 ss., regarding the ECJ's institutional position and role.

[8]The 'Lords of the Treaties', according to the very well-known expression used by the German Federal Constitutional Court in its *Maastricht* decision of 12 October 1993.

unification of Italy could be useful. However, apart from the fact that the preceding analysis has sought to consider the issues being examined from a contemporary perspective, it is my belief that there is still an important limit on the possibility of performing useful historical comparisons here. If we take for example the specific case of Italian unification, the solution to the problems of the 'transitional law' posed at that time were easier to solve, as there was a clear, ultimate goal in mind: unification. Instead, in the case of EU law that clear final objective (the United States of Europe?) is not there and, in fact, never has been.[9]

In this specific context, therefore, the contribution of 'systematization' that can be asked of the ECJ is solely to provide a teleological interpretation in relation to the goal that is explicitly stated in the Preamble of the EC Treaty (now both in the Preambles of the TEU and TFEU).[10] This consists of '*an ever closer union among the peoples of Europe*' that, from Maastricht onwards (and, eventually, even in the Treaty of Lisbon) has been linked to the need to ensure a higher level of effectiveness of the EU law in force.[11]

Therefore I have no doubt that the ever greater effort made by the ECJ in its jurisprudence, to ensure the *effet utile* of the direct effect of EU substantive law -in an unchanged context of 'procedural autonomy' of the Member States- should be interpreted in such a perspective. As a consequence, the national procedural law becomes ever more 'functionalized' to the requirements of the effectiveness of EU substantive law, and thus procedural autonomy reveals its inner essence of 'functionalized procedural competence.'

---

[9]As is in fact known, between the federalist approach of Altiero Spinelli and the 'functionalist' one of Jean Monnet, the latter has prevailed. Although in the clear perspective of political integration, the method that tends to favour development on concrete goals of an economic content has therefore prevailed over the purely political and general dimension.

[10]Which has stated, since 1957, that the Member States are '*Determined to lay the foundations of an ever closer union among the peoples of Europe.*'

[11]On this point, see in particular Chap. 3, para. 3.3.

References[12]

R. Abraham, *Les principes généraux de la protection juridictionnelle administrative en Europe: L'influence des jurisprudences européennes*, in *European Review of Public Law*, 1997, p. 577 ff

R. Adam, A. Tizzano, *Lineamenti di diritto dell'Unione europea*, Giappichelli, Turin, 2008

M. Accetto, S. Zleptnig, *The Principle of Effectiveness: Rethinking Its Role in Community Law*, in *European Public Law*, 2005/3, p. 375 ff

A. Adinolfi, *The Judicial Application of Community Law in Italy*, in *Common Market Law Review*, 1998, p. 1313 ff

A. Adinolfi, *La tutela giurisdizionale nazionale delle situazioni soggettive individuali conferite dal diritto comunitario*, in *Il Diritto dell'Unione europea*, 2001/1, p. 41 ff

R. Alonso García, *Sistema Jurídico de la Unión Europea*, Thomson-Civitas, Cizur Menor (Navarra), 2007

R. Alonso García, *Cuestión prejudicial comunitaria y autonomía procesal nacional: a propósito del asunto Cartesio, STJCE de 16 de diciembre de 2008 (C-210/06)*, in *Revista española de Derecho Europeo*, 2009, p. 197 ff

S. Amadeo, *Norme comunitarie, posizioni giuridiche soggettive e giudizi interni*, Giuffré, Milan, 2002

A. Angeletti, *Ordinamento comunitario e diritto interno nel progetto di riforma del processo amministrativo: la tutela dei diritti e degli interessi*, in *Giurisprudenza italiana*, 1992/4, p. 368 ff

C. Ardanese, *La direttiva "ricorsi" 2007/66/CE. Rilevanza sul regime giuridico del contratto*, in *Giustizia amministrativa (http://www.giustamm.it)*, 2008/11, p. 1 ff

A. Arnull, *The Evolution of the Court's Jurisdiction under Art. 177 EEC*, in *European Law Review*, 1993, p. 129 ff

A. Arnull, *The European Union and its Court of Justice*, Oxford, New York, 2nd. Ed., 2006.

A. Arnull, *Case C-432/05, Unibet*, in *Common Market Law Review*, 2007, p. 1763 ff

F. Astone, *Integrazione giuridica europea e giustizia amministrativa: contributo allo studio dell'influenza manifestata dal diritto europeo sul sistema di giustizia amministrativa italiano e sui poteri del giudice amministrativo*, ESI, Naples, 1999

[12]The literature on the subject is vast and, therefore, it is almost impossible to provide a comprehensive guide on the European studies that have dealt with the issues addressed here. This list is limited, then, to the literature (in Italian, French, English, German and Spanish) that was my specific point of reference while writing this book. In footnotes, the references of this literature are abbreviated (with the indication of the author, title and reference page) and limited to the basic information.

V. Atripaldi, *Leale cooperazione comunitaria ed obbligo degli stati al riesame degli atti amministrativi definitivi contrari al diritto comunitario*, in *Diritto pubblico comparato ed europeo*, 2004/2, p. 883 ff

L. Azoulay, *The Court of Justice and the Administrative Governance*, in *European Law Journal*, 2001/4, p. 425 ff

A. Barav, *La plénitude des compétences du juge national en sa qualité de juge communautaire*, in *L'Europe et le droit. Mélanges en hommage à Jean Boulouis*, Dalloz, Paris, 1991, p. 1 ff

A. Barav, *Primauté*, in A. Barav, Ch. Philip, *Dictionnaire juridique des Communautés européennes*, PUF, Paris, 1993, p. 855 ff

A. Barav, *Renvoi préjudiciel*, in A. Barav, Ch. Philip, *Dictionnaire juridique des Communautés européennes*, PUF, Paris, 1993, p. 926 ff

G. Barbagallo, *Influenze dell'ordinamento comunitario sulla tutela giurisdizionale*, in *Sovranazionalità europea, posizioni soggettive e normazione*, in *Quaderni del Consiglio di Stato*, Giappichelli, Turin, 2000, p. 27 ff

E.M. Barbieri, *Norme comunitarie self-executing e decorrenza dei termini di prescrizione e decadenza*, in *Rivista italiana di diritto pubblico comunitario*, 1995/1, p. 73 ff

E.M. Barbieri, *Poteri del giudice amministrativo e diritto comunitario*, in *Rivista italiana di diritto pubblico comunitario*, 1996/3-4, p. 692 ff

E.M. Barbieri, *Poteri dei giudici nazionali e situazioni giuridiche soggettive di diritto comunitario*, in *Rivista italiana di diritto pubblico comunitario*, 1997, p. 144 ff

E.M. Barbieri, *Diritto comunitario, processo amministrativo e tutela* ante causam, in *Rivista italiana di diritto pubblico comunitario*, 2003/5, p. 1287 ff

C. Barnard, E. Sharpston, *The Changing Face of Article 177 References*, in *Common Market Law Review*, 1997, p. 1113 ff

A. Barone, *Giustizia comunitaria e funzioni interne*, Cacucci, Bari, 2008

A. Bartolini, S. Fantini, *La nuova direttiva ricorsi*, in *Urbanistica e appalti*, 2008/10, p. 1093 ff

M.E. Bartoloni, *La competenza della Corte di giustizia ad interpretare il diritto nazionale "modellato" sulla normativa comunitaria*, in *Il Diritto dell'Unione europea*, 2001/2-3, p. 311 ff

N. Bassi, *Principio di legalità e poteri amministrativi impliciti*, Giuffré, Milan, 2001

N. Bassi, *Mutuo riconoscimento e tutela giurisdizionale. La circolazione degli effetti del provvedimento amministrativo straniero fra diritto europeo e protezione degli interessi del terzo*, Giuffré, Milan, 2008

E. Bernard, *Entre monologue et dialogue de sourds... Les dérives du « dialogue des juges » dans le cadre de la procédure préjudicielle?* in *Europe*, 2009/2, p. 21

G. Biagioni, *Norme processuali e principio di effettività: ulteriori sviluppi nella giurisprudenza comunitaria*, in *Il Diritto dell'Unione europea*, 2004/1, p. 201 ff

P. Biavati, *Diritto comunitario e diritto processuale civile italiano fra attrazione, autonomia e resistenze*, in *Il Diritto dell'Unione europea*, 2000/4, p. 717 ff

P. Biavati, *Diritto processuale dell'Unione europea*, Giuffré, Milan, 2005

P. Biavati, *La sentenza Lucchini: il giudicato nazionale cede al diritto comunitario*, in *Rassegna Tributaria*, 2007, p. 1579 ff

A. Biondi, *The European Court of Justice and certain national procedural limitations: not such a tough relationship*, in *Common Market Law Review*, 1999, p. 1271 ff

A. Biondi, *Case C-119/05, Lucchini*, in *Common Market Law Review*, 2008, p. 1459 ff

M. Blanquet, *L'article 5 du Traité CEE. Recherche sur les obligations de fidélité des Etat membres de la Communauté européenne*, Librairie générale de droit et jurisprudence, Paris, 1994

A. Bleckmann, *Art. 5 EWG-Vertrag und die Gemeinschaftstreue*, in *Deutsches Verwaltungsblatt*, 1976, p. 483 ff

A. Bleckmann, *Die Rechtsprechung des Europäischen Gerichtshof zur Gemeinschaftstreue*, in *Recht der internationalen Wirtschaft/Außenwirtschaftsdienst des Betriebs-Beraters (RIW/AWD)*, 1981, p. 653 ff

A. Bleckmann, Ph. Delannay e.a. (eds.), *Les recours des individus devant les instances nationales en cas de violation du droit européen*, Institut d'études européennes, Larcier, Brussels, 1978

C. Blumann, L. Dubouis, *Droit institutionnel de l'Union européenne*, 3rd. Ed., Litec - JurisClasseur (LexisNexis), Paris, 2007
J-D. Braun, J. Kühling, *Article 87 EC and the Community Courts: from Revolution to Evolution*, in *Common Market Law Review*, 2008, p. 465 ff
M. Brenner, *Determinanten verwaltungsrechtlicher Rechtsschutzgewährleistung in Europa*, in *Landes- und Kommunalverwaltung*, 2002/7, p. 304 ff
W. Buch, *Die Europäisierung des verwaltungsgerichtlichen vorläufigen Rechtsschutzes*, Nomos, Baden-Baden, 2000
M. Burgi, *Verwaltungsprozess und Europarecht. Eine systematische Darstellung*, Beck, Munich, 1996
V. Caianiello, *Dalla giustizia amministrativa al diritto processuale amministrativo*, in *Diritto processuale amministrativo*, 1994, p. 193 ff
C. Calabrò, *Giudicato III) Diritto processuale amministrativo*, in *Enc. giur. Treccani*, vol. XV, Treccani, Rome, 2002, p. 1 ff
Ch. Callies, *Kohärenz und Konvergenz beim europäischen Individualrechtsschutz. Der Zugang zum Gericht im Lichte des Grundrechts auf effektiven Rechtsschutz*, in *Neue Juristiche Wochenschrift*, 2002/49, p. 3577 ff
Ch. Callies, *Feinstaub im Rechtsschutz deutscher Verwaltungsgerichte. Europarechtliche Vorgaben für die Klagebefugnis vor deutschen Gerichten und ihre dogmatische Verarbeitung*, in *Neue Zeitschrift für Verwaltungsrecht*, 2006/1, p. 1 ff
E. Cannizzaro, *Sui rapporti fra sistemi processuali nazionali e diritto dell'Unione europea*, in *Il Diritto dell'Unione europea*, 2008/3, p. 447 ff
F. Capotorti, *Il diritto comunitario dal punto di vista del giudice nazionale*, in *Rivista di diritto internazionale privato e processuale*, 1977, p. 497 ff
F. Capotorti, *Sull'obbligo del rinvio alla Corte di giustizia per l'interpretazione a titolo pregiudiziale a norma del comma 3 dell'art. 177 del Trattato CEE*, in *Giurisprudenza italiana*, 1983/7, p. 1007 ff
R. Caranta, *Effettività della garanzia giurisdizionale nei confronti della pubblica amministrazione e diritto comunitario: il problema della tutela cautelare*, in *Il Foro amministrativo*, 1991, p. 1885 ff
R. Caranta, *Giustizia amministrativa e diritto comunitario*, Jovene, Naples, 1992
R. Caranta, *La responsabilità oggettiva dei pubblici poteri per violazioni del diritto comunitario*, in *Giurisprudenza italiana*, 1992, I, 1, p. 1169 ff
R. Caranta, *Diritto comunitario e tutela cautelare: dall'effettività allo "ius commune"*, in *Giurisprudenza italiana*, 1994, I, p. 353 ff
R. Caranta, *Judicial protection against Member States: a new* ius commune *takes shape*, in *Common Market Law Review*, 1995, p. 703 ff
R. Caranta, *L'ampliamento degli strumenti di tutela cautelare e la progressiva "comunitarizzazione" delle regole processuali nazionali*, in *Il Foro amministrativo*, 1996, p. 2543 ff
R. Caranta, *Impulso di parte e iniziativa del giudice nell'applicazione del diritto comunitario*, in *Giurisprudenza italiana*, 1996, I, 1, p. 1289 ff
R. Caranta, *Tutela giurisdizionale effettiva delle situazioni giuridiche soggettive di origine comunitaria ed incisività del sindacato del giudice nazionale* (Kontrolldichte), in *Rivista italiana di diritto pubblico comunitario*, 1999, p. 503 ff
R. Caranta, *Valutazioni dell'amministrazione e sindacato del giudice*, in *Quaderni del Consiglio di Stato*, Giappichelli, Turin, 2000, p. 39 ff
R. Caranta, *Coordinamento e divisione dei compiti tra Corte di giustizia delle comunità europee e giudici nazionali nelle ipotesi di coamministrazione: il caso dei prodotti modificati geneticamente*, in *Rivista italiana di diritto pubblico comunitario*, 2000/5, p. 1133 ff
R. Caranta, *Diritto comunitario e tutela giuridica di fronte al giudice amministrativo italiano*, in *Rivista trimestrale di diritto pubblico*, 2000/1, p. 81 ff
R. Caranta, *Commento alla sentenza in causa C-453/00, Kühne & Heitz*, in *Urbanistica e appalti*, 2004, p. 1154 ff

R. Caranta, *La tutela giurisdizionale (italiana, sotto l'influenza comunitaria)*, in M.P. Chiti and G. Greco (eds.), *Trattato di diritto amministrativo europeo* (coord. by G.F. Cartei and D.U. Galetta), Giuffrè, Milan, 2nd. Ed., 2007, General Part, Volume II, p. 1031 ff
S. Cassese, *Grandezza e insuccessi del giudice amministrativo italiano*, in *Studi in onore di G. Guarino*, Giuffré, Milan, 1998, Vol. I, p. 543 ff
S. Cassese, *La signoria comunitaria sul diritto amministrativo*, in *Rivista italiana di diritto pubblico comunitario*, 2002/2-3, p. 291 ff
S. Cassese, *Diritto amministrativo europeo e diritto amministrativo nazionale: signoria o integrazione?* in *Rivista italiana di diritto pubblico comunitario*, 2004/5, p. 1135 ff
S. Cassese, *Quando gli ordinamenti si scontrano. Dal dialogo alla cooperazione tra le Corti*, at www.irpa.eu.
J. Cavallini, *Le juge national du provisoire face au droit communautaire. Les contentieux français et anglais,* Bruylant, Brussels, 1995
A. Celotto, *Le "modalità" di prevalenza delle norme comunitarie sulle norme interne: spunti ricostruttivi*, in *Rivista italiana di diritto pubblico comunitario*, 1999/6, p. 1473 ff
A. Cerri, *L'integrazione europea nella giurisprudenza delle Corti*, in *Rivista italiana di diritto pubblico comunitario*, 1999/6, p. 1485 ff
V. Cerulli Irelli, *I rapporti tra ordinamento dell'Unione europea e ordinamento interno*, in F. Bassanini, G. Tiberi, *Le nuove istituzioni europee. Commento al Trattato di Lisbona*, Quaderni Astrid, Il Mulino, Bologna, 2008, p. 383 ff
V. Cerulli Irelli, *Trasformazioni del sistema di tutela giurisdizionale nelle controversie di diritto pubblico per effetto della giurisprudenza europea*, in *Rivista italiana di diritto pubblico comunitario*, 2008/2, p. 433 ff
D. Chalmers, *The Much Ado about Judicial Politics in the United Kingdom: A Statistical Analysis of Reported Decisions of United Kingdom Courts Invoking EU Law 1973–1998*. Harvard Jean Monnet Working Paper, n. 1/2000, at http://www.jeanmonnetprogram.org/papers
E. Chiti, *Misure cautelari positive e effettività del diritto comunitario*, in *Giornale di diritto amministrativo*, 1996, p. 338 ff
E. Chiti, *Giudizio cautelare ed innovazioni comunitarie*, in *Giornale di diritto amministrativo*, 1997, p. 1085 ff
M.P. Chiti, *L'influenza dei valori costituzionali sul diritto processuale amministrativo*, in *Diritto processuale amministrativo*, 1984, p. 177 ff
M.P. Chiti, *I signori del diritto comunitario: la Corte di giustizia e lo sviluppo del diritto amministrativo europeo*, in *Rivista trimestrale di diritto pubblico*, 1991, p. 796 ff
M.P. Chiti, *Implicazioni amministrative della integrazione europea*, in *Rivista italiana di diritto pubblico comunitario*, 1992, p. 1175 ff
M.P. Chiti, *Towards a Unified Judicial Protection in Europe?* in *European Review of Public Law*, 1997, p. 553 ff
M.P. Chiti, *L'effettività della tutela giurisdizionale tra riforme nazionali e influenza del diritto comunitario*, in *Diritto processuale amministrativo*, 1998, p. 499 ff
M. P. Chiti, *La giurisdizione*, in F. Bassanini, G. Tiberi, *Le nuove istituzioni europee. Commento al Trattato di Lisbona*, Quaderni Astrid, Il Mulino, Bologna, 2008, p. 349 ff
M.P. Chiti, *Diritto amministrativo europeo*,Giuffré, Milan, 2008
M.P. Chiti, *Le peculiarità dell'invalidità amministrativa per anticomunitarietà*, in *Rivista italiana di diritto pubblico comunitario*, 2008/2, p. 477 ff
F. Cintioli, *Orientamenti della Corte di giustizia in tema di accesso al fatto del giudice amministrativo nazionale*, in *Quaderni del Consiglio di Stato*, Giappichelli, Turin, 2000, p. 51 ff
M. Clarich, *La responsabilità nel sistema comunitario*, in M.P. Chiti, G. Greco (eds.), *Trattato di diritto amministrativo europeo* (coord. by G.F. Cartei and D.U. Galetta), Giuffrè, Milan, 2nd. Ed., 2007, General Part, Vol. II, p. 589 ff
C.D. Classen, *Die Europäisierung der Verwaltungsgerichtsbarkeit*, Mohr Siebeck, Tübingen, 1996
G. Cocco, *L'insostenibile leggerezza del diritto italiano*, in *Rivista italiana di diritto pubblico comunitario*, 1996/3-4, p. 629 ff

G. Cogliandro, *Il rinvio pregiudiziale sull'interpretazione del diritto comunitario*, in *Il Foro amministrativo*, 1989, p. 1067 ff
R. Colonna, *Giudicato e ius superveniens retroattivo: un'armonizzazione difficile*, in *Diritto processuale amministrativo*, 1995, p. 255 ff
C. Consolo, *L'ordinamento comunitario quale fondamento per la tutela cautelare del giudice nazionale (in via di disapplicazione di norme legislative interne)*, in *Diritto processuale amministrativo*, 1991, p. 255 ff
C. Consolo, *La sentenza Lucchini della Corte di giustizia: quale possibile adattamento degli ordinamenti processuali interni e in specie del nostro?* in *Riv. dir. proc.*, 2008, p. 224 ff
R. Conti, *Il principio di effettività della tutela giurisdizionale ed il ruolo del giudice: l'interpretazione conforme*, in *Politica del diritto*, 2007, p. 377 ff
G. Corso, *Per una giustizia amministrativa più celere*, in *Giustizia amministrativa*, at hptt://www.giust.it. 7 August, 1999
F. Cortese, *Il riesame di decisioni amministrative definitive tra obbligo di cooperazione e certezza del diritto*, in *Rivista italiana di diritto pubbico comunitario*, 2008/6, p. 1527 ff
V. Costantinesco, *L'art. 5 CEE. De la bonne foi à la loyauté communautaire*, in *Du droit international au droit de l'intégration: Liber Amicorum Pierre Pescatore*, Nomos, Baden-Baden, 1987, p. 87 ff
P. Craig, *Sovereignty of the United Kingdom Parliament after Factortame*, in *Yearbook of European Law*, 1991, p. 221 ff
P. Craig, *EU Administrative Law*, Oxford, New York, 2006
M. D'Alberti, *Regole e rimedi: convergenze fra i diritti amministrativi d'Europa*, in *Rivista trimestrale di diritto pubblico*, 1992/4, p. 1048 ff
L. Daniele, *L'effettività della giustizia amministrativa nell'applicazione del diritto comunitario europeo*, in *Rivista italiana di diritto pubblico comunitario*, 1996, p. 1385 ff
L. Daniele, *Diritto dell'Unione europea*, Giuffré, Milan, 2008
Th. von Danwitz, *Die Garantie effektiven Rechtsschutzes im Recht der Europäischen Gemeinschaft. Zur Verbesserung des Individualrechtsschutzes vor dem EuGH*, in *Neue Juristische Wochenschrift*, 1993/17, p. 1108 ff
Th. von Danwitz, *Verwaltungsrechtliches System und Europäische Integration*, Mohr Siebeck, Tübingen, 1996
Th. von Danwitz, *Die Eigenverantwortung der Mitgliedstaaten für die Durchführung von Gemeinschaftsrecht*, in *Deutsches Verwaltungsblatt*, 1998, p. 421 ff
Th. von Danwitz, *Funktionsbedingungen der Rechtsprechung des Europäischen Gerichten*, in *Europarecht*, 2008/6, p. 769 ff
Th. Von Danwitz, *Europäisches Veraltungsrecht*, Springer, Berlin, 2008
G. de Burca, A. Ryall, *The ECJ and Judicial Review of National Administrative Procedure in the Field of the EIA*, in K-H. Ladeur (eds.), *The Europeanisation of Administrative Law. Transforming national decision-making procedures*, Ashgate, Dartmouth, 2002, p. 145 ff
M. Dederichs, *Die Methodik des Gerichtshofes der Europäischen Gemeinschaften*, in *Europarecht*, 2004/2, p. 345 ff
D. Del Gaizo, *La tutela delle posizioni soggettive nei confronti delle istituzioni comunitarie: il ruolo dei giudici nazionali*, in *Quaderni del Consiglio di Stato*, Giappichelli, Turin, 2000, p. 65 ff
G. Della Cananea, *I procedimenti amministrativi dell'Unione europea*, in M.P. Chiti and G. Greco (eds.), *Trattato di diritto amministrativo europeo* (coord. by G.F. Cartei and D.U. Galetta), Giuffrè, Milan, 2nd. Ed., 2007, General Part, Vol. I, p. 497 ff
J.S. Delicostopoulos, *Towards European Procedural Primacy in National Legal Systems*, in *European Law Journal*, 2003/5, p. 599 ff
G. De Michele, *La giustizia amministrativa nella prospettiva comunitaria*, in *Rivista italiana di diritto pubblico comunitario*, 1995, p. 87 ff
D. De Pretis, *La tutela giurisdizionale amministrativa in Europa fra integrazione e diversità*, in *Rivista italiana di diritto pubblico comunitario*, 2005/1, p. 1 ff

C. Di Seri, *La responsabilità del giudice nell'attività interpretativa: una discriminazione a rovescio?* in *Rivista italiana di diritto pubblico comunitario*, 2006/6, p. 1116 ff

G. Dolso, S. Amadeo, *Il Consiglio di Stato tra Corte Costituzionale e Corte di giustizia*, in *Giurisprudenza costituzionale*, 2006/1, p. 785 ff

O. Dörr, *Rechtsprechungskonkurrenz zwischen nationalen und europäischen Verfassungsgerichten*, in *Deutsches Verwaltungsblatt*, 2006/17, p. 1088 ff

O. Dörr, *Der europäisierte Rechtsschutzauftrag deutscher Gerichte*, Mohr Siebeck, Tübingen, 2003

M. Dougan, *National Remedies before the Court of Justice. Issues of Harmonisation and Differentiation*, Oxford, New York, 2004

O. Dubos, *Les juridictions nationales, juge communautaire*, Dalloz, Paris, 2001

Th. Dünchheim, *Verwaltungsprozessrecht unter europäischem Einfluss*, Duncker & Humblot, Berlin, 2003

Th. Dünchheim, *Die Europäisierung des Verwaltungsprozessrechts und die Notwendigkeit europäischer Gerichtskooperation*, in *Verwaltungsrundschau*, 2003, p. 361 ff

D. Ehle, *Zum Rechtsschutz und Verfahren im Europäischen Gemeinschaftsrecht*, in *Agrarrecht*, 1989/3, p. 11 ff

D. Ehlers, *Die Europäisierung des Verwaltungsprozeßrechts*, Carl Heymanns, Cologne, 1999

Th. Eilmansberger, *The relationship between rights and remedies in EC Law: in search of the missing link*, in *Common Market Law Review*, 2004, p. 1199 ff

M. Eliantonio, *Europeanisation of Administrative Justice? The influence of ECJ's Case Law in Italy, Germany and England*, Europa Law Publishing, Groningen, 2008

G. Falcon, *Dal diritto amministrativo nazionale al diritto amministrativo comunitario*, in *Rivista italiana di diritto pubblico comunitario*, 1991, p. 351 ff

G. Falcon, *Alcune osservazioni sullo sviluppo del diritto amministrativo comunitario*, in *Rivista trimestrale di diritto pubblico*, 1993, p. 74 ff

G. Falcon, *Giustizia comunitaria e giustizia amministrativa*, in *Diritto amministrativo comunitario*, Maggioli, Rimini, 1994, p. 271 ff

G. Falcon, *Separazione e coordinamento tra giurisdizioni europee e giurisdizioni nazionali nella tutela avverso gli atti lesivi di situazioni soggettive europee*, in *Rivista italiana di diritto pubblico comunitario*, 2004/5, p. 1153 ff

G. Falcon, *Provvedimenti, diritto amministrativo e tutela giurisdizionale nel sistema comunitario*, in G. Guzzetta (eds.), *Le forma dell'azione comunitaria nella prospettiva della Costituzione europea*, CEDAM, Padua, 2005, p. 91 ff

G. Falcon, *La tutela giurisdizionale*, in M.P. Chiti and G. Greco (eds.), *Trattato di diritto amministrativo europeo* (coord. by G.F. Cartei and D.U. Galetta), Giuffré, Milan, 2nd. Ed., 2007, General Part, Vol. II, p. 697 ff

M. Filippi, *La giurisprudenza amministrativa a contenuto comunitario*, in *Rivista italiana di diritto pubblico comunitario*, 1993, p. 1181 ff

L. Flynn, *Whatever Happened to Emmott? The Perfecting of Community Rules on National Time-Limits*, in C. Kilpatrick, T. Novitz, P. Skidmore (eds.), *The future of remedies in Europe*, Oxford University Press, Oxford-New York, 2000, p. 51 ff

E. Fontana, *Intorno a qualche limite ordinamentale all'attuazione del diritto comunitario*, in *Giustizia civile*, 2007/11, p. 2569 ff

C. Franchini, *Nuovi modelli di azione comunitaria e tutela giurisdizionale*, in *Sovranazionalità europea, posizioni soggettive e normazione*, in *Quaderni del Consiglio di Stato*, Giappichelli, Turin, 2000, p. 13 ff

M. Fromont, *L'influence des droits française et allemande sur les conditions de recevabilité du recours en annulation devant la Court de justice des Communautés européens*, in *Revue trimestrielle de droit européen*, 1966, p. 47 ff

M. Fromont, *Die Annäherung der Verwaltungsgerichtsbarkeiten in Europa. Die Befugnisse des Verwaltungsrichters gegenüber der Verwaltung*, in E. Schmidt-Aßmann, D. Sellner e.a., *Festgabe 50 Jahre Bundesverwaltungsgericht*, Carl Heymanns, Cologne e.a., 2003, p. 93 ff

D.U. Galetta, *Principio di proporzionalità e sindacato giurisdizionale nel diritto amministrativo*, Giuffré, Milan, 1998

D.U. Galetta, *Giustizia amministrativa italiana e diritto comunitario: problemi e prospettive di sviluppo nell'ottica di una giustizia amministrativa europea*, in *Rivista italiana di diritto pubblico comunitario*, 1999/5, pp. 1003

D.U. Galetta, *Una sentenza storica sul principio di proporzionalità con talune ombre in ordine al rinvio pregiudiziale alla Corte di giustizia*, in *Rivista italiana di diritto pubblico comunitario*, 2000/2, p. 459 ff

D.U. Galetta, *La previsione di cui all'articolo 3, comma 1, cpv. 1, della legge di revisione del titolo V della costituzione come definitivo superamento della teoria dualista degli ordinamenti*, in *Problemi del federalismo*, Giuffré, Milan, 2001, p. 293 ff

D.U. Galetta, *Vizi procedurali e vizi sostanziali al vaglio della Corte di giustizia (che non si pronuncia sulla questione)*, in *Rivista italiana di diritto pubblico comunitario*, 2004/1, p. 317 ff

D.U. Galetta, *Autotutela decisoria e diritto comunitario*, in G. Falcon (eds.), *Il diritto amministrativo dei Paesi europei tra omogeneizzazione e diversità culturali*, CEDAM, Padua, 2005, p. 39 ff (also, in *Rivista italiana di diritto pubblico comunitario*, 2005/1, p. 35 ff)

D.U. Galetta, *I procedimenti di riesame*, in V. Cerulli Irelli (eds.), *La disciplina generale dell'azione amministrativa*, Jovene, Naples, 2006, pp. 393 ff

D.U. Galetta, *Le Principe de proportionnalité*, in J.B. Auby, J. Dutheil de la Rochère (eds.), *Droit Administratif Européen*, Bruylant, Bruxelles, 2007, p. 357 ff

D.U. Galetta, *La tutela dell'affidamento nella prospettiva del diritto amministrativo italiano, tedesco e comunitario: un'analisi comparata*, in *Diritto Amministrativo*, 2008/4, p. 757 ff

D.U. Galetta, *Riflessioni sulla più recente giurisprudenza comunitaria in materia di giudicato nazionale (ovvero sull'autonomia procedurale come competenza procedurale funzionalizzata)*, in *Il Diritto dell'Unione europea*, 2009/4, p. 961 ff

C.E. Gallo, *La giustizia amministrativa fra modello costituzionale e principi comunitari*, at www.diritto-amministrativo.org

E. García de Enterría, *Perspectivas de las justicias administrativas nacionales en el ámbito de la Unión Europea*, in *Rivista trimestrale di diritto pubblico*, 1999, p. 1 ff

G. Gattinara, *La precisazione del ruolo comunitario delle amministrazioni nazionali*, in *Diritto comunitario e degli scambi internazionali*, 2004, p. 496 ff

A. Gatto, *I poteri del giudice amministrativo rispetto a provvedimenti individuali e concreti contrastanti con il diritto comunitario*, in *Rivista italiana di diritto pubblico comunitario*, 2002/6, p. 1429 ff

G. Gaja, *L'esigenza di interpretare le norme nazionali in conformità con il diritto comunitario*, in S.P. Panunzio, E. Sciso (eds.), *Le riforme istituzionali e la partecipazione dell'Italia all'Unione Europea*, Giuffré, Milan, 2002, p. 133 ff

M. Gnes, *Giudice amministrativo e diritto comunitario*, in *Rivista trimestrale di diritto pubblico*, 1999/2, p. 331 ff

E. Grabitz, *Europäisches Verwaltungsrecht. Gemeinschaftsrechtliche Grundsätze des Verwaltungsrechts*, in *Neue Juristiche Wochenschrift*, 1989/29, p. 1776 ff

M. Grandinetti, S. Monzani, *L'effettività della tutela giurisdizionale nell'ottica comunitaria: riflessioni in ordine alla tutela cautelare e alla restituzione di tributi riscossi in violazione del diritto comunitario*, in *Rivista italiana di diritto pubblico comunitario*, 2008/3-4, p. 927 ff

R. Grappiolo, *La giurisprudenza della Corte di giustizia sul rinvio pregiudiziale ai sensi dell'art. 177 del Trattato CEE*, in *Diritto comunitario e degli scambi internazionali*, 1992/1-2, p. 63 ff

G. Greco, *Il diritto comunitario propulsore del diritto amministrativo europeo*, in *Rivista trimestrale di diritto pubblico*, 1993, p. 85 ff

G. Greco, *L'effettività della giustizia amministrativa italiana nel quadro del diritto europeo*, in *Rivista italiana di diritto pubblico comunitario*, 1996/3-4, p. 797 ff

G. Greco, *I rapporti tra ordinamento comunitario e nazionale*, in M.P. Chiti and G. Greco (eds.), *Trattato di diritto amministrativo europeo* (coord. by G.F. Cartei and D.U. Galetta), Giuffré, Milan, 2nd. Ed., 2007, General Part, Vol. II, p. 827 ff

G. Greco, *L'incidenza del diritto comunitario sugli atti amministrativi nazionali*, in M.P. Chiti and G. Greco (eds.), *Trattato di diritto amministrativo europeo* (coord. by G.F. Cartei and D.U. Galetta), Giuffrè, Milan, 2nd. Ed., 2007, General Part, Vol. II, p. 933 ff

G. Greco, *Illegittimità comunitaria e pari dignità degli ordinamenti*, in *Rivista italiana di diritto pubblico comunitario*, 2008/2, p. 505 ff

G. Greco, *La direttiva 2007/66/CE: illegittimità comunitaria, sorte del contratto ed effetti collaterali indotti*, in *Rivista italiana di diritto pubblico comunitario*, 2008/5, p. 1029 ff

G. Greco, *Superprimato del diritto europeo: le direttive sui mezzi di ricorso vincolano tutti, ma non la Commissione e la Corte di Giustizia*, in *Rivista italiana di diritto pubblico comunitario*, 2009/2, p. 431 ff

F. Grévisse, J.C. Bonichot, *Les incidences du droit communautaire sur l'organisation et l'exercice de la fonction juridictionnelle dans les Etat membres*, in *L'Europe et le droit. Mélanges en hommage à Jean Boulouis*, Dalloz, Paris, 1991, p. 297 ff

N. Gross, *Le renvoi préjudiciel devant la Cour de Justice des Communautés Européennes – Contraintes, Hésitation et Refus*, in *La France, L'Europe et le Monde. Mélanges en l'honneur de Jean Charpentier*, Pedone, Paris, 2009, p. 331 ff

G. Haibach, *Gemeinschaftsrecht und vorläufiger Rechtsschutz durch mitgliedstaatliche Gerichte*, Beck, Munich, 1995

C. Harlow, *Voices of Difference in a Plural Community*. Harvard Jean Monnet Working Paper, n. 3/2000, at http://www.jeanmonnetprogram.org/papers

C. Harlow, *A Common European Law of Remedies*, in C. Kilpatrick, T. Novitz, P. Skidmore (eds.), *The future of remedies in Europe*, Oxford University Press, Oxford-New York, 2000, p. 69 ff

A. Hatje, *Die gemeinschaftsrechtliche Steuerung der Wirtschaftsverwaltung: Grundlagen, Erscheinungsformen, verfassungsrechtliche Grenzen am Beispiel der Bundesrepublik Deutschland*, Nomos, Baden-Baden, 1998

A. Hatje, *Rechtssicherheit und Vertrauensschutz – Wechselseitige Einwirkungen zwischen Europäischem Gemeinschaftsrecht und deutschem Verfassungs- und Verwaltungsrecht*, in J. Schwarze (eds.), *Bestand und Perspektiven des Europäischen Verwaltungsrechts. Rechtsvergleichende Analysen*, Nomos, Baden-Baden, 2008

A. Hatje, *Artikel 10 (Verpflichtung der Mitgliedstaaten)*, in J. Schwarze (eds.), *EU-Kommentar*, Nomos, Baden-Baden, 2nd. Ed., 2009, p. 314 ff

S. Hegels, *EG-Eigenverwaltungsrecht und Gemeinschaftsverwaltungsrecht. Europäisches Verwaltungsrecht für den direkten und den indirekten Gemeinschaftsrechtsvollzug*, Nomos, Baden-Baden, 2001

E. Herlin-Karnell, *An exercise in effectiveness?* in *European Business Law Review*, 2007, p. 1181

H.C.H. Hofmann, A. Türk, *The Development of Integrated Administration in the EU and its Consequences*, in *European Law Journal*, 2007, p. 253 ff

J. Hofmann, *Rechtsschutz und Haftung im Europäischen Verwaltungsverbund*, in E. Schmidt-Aßmann, B. Schöndorf-Haubold (eds.), *Der Europäische Verwaltungsverbund*, Mohr Siebeck, Tübingen, 2005, p. 353 ff

M. Huber, *Die Europäisierung des verwaltungsgerichtlichen Rechtsschutzes*, in *Bayerisches Verwaltungsblatt*, 2001, p. 577 ff

C. Iannone, *Art. 10 TCE*, in A. Tizzano (eds.), *Trattati dell'Unione Europea e della Comunità Europea*, Giuffrè, Milan, 2004, p. 219 ff

M. Interlandi, *Annullamento d'ufficio e aiuti di Stato illegittimi: la difficile convergenza tra effettività comunitaria e autonomia dei sistemi normativi nazionali*, in *Nuove autonomie*, 2006, p. 823 ff

V. Italia, *Il ragionamento giuridico*, Giuffrè, Milan, 2009

J.P. Jacqué, *Droit institutionnel de l'Union européenne*, 3rd. Ed., Dalloz, Paris, 2004

H.D. Jarass, *Konflikte zwischen EG-Recht und nationalen Recht von den Gerichten der Mitgliedstaaten*, in *Deutsches Verwaltungsblatt*, 1995, p. 954 ff

R. Joliet, *L'article 177 du Traité CEE et le renvoi prejudiciel*, in *Rivista di Diritto europeo*, 1991, p. 591 ff

P. Kalbe, *Gemeinschaftsrecht und nationale Rechtsbehelfsfristen*, in *Zeitschrift für Zölle und Verbrauchsteuern*, 1977, p. 360 ff

C.N. Kakouris, *Do the Member States possess Judicial Procedural "Autonomy"?* in *Common Market Law Review*, 1997, p. 1389 ff

G. Kalflèche, *La modification des directives «recours» en matière de marchés publics. Une boule de cristal pour le contentieux des contracts publics*, in *Europe*, 2008/4, p. 4 ff

C. Kilpatrick, *The Future of Remedies in Europe*, in C. Kilpatrick, T. Novitz, P. Skidmore (eds.), *The future of remedies in Europe*, Oxford University Press, Oxford-New York, 2000, p. 1 ff

C. Kilpatrick, *Turning Remedies Around: A Sectoral Analysis of the Court of Justice*, in G. de Burca, J.H.H. Weiler (eds.), *The European Court of Justice*, Oxford University Press, Oxford-New York, 2001, p. 143 ff

E. Klein, *L'influenza del diritto comunitario sul diritto amministrativo degli Stati membri*, in *Rivista italiana di diritto pubblico comunitario*, 1993, p. 683 ff

M. Kment, *Die Stellung nationaler Unbeachtlichtkeits-, Heilungs- und Präklusionsvorschriften im europäischen Recht*, in *Europarecht*, 2006/2, p. 201 ff

J. Kokott, *Europäisierung des Verwaltungsprozessrechts*, in *Die Verwaltung*, 1998, p. 335 ff

A. P. Komninos, *Case C-126/97, Eco Swiss*, in *Common Market Law Reviev*, 2000, p. 459 ff

T. Koopmans, *La procédure préjudicielle – victime de son succès?* in *Du droit international au droit de l'intégration: Liber Amicorum Pierre Pescatore*, Nomos, Baden-Baden, 1987, p. 347 ff

R. Kovar, *Droit communautaire et droit procédural national*, in *Cahiers de droit européenne*, 1977, p. 230 ff

R. Kovar, *Voies de droit ouvertes aux individus devant les instances nationales en cas de violation des normes et décision du droit communautaire*, in A. Bleckmann, Ph. Delannay e.a. (eds.), *Les recours des individus devant les instances nationales en cas de violation du droit européen*, Larcier, Brussels, 1978, p. 245 ff

R. Kovar, *Immédiateté du droit communautaire*, in *Juris Classeur-Europe*, 1981, Issue 432, p. 1 ff

R. Kovar, *Le droit national d'exécution du droit communautaire: essai d'une théorie de l'« écran communautaire »*, in *L'Europe et le droit. Mélanges en hommage a Jean Boulouis*, Dalloz, Paris, 1991, p. 341 ff

R. Kovar, *La contribution de la Cour de justice à l'édification de l'ordre juridique communautaire. Cours général de droit communautaire*, in *Collected courses of the Academy of European Law*, Vol. IV, Book 1 - European Community Law, Oxford University Press, Oxford-New York, 1993, p. 15 ff

R. Kovar, *L'interprétation des droits nationaux en conformité avec le droit communautaire*, in *La France, L'Europe et le Monde. Mélanges en l'honneur de Jean Charpentier*, Pedone, Paris, 2009, p. 381 ff

C. Kremer, *Effektuierung des europäischen Beihilferechts durch die Begrenzung der Rechtskraft*, in *Europäische Zeitschrift für Wirtschaftsrecht*, 2007/23, p. 726 ff

C. Kremer, *Gemeinschaftsrechtliche Grenzen der Rechtskraft*, in *Europarecht*, 2007, p. 479 ff

K-H. Ladeur, *Supra und transnationale Tendenzen in der Europäisierung des Verwaltungsrechtes – Eine Skizze*, in *Europarecht*, 1995/3, p. 227 ff

K-H. Ladeur, *Conflict and Cooperation between European Law and the General Administrative Law of the Member States*, in K-H. Ladeur (eds.), *The Europeanisation of Administrative Law. Transforming national decision-making procedures*, Ashgate, Dartmouth, 2002, p. 1 ff

K-H. Ladeur, R. Prelle, *Judicial Control of Administrative Procedural Mistakes in Germany: A Comparative European View of Environmental Impact Assessments*, in K-H. Ladeur (eds.), *The Europeaanisation of Administrative Law. Transforming national decision-making procedures*, Ashgate, Dartmouth, 2002, p. 93 ff

K.P.E. Lasok, T. Millet, A. Howard, *Judicial Control in the EU: Procedures and Principles*, Oxford University Press, Oxford-New York, 2004

H. Lecheler, *Der Beitrag der allgemeinen Rechtsgrundsätze zur Europäischen Integration – Rückblick und Ausblick*, in *Zeitschrift für Europarechtliche Studien*, 2003/3, p. 337 ff

K. Lenaerts, *The Rule of Law and the Coherence of the Judicial System of the European Union*, in *Common Market Law Review*, 2007, p. 1625 ff

K. Lenaerts, D. Gerard, *Decentralisation of EC Competition Law Enforcement: Judges in the Frontline*, in *Common Market Law Review*, 2004, p. 313 ff

K. Lenaerts, T. Corthaut, *Towards an Internally Consistent Doctrine of Invoking Norms of EU Law*, in S. Prechal, B. van Roermund (eds.), *The Coherence of EU Law. The search for Unity in Divergent Concepts*, Oxford University Press, Oxford-New York, 2008, p. 495 ff

R. Lecourt, *L'Europe des juges*, Bruylant, Bruxelles, 2008 (re-edition of the book published in 1976)

L. Limberti, *Principio di effettività della tutela giurisdizionale e diritto comunitario: a proposito del potere del giudice nazionale di concedere provvedimenti cautelari "positivi"*, in *Rivista italiana di diritto pubblico comunitario*, 1996, p. 991 ff

J.F. Lindner, *Individualrechtsschutz im europäischen Gemeinschaftsrecht. Ein systematischer Überblick*, in *Juristiche Schulung*, 2008/1, p. 1 ff

M. Lipari, *Annullamento dell'aggiudicazione ed effetti del contratto: la parola al diritto comunitario*, in *Giustizia amministrativa*, 2008, p. 1 ff, at www.giustamm.it

J.V. Louis, Th. Ronse, *L'ordre juridique de l'Union européenne*, Bruylant, Genève, Bruxelles, Paris, 2005

M. Ludwigs, *Die Arcor-Entscheidung des EuGH: Ein Beitrag zur Stärkung der mitgliedstaatlichen Verfahrensautonomie*, in *Neue Zeitschrift für Verwaltungsrecht*, 2007/5, p. 549 ff

F.P. Luiso, *La responsabilità civile del magistrato*, in *Judicium*, 2007, p. 1 ff, at www.judicium.it

M. Poiares Maduro, *The Scope of European Remedies: The Case of Purely Internal Situations and Reverse Discrimination*, in C. Kilpatrick, T. Novitz, P. Skidmore (eds.), *The future of remedies in Europe*, Oxford University Press, Oxford-New York, 2000, p. 117 ff

S. Magiera, *Die Durchsetzung des Gemeinschaftsrechts im europäischen Integrationsprozeß*, in *Die Öffentliche Verwaltung*, 1998/5, p. 173 ff

C. Malinconico, *Il recupero degli aiuti di Stato tra preclusioni processuali nazionali e limiti alla proposizione d'ufficio del ricorso pregiudiziale alla Corte di giustizia*, in *Diritto processuale amministrativo*, 2005/3, p. 805 ff

Ph. Manin, *La place de la diversité dans le Traité sur l'Union européenne*, in *La France, L'Europe et le Monde. Mélanges en l'honneur de Jean Charpentier*, Pedone, Paris, 2009, p. 395 ff

B. Marchetti, *Sul potere di annullamento d'ufficio, la Corte ribadisce l'autonomia procedurale degli Stati membri, ma si sbilancia un po'*, in *Rivista italiana di diritto pubblico comunitario*, 2006/6, p. 1132 ff

G. Mari, *La forza di giudicato delle decisioni dei giudici nazionali di ultima istanza nella giurisprudenza comunitaria*, in *Rivista italiana di diritto pubblico comunitario*, 2004/3-4, p. 1007 ff

G. Martinico, *L'integrazione silente. La funzione interpretativa della Corte di giustizia e il diritto costituzionale europeo*, Novene, Naples, 2009

A. Marzano, *Sulla ripetibilità delle somme indebitamente corrisposte per tasse di effetto equivalente ai dazi doganali*, in *Rassegna dell'Avvocatura di Stato*, 1977, II, p. 71 ff

A. Massera (eds.), *Le tutele procedimentali. Profili di diritto comparato*, Jovene, Naples, 2007

R. Mastroianni, *Rilevanza delle questioni pregiudiziali e dovere di collaborazione tra giudici nazionali e Corte di giustizia: la sentenza sulle "telepromozioni"*, in *Il Diritto dell'Unione europea*, 1997/1-2, p. 191 ff

A. Masucci, *La lunga marcia della Corte di Lussemburgo verso una tutela cautelare europea*, in *Rivista italiana di diritto pubbico comunitario*, 1996, p. 1155 ff

B.G. Mattarella, *Autotutela amministrativa e principio di legalità*, in *Rivista italiana di diritto pubblico comunitario*, 2007/6, p. 1223 ff

J. McKendrick, *Modifying Procedural Autonomy: Better Protection for Community Rights*, in *European Review of Private Law*, 2000/4, p. 565 ff

R. Mehdi, *L'autonomie institutionnelle et procédurale et le droit administratif*, in J.B. Auby, J. Dutheil de la Rochère (eds.), *Droit Administratif Européen*, Bruylant, Brussels, 2007, p. 685 ff

S. Menchini, *Il nuovo assetto delle tutele giurisdizionali avverso gli atti amministrativi illegittimi*, in *Diritto pubblico*, 2008, p. 81 ff

P. Mengozzi, *L'applicazione del diritto comunitario e l'evolversi della giurisprudenza della Corte di giustizia nella direzione di una chiamata dei giudici nazionali ad assicurare una efficace tutela dei diritti da esso attribuiti ai cittadini degli stati membri*, in L. Vandelli, C. Bottari, D. Donati (eds.), *Diritto amministrativo comunitario*, Maggioli, Rimini, 1994, p. 29 ff

J. Mertens de Wilmars, *L'efficacité des différentes techniques nationales de protection juridique contre les violations du droit communautaire par les autorités nationales et les particuliers*, in *Cahiers de droit européen*, 1981, p. 379 ff

V. Michel, *2004: Le défi de la répartition des compétences*, in *Cahier de droit européen*, 2003, p. 17 ff

E. Minozzi, *Norme nazionali di rinvio al diritto comunitario per la disciplina di situazioni puramente interne e competenza della Corte di giustizia*, in *Diritto e pratica tributaria*, 1998, II, p. 1103 ff

C. Modica, *Giustizia amministrativa comunitaria e modelli di processo amministrativo*, Report on the Lecce Conference, 21-22 November 1997, in *Diritto & Diritti*, at hptt://www.diritto.it

Ch. Möllers, *Tertiäre exekutive Rechtssetzung im Europarecht*, in E. Schmidt-Aßmann, B. Schöndorf-Haubold (eds.), *Der Europäische Verwaltungsverbund*, Mohr Siebeck, Tübingen, 2005, p. 293 ff

G. Montedoro, *Il giudizio amministrativo fra annullamento e disapplicazione (ovvero dell'"insostenibile leggerezza" del processo impugnatorio)*, in *Rivista italiana di diritto pubblico comunitario*, 2008/2, p. 519 ff

G. Morbidelli, *La tutela giurisdizionale dei diritti nell'ordinamento comunitario. Quaderni della Rivista "Il Diritto dell'Unione Europea"*, Giuffré, Milan, 2001

G. Morbidelli, *Controlimiti o contro la pregiudiziale comunitaria*, in *Giurisprudenza costituzionale*, 2005, p. 3404 ff

G. Morbidelli, *Corte Costitituzionale e Corti europee: la tutela dei diritti (dal punto di vista della Corte del Lussemburgo)*, in *Diritto processuale amministrativo* 2006/2, p. 285 ff

S. Morettini, *L'effettività del diritto comunitario ed il processo amministrativo negli Stati membri*, in *Rivista trimestrale di diritto pubblico*, 2007/3, p. 723 ff

C. Morviducci, Fumus bonis iuris *e misure cautelari nel processo comunitario*, in *Rivista italiana di diritto pubblico comunitario*, 1999/3-4, p. 705 ff

J.-D. Mouton, *Effet utile*, in A. Barav, Ch. Philip (comp.), *Dictionnaire juridique des Communautés européennes*, PUF, Paris, 1993, p. 449 ff

R. Murgia, *Il rinvio pregiudiziale interpretativo davanti alla Corte di giustizia della C.E.*, in *Diritto processuale amministrativo*, 2006/2, p. 441 ff

M. Muscardini, *Potere cautelare dei giudici nazionali in materie disciplinate dal diritto comunitario*, in *Rivista italiana di diritto pubblico comunitario*, 1991, p. 1042 ff

L. Musselli, *La giustizia amministrativa dell'ordinamento comunitario*, Giappichelli, Turin, 2000

B. Nascimbene, *Il diritto comunitario nel futuro*, in *Rivista di diritto internazionale privato e processuale*, 1993/4, p. 857 ff

B. Nascimbene (eds.), *Il processo comunitario dopo Nizza*, Giuffré, Milan, 2003

B. Nascimbene, M. Condinanzi, *Giurisprudenza di diritto comunitario. Casi scelti*, Giuffré, Milan, 2007

A. Negrelli, *Il primato del diritto comunitario e il giudicato nazionale: un confronto che si poteva evitare o risolvere altrimenti*, in *Rivista italiana di diritto pubblico comunitario*, 2008/5, p. 1217 ff

M. Nigro, *Giustizia amministrativa*, Il Mulino, Bologna, 2002, 6th. Ed. (edited by E. Cardi and A. Nigro)

C. Nizzo, *L'art. 5 del Trattato CE e la clausola generale di buona fede nell'integrazione europea*, in *Il Diritto dell'Unione europea*, 1997/3, p. 381 ff

C. Nizzo, *La Corte di giustizia e la competenza ad interpretare, in via pregiudiziale, norme nazionali modellate su disposizioni comunitarie*, in *Diritto comm. internaz.*, 1997, p. 998 ff

O.M. Papadopoulou, *Vers une protection juridictionnelle commune en Europe : la directive « Recours » 89/665/CEE*, in *Rivista italiana di diritto pubblico comunitario*, 1997/5, p. 947 ff
P. Pescatore, *L'Ordre juridique des Communautés européennes*, Liège, 2nd. Ed., 1973 (republished in a new edition Bruylant, Bruxelles, 2006)
P. Pescatore, *Il rinvio pregiudiziale di cui all'art. 177 del Trattato CEE e la cooperazione tra la Corte ed i giudici nazionali*, in *Il Foro italiano*, 1986/1, c. 26 ff
P.M. Piacentini, *L'apporto dei "grandi corpi" alla normazione nazionale e comunitaria*, in *Quaderni del Consiglio di Stato*, Giappichelli, Turin, 2000, p. 145 ff
F. Picod, *Article I-29*, in L. Burgorgue-Larsen, A. Levade, F. Picod (eds.), *Traité établissant une Constitution pour l'Europe. Commentaire article par article*, Vol. I, Bruylant, Brussels, 2007, p. 384 ff
E. Picozza, *Alcune riflessioni circa la rilevanza del diritto comunitario sui principi del diritto amministrativo italiano*, in *Rivista italiana di diritto pubblico comunitario*, 1992, p. 1209 ff
E. Picozza, *Il regime giuridico del procedimento amministrativo comunitario*, in *Rivista italiana di diritto pubblico comunitario*, 1994, p. 321 ff
E. Picozza, *L'effettività della tutela giurisdizionale nel processo amministrativo, rispetto al diritto comunitario*, in Id. (eds.), *Processo amministrativo e diritto comunitario*, CEDAM, Padua, 1997, p. 1 ff
E. Picozza, *La C.T.U., tra processo amministrativo ed effettività del diritto comunitario*, in *Convivenza nella libertà. Scritti in onore di Giuseppe Abbamonte*, Jovene, Naples, 1999, p. 1137 ff
E. Picozza, *Diritto amministrativo e diritto comunitario*, Giappichelli, Turin, 2004
E. Picozza, *Le situazioni giuridiche soggettive*, in M.P. Chiti and G. Greco (eds.), *Trattato di diritto amministrativo europeo* (coord. by G.F. Cartei and D.U. Galetta), Giuffré, Milan, 2nd. Ed., 2007, General Part, Vol. II, p. 903 ff
F. Poilvache, *Compétence préjudicielle et dispositions nationales inspirées du droit communautaire*, in *Journal des tribunaux /Droit européen*, 1998, p.121 ff
V. Poli, *Funzione nomofilattica e certezza del diritto: la vincolatività delle decisioni del giudice superiore nazionale-comunitario*, in *Quaderni del Consiglio di Stato*, Giappichelli, Turin, 2000, p. 213 ff
O. Porchia, *Il procedimento di controllo degli aiuti pubblici alle imprese. Tra ordinamento comunitario e ordinamento interno*, Jovene, Naples, 2001
O. Porchia, *I principi dell'ordinamento europeo. La cooperazione pluridirezionale*, Zanichelli, Bologna, 2008
M. Potacs, *Bestandskraft staatlicher Verwaltungsakte oder Effektivität des Gemeinschaftsrecht?* in *Europarecht*, 2004/4, p. 595 ff
S. Prechal, *Community Law in National Courts: The Lessons From Vam Schijndel*, in *Common Market Law Review*, 1998, p. 681 ff
S. Prechal, N. Shelkoplyas, *National Procedures, Public Policy and EC-Law. From Van Schijndel to Eco Swiss and Beyond*, in *European Review of Private Law*, 2004/5, p. 589 ff
M. Protto, *L'effettività della tutela giurisdizionale nelle procedure di aggiudicazione di pubblici appalti. Studio sull'influsso dell'integrazione europea sulla tutela giurisdizionale degli operatori economici nei confronti delle amministrazioni nazionali*, Giuffré, Milan, 1997
M. Protto, *Giurisdizione nazionale ed effettività della tutela giurisdizionale delle situazioni soggettive di matrice comunitaria*, in *Urbanistica e Appalti*, 1998, IV, p. 444 ff
M. Protto, *Valutazioni tecniche, giudice nazionale e diritto comunitario*, in *Giurisprudenza italiana*, 1999, p. 834 ff
W. Pühs, *Der Vollzug von Gemeinschaftsrecht. Formen und Grenzen eines effektiven Gemeinschaftsrechtsvollzugs und Überlegungen zu seiner Effektuierung*, Duncker & Humblot, Berlin, 1997
R. Quadri, *Articolo 5 CEE*, in R. Quadri, R. Monaco, A. Trabucchi (eds.), *Commentario CEE*, Giuffré, Milan, 1965, Vol I, p. 51 ff

L. Raimondi, *Atti nazionali inoppugnabili e diritto comunitario tra principio di effettività e competenze di attribuzione*, in *Il diritto dell'Unione Europea*, 2008/4, p. 773 ff

G. Raiti, *La collaborazione giudiziaria nell'esperienza del rinvio pregiudiziale comunitario*, Giuffré, Milan, 2003

C. Rasia, *Il controllo della Commissione europea sull'interpretazione del diritto comunitario da parte delle corti supreme degli Stati membri*, in *Rivista trimestrale di diritto e procedura civile*, 2005/3, p. 1025 ff

C. Rasia, *Responsabilità dello Stato per violazione del diritto comunitario da parte del giudice supremo: il caso Traghetti del Mediterraneo contro Italia*, in *Rivista trimestrale di diritto e procedura civile*, 2007, p. 1025 ff

H. Rasmussen, *Remedying the Crumbling EC Judicial System*, in *Common Market Law Review*, 2000, p. 1071 ff

R. Rawlings, *Engaged Elites: Citizen Action and Institutional Attitudes in Commission Enforcement*, in C. Kilpatrick, T. Novitz, P. Skidmore (eds.), *The future of remedies in Europe*, Oxford University Press, Oxford-New York, 2000, p. 267 ff

G. Recchia, *Ordinamenti europei di giustizia amministrativa*, in G. Santaniello (eds.), *Trattato di diritto amministrativo*, Vol. XXV, CEDAM, Padua, 1996

G. Recchia, *Profili metodologici nell'attuazione amministrativa del diritto comunitario*, in *Rivista italiana di diritto pubblico comunitario*, 1998, p. 1105 ff

H-W. Rengeling, *Deutsches und europäisches Verwaltungsrecht: wechselseitige Einwirkungen*, in *VVDStRL*, 1994, 53, p. 202

J. Rideau, *Droit institutionnel de l'Union et des Communautés européennes*, 5th. Ed.,: LGDJ, Paris, 2006

E. Rinaldi, *Miracoli dei polli olandesi: la* primauté *del diritto comunitario va "oltre" il giudicato nazionale "anticomunitario". E all'Amministrazione spetta il compito di rimediare*, in *Rivista italiana di diritto pubblico comunitario*, 2005/2, p. 651 ff

D. Ritleng, *Le retrait des actes administratifs contraires au droit communautaire*, in J. Schwarze (eds.), *Bestand und Perspektiven des Europäischen Verwaltungsrechts. Rechtsvergleichende Analysen*, Nomos, Baden-Baden, 2008, p. 237 ff

V. Röben, *Die Einwirkung der Rechtsprechung des Europäischen Gerichtshofs auf das Mitgliedstaatliche Verfahren in öffentlich-rechtlichen Streitigkeiten*, Duncker & Humblot, Berlin, 1998

C. Rodríguez Iglesias, *Sui limiti all'autonomia procedimentale e processuale degli Stati membri nell'applicazione del diritto comunitario*, in *Rivista italiana di diritto pubblico comunitario*, 2001/1, p. 5 ff

H. Ch. Röhl, *Die anfechtbare Entscheidung nach Art. 230 Abs. 4 EGV als Rechtsschutzform,* in E. Schmidt-Aßmann, B. Schöndorf-Haubold (eds.), *Der Europäische Verwaltungsverbund*, Mohr Siebeck, Tübingen, 2005, p. 319 ff

H.Ch. Röhl, *Verantwortung und Effizienz in der Mehrebenenverwaltung*, in *Deutsches Verwaltungsblatt*, 2006/17, p. 1070 ff

R. Romboli, *Il ruolo del giudice in rapporto all'evoluzione del sistema delle fonti ed alla disciplina dell'ordinamento giudiziario*, in *Quaderni dell'Associazione per gli studi e le ricerche parlamentari*, Giappichelli, Turin, 2006 and at www.associazionedeicostituzionalisti.it

M. Rossi, W. Kahl, *Grundsatz der loyalen Zusammenarbeit (Art. 10 EGV),* in Ch. Callies. M. Ruffert (eds.), *Das Verfassungsrecht der Europäischen Union,* Neuwied, Luchterhand, 2007, 3rd. Ed., para. 1 ff

M. Ruffert, *Rights and Remedies in European Community Law: A Comparative View*, in *Common Market Law Review*, 1997/2, p. 307 ff

A. Russo, *E'sempre più "diffuso" il controllo di conformità al diritto comunitario ad opera del giudice nazionale?* in *Rivista italiana di diritto pubblico comunitario*, 1996/3-4, p. 701 ff

L. Saltari, *La legalità comunitaria prevale sulla certezza (nazionale) del diritto*, in *Giornale di diritto amministrativo*, 2007, p. 477 ff

M.A. Sandulli, *La giustizia cautelare sugli interessi legittimi "apre" all'art. 700 c.p.c.?* in *Giustizia civile*, 1998, II, p. 235 ff

M.A. Sandulli, *Diritto europeo e processo amministrativo*, in *Rivista italiana di diritto pubblico comunitario*, 2008/1, p. 37 ff

M.A. Sandulli, *Il processo amministrativo superaccelerato e i nuovi contratti ricorso-resistenti*, in *Federalismi.it* (available at http://www.federalismi.it), 2009/4, p. 1 ff

A. Santa Maria, *Il rinvio pregiudiziale nella nuova disciplina a seguito del Trattato di Nizza*, in *Diritto del commercio internazionale*, 2003, p. 367 ff

F. Satta, *Annullamento dell'aggiudicazione: la fine di un problema*, in *Giustizia amministrativa* (available at http://www.giustamm.it), 2008/11, p. 1 ff

D. Savy, *La leale cooperazione nella disciplina antitrust e nel nuovo regolamento CE n. 1/2003 del Consiglio*, in *Diritto pubblico comparato ed europeo*, 2003/2, p. 913 ff

W. Schenk, *Die Leistungsverwaltung der EG als Herausforderung für das Europäische Verwaltungsrecht*, in E. Schmidt-Aßmann, B. Schöndorf-Haubold (eds.), *Der Europäische Verwaltungsverbund*, Mohr Siebeck, Tübingen, 2005, p. 265 ff

C. Schepisi, *Sull'applicabilità d'ufficio delle norme comunitarie da parte dei giudici nazionali*, in *Il Diritto dell'Unione europea*, 1997/4, p. 811 ff

C. Schepisi, *Rinvio pregiudiziale obbligatorio ed effettività della tutela giurisdizionale*, EUT, Trieste, 2003

G. Scheuing, *Europäisierung des Verwaltungsrechts*, in *Die Verwaltung*, 2001, p. 107 ff

E. Schmidt-Aßmann, *Deutsches und europäisches Verwaltungsrecht*, in *Deutsches Verwaltungsblatt*, 1993, p. 924 ff

E. Schmidt-Aßmann, *Verwaltungskooperation und Verwaltungskooperationsrecht in der Europäischen Gemeinschaft*, in *Europarecht*, 1996/3, p. 271 ff

E. Schmidt-Aßmann, *Verwaltungsverfahren und Verwaltungskultur*, in *Neue Zeitschrift für Verwaltungsrecht*, 2007/1, p. 40 ff

F. Schoch, *Die Europäisierung des verwaltungsgerichtlichen vorläufigen Rechtsschutzes*, in *Deutsches Verwaltungsblatt*, 1997, p. 289 ff

B. Schöndorf-Haubold, *Gemeinsame Europäischen Verwaltung: die Strukturfonds der Europäischen Gemeinschaft*, in E. Schmidt-Aßmann, B. Schöndorf-Haubold (eds.), *Der Europäische Verwaltungsverbund*, Mohr Siebeck, Tübingen, 2005, p. 25 ff

R. Scholz, *Zum Verhältnis vom europäischen Gemeinschaftsrecht und nationalem Verwaltungsverfahrensrecht. Zur Rechtsprechung des EuGH im Fall "Alcan"*, in *Die öffentliche Verwaltung*, 1998, p. 261 ff

J. Schwarze, *Der Beitrag des Europäischen Gerichtshofs zur Europäisierung des Verwaltungsrechts*, in *Europarecht*, 1997/4, p. 419 ff

J. Schwarze, *Europäische Rahmenbedingungen für die Verwaltungsgerichtsbarkeit*, in *Neue Zeitschrift für Verwaltungsrecht*, 2000/3, p. 241 ff

J. Schwarze, *Rules and general principles of European Administrative Law*, in *Rivista italiana di diritto pubblico comunitario*, 2004/5, p. 1219 ff

J. Schwarze, *Il controllo giurisdizionale sul procedimento amministrativo europeo*, in F. Bignami and S. Cassese (eds.), *Il procedimento amministrativo nel diritto europeo*, Giuffré, Milan, 2004, p. 125 ff

J. Schwarze, *Europäisches Verwaltungsrecht. Entstehung und Entwicklung im Rahmen der Europäischen Gemeinschaft*, Nomos, Baden-Baden, 2nd. Ed., 2006

J. Schwarze, *Legal protection by and within the administrative procedure. Some observations on the legal situation in German and European Community Law*, in A. Massera (eds.), *Le tutele procedimentali. Profili di diritto comparato*, Jovene, Naples, 2007, p. 51 ff

J. Schwarze, *Artikel 234 (Vorabentscheidung)*, in J. Schwarze (eds.), *EU-Kommentar*, Nomos, Baden-Baden, 2nd. Ed., 2009, p. 1807 ff

A. Scognamiglio, *Ancora un intervento della Corte di giustizia in tema di tutela cautelare*, in *Il Foro amministrativo*, 1997, p. 384 ff

H. Sendler, *Über richterliche Kontrolldichte in Deutschland und anderswo*, in *Neue Juristische Wochenschrift*, 1994, p. 1516 ff

D. Simon, *Lex exigences de la primauté du droit communautaire; continuité ou métamorphoses?* in *L'Europe et le droit. Mélanges en hommage a Jean Boulouis*, Dalloz, Paris, 1991, p.481 ff
D. Simon, *Le système juridique communautaire*, 3rd. Ed., PUF, Paris, 2001
D. Simon, *Autorité de chose jugée de l'arrêt d'une juridiction nationale devenu définitif*, in *Juris Classeur-Europe*, 2007/10, n. 235, p. 12 ff
D. Simon, *L'autonomisation du contrôle d'euro-compatibilité: une rupture épistémologique dans les rapports de systèmes ?* in *La France, L'Europe et le Monde. Mélanges en l'honneur de Jean Charpentier*, Pedone, Paris, 2009, p. 497 ff
V. Skouris, *L'influence du droit national et de la jurisprudence des juridictions des Etats membres sur l'interprétation du droit communautaire*, in *Il Diritto dell'Unione europea*, 2008/2, p. 239 ff
K.P. Sommermann, *Europäisches Verwaltungsrecht oder Europäisierung des Verwaltungsrechts?* in *Deutsches Verwaltungsblatt*, 1996, p. 889 ff
K.P. Sommermann, *Konvergenzen im Verwaltungsverfahrens- und Verwaltungsprozeßrecht europäischer Staaten*, in *Die öffentliche Verwaltung*, 2002, p. 133 ff
F. Sorrentino, *L'art. 177 del Trattato di Roma nel rapporto tra ordinamento comunitario e ordinamenti interni*, in *Studi in onore di Manlio Mazziotti di Celso*, CEDAM, Padua, 1995, Vol. II, p. 737 ff
K. Stern, *Die Einwirkung des europäischen Gemeinschaftsrechts auf die Verwaltungsgerichtsbarkeit*, in *Juristiche Schulung*, 1998, p. 769 ff
A. Stone Sweet, Th. L. Brunell, *The European Court and the National Courts: A Statistical Analysis of Preliminary References, 1961–95*. Harvard Jean Monnet Working Paper, n. 14/1997, at http://www.jeanmonnetprogram.org/papers
M. Taborowski, *Case C-329/04 e C-422/04, Arcor e.a.*, in *Common Market Law Review*, 2007, p. 1463 ff
S. Tarullo, *Il giusto processo amministrativo. Studio sull'effettività della tutela giurisdizionale nella prospettiva europea*, Giuffré, Milan, 2004
S. Tarullo, *Giusto processo (diritto processuale amministrativo)*, in *Annali dell'Enciclopedia del Diritto*, II, Volume I, Giuffré, Milan, 2007, p. 376 ff
S. Tassone, *Sulla responsabilità dello Stato membro per omessa attuazione di direttive comunitarie nell'ordinamento interno*, in *Responsabilità civile e previdenza*, 1992, p. 847 ff
G. Tesauro, *Tutela cautelare e diritto comunitario*, in *Rivista italiana di diritto pubblico comunitario*, 1992, p. 125 ff
G. Tesauro, *Diritto comunitario*, 5th. Ed., CEDAM, Padua, 2008
A. Tizzano, *La tutela dei privati nei confronti degli Stati membri dell'Unione europea*, in *Il Foro italiano*, 1995, IV, c. 13 ff
A. Tizzano, *Qualche riflessione sul contributo della Corte di Giustizia allo sviluppo del sistema comunitario*, in *Il diritto dell'Unione Europea*, 2009/1, p. 141 ff
L. Torchia, *Diritto amministrativo nazionale e diritto comunitario: sviluppi recenti del processo di ibridazione*, in *Rivista italiana di diritto pubblico comunitario*, 1997, p. 845 ff
A. Travi, *Il giudicato amministrativo*, in *Diritto processuale amministrativo*, 2006/4, p. 912 ff
T. Tridimas, *Knocking on Heaven's door: Fragmentation, Efficiency and Defiance in the Preliminary Reference Procedure*, in *Common Market Law Review*, 2003, p. 9 ff
T. Tridimas, *Enforcing Community Rights in National Courts: Some Recent Development*, in C. Kilpatrick, T. Novitz, P. Skidmore (eds.), *The future of remedies in Europe*, Oxford University Press, Oxford-New York, 2000, p. 35 ff
N. Trocker, *"Civil Law" e "Common Law" nella formazione del diritto processuale europeo*, in *Rivista italiana di diritto pubblico comunitario*, 2007/2, p. 421 ff
W. van Gerven, *Bridging the gap between Community and National Laws: towards a principle of homogeneity in the field of legal remedies?* in *Common Market Law Review*, 1995, p. 679 ff
W. van Gerven, *Of Rights, Remedies and Procedures*, in *Common Market Law Review*, 2000, p. 501 ff

L. Wagner, *Aides d'Etat: la Commission européenne confrontée au risque systémique*, in *Europe*, 2009/1, p. 4 ff

P.J. Wattel, *Köbler, Cilfit and Welthgrove: we can't go on meeting like this*, in *Common Market Law Review*, 2004, p. 177 ff

P.J. Wattel, *National Procedural Autonomy and Effectiveness of EC Law: Challenge the Charge, File for Restitution, Sue for Damages*, in *Legal Issues of Economic Integration*, 2008, p. 109 ff

S. Weatherill, *Addressing Problems of Imbalanced Implementation in EC Law: Remedies in an Institutional Perspective*, in C. Kilpatrick, T. Novitz, P. Skidmore (eds.), *The future of remedies in Europe*, Oxford University Press, Oxford-New York, 2000, p. 87 ff

A. Weber, *Sviluppi nel diritto amministrativo europeo*, in *Rivista italiana di diritto pubblico comunitario*, 1998, p. 589 ff

E. Werlauff, *Common European Procedural law. European Law Requirements Imposed on National Administration of Justice*, DJOF Publishing, Copenhagen, 1999

F. Wettner, *Das allgemeine Verfahrensrecht der gemeinschaftlichen Amtshilfe*, in E. Schmidt-Aßmann, B. Schöndorf-Haubold (eds.), *Der Europäische Verwaltungsverbund*, Mohr Siebeck, Tübingen, 2005, p. 181 ff

G. Winter, *Kompetenzverteilung und Legitimation in der Europäischen Mehrebenenverwaltung*, in *Europarecht*, 2005, p. 255 ff

J. Ziller, *La dialectique du contentieux européen: le cas des recours contre les actes normatifs*, in *Les droits individuels et le juge en Europe. Mélanges en l'honneur de Michel Fromont*, Presses universitaires de Strasbourg, Strasbourg, 2001, p. 443 ff

J. Ziller, J. Lotarski, *Institutions et organes judiciaires*, in B. de Witte (eds.), *Ten Reflections on the Constitutional Treaty for Europe*, European University Union, Robert Schuman Center for Advanced Studies and Academy of European Law, Florence, 2003, p. 67 ff

J. Ziller, *Separation of Powers in the European Union's Intertwined System of Government. A Treaty Based Analysis for the Use of Political Scientists and Constitutional Lawyers*, in *Il Politico*, 2008/3, p. 133 ff

J. Ziller, *Bases juridiques et compétences en droit de l'Union européenne*, in *Union de droit, Union des droits – Mélanges en l'honneur de Philippe Manin*, Pedone, Paris, 2009

B. Zuffi, *Il caso Lucchini infrange l'autorità del giudicato nazionale nel campo degli aiuti statali*, in *Giurisprudenza italiana*, 2008, p. 382 ff

M. Zuleeg, *Die föderativen Grundsätze der Europäischen Union*, in *Neue Juristische Wochenschrift*, 2000, p. 2846 ff

M. Zuleeg, *Art. 10: Verpflichtungen der Mitgliedstaaten*, in H. von der Groeben, J. Schwarze (eds.), *Vertrag über die Europäische Union und Verträge zur Gründung der Europäischen Gemeinschaft*, Nomos, Baden-Baden, 6th. Ed., 2003, p. 668 ff

M. Zuleeg, *Der rechtliche Zusammenhalt der Europäischen Union*, Nomos, Baden-Baden, 2004

Table of Cases of the ECJ

5 February 1963. Case 26-62. van Gend & Loos. *European Court reports* 1963 Page 00001, 85.
15 July 1964. Case 6/64. Costa v E.N.E.L. *European Court reports* 1964 Page 00585, 15.
4 April 1968. Case 34/67. Lück. *European Court reports* 1968, Page 00245, 11.
19 December 1968. Case 13-68. Salgoil. *European Court reports* 1968, Page 00453, 12.
24 June 1969. Case 29-68. Eierkontor. *European Court reports* 1969 Page 00165, 87.
10 December 1969. Joined cases 6 and 11-69. Commission of the European Communities v French Republic. *European Court reports* 1969 Page 00523, 31.
6 October 1970. Case 9-70. Grad. *European Court reports* 1970 Page 00825, 15.
6 June 1972. Case 94-71. Schlüter & Maack. *European Court reports* 1972 Page 00307, 79.
7 February 1973. Case 39-72. Commission of the European Communities v Italian Republic. *European Court reports* 1973 Page 00101, 31.
11 December 1973. Case 120-73. Lorenz. *European Court reports* 1973 Page 01471, 11.
11 December 1973. Case 121/73. Markmann. *European Court reports* 1973 Page 01495, 11.
11 December 1973. Case 141/73. Loyrey. *European Court reports* 1973 Page 01527, 11.
16 January 1974. Case 166-73. Rheinmühlen. *European Court reports* 1974 Page 00033, 72.
4 December 1974. Case 41-74. van Duyn. *European Court reports* 1974 Page 01337, 43.
8 April 1976. Case 43-75. Defrenne. *European Court reports* 1976 Page 00455, 87.
16 December 1976. Case 33/76. Rewe. *European Court reports* 1976 Page 01989, 8, 103, 115.
16 December 1976. Case 45-76. Comet. *European Court reports* 1976 Page 02043, 11.
9 March 1978. Case 106/77. Amministrazione delle Finanze dello Stato v Simmenthal SpA. *European Court reports* 1978 Page 00629, 80.

23 February 1994. Case C-236/92. Comitato di Coordinamento per la Difesa della Cava and others. *European Court reports* 1994 Page I-00483, 20.
6 December 1994. Case C-410/92. Johnson. *European Court reports* 1994 Page I-05483, 46.
9 November 1995. Case C-465/93. Atlanta. *European Court reports* 1995 Page I-03761, 71.
14 December 1995. Case C-312/93. Peterbroeck. *European Court reports* 1995 Page I-04599, 71.
14 December 1995. Joined cases C-430/93 and C-431/93. van Schijndel. *European Court reports* 1995 Page I-04705, 48.
24 October 1996. Case C-72/95. Kraaijeveld. *European Court reports* 1996 Page I-05403, 50.
20 March 1997. Case C-24/95. Alcan. *European Court reports* 1997 Page I-01591, 53.
10 July 1997. Case C-261/95. Palmisani. *European Court reports* 1997 Page I-04025, 25.
17 July 1997. Case C-28/95. Leur-Bloem. *European Court reports* 1997 Page I-04161, 27.
17 July 1997. Case C-130/95. Giloy. *European Court reports* 1997 Page I-04291, 27.
2 December 1997. Case C-188/95. Fantask. *European Court reports* 1997 Page I-06783, 37.
18 December 1997. Case C-129/96. Inter-Environnement Wallonie. *European Court reports* 1997 Page I-07411, 108.
16 June 1998. Case C-53/96. Hermès. *European Court reports* 1998 Page I-03603, 27.
1 December 1998. Case C-326/96. Levez. *European Court reports* 1998 Page I-07835, 24.
21 January 1999. Case C-120/97. Upjohn. *European Court reports* 1999 Page I-00223, 77.
1 June 1999. Case C-126/97. Eco Swiss. *European Court reports* 1999 Page I-03055, 50.
5 October 2000. Case C-376/98. Federal Republic of Germany v European Parliament and Council of the European Union. *European Court reports* 2000 Page I-08419, 10.
14 December 2000. Case C-344/98. Masterfoods. *European Court reports* 2000 Page I-11369, 93.
11 January 2001. Case C-1/99. Kofisa. *European Court reports* 2001 Page I-00207, 27.
13 March 2001. Case C-379/98. Preussen-Elektra. *European Court reports* 2001 Page I-02099, 96.
20 September 2001. Case C-453/99. Courage. *European Court reports* 2001 Page I-06297, 37.
15 January 2002. Case C-43/00. Andersen. *European Court reports* 2002 Page I-00379, 27.
22 January 2002. Case C-390/99. Canal Satélite Digital SL. *European Court reports* 2002 Page I-00607, 96.

18 July 2007. Case C-503/04. Commission of the European Communities v Federal Republic of Germany. *European Court reports* 2007 Page I-06153, 109.
11 December 2007. Case C-280/06. Philip Morris. *European Court reports* 2007 Page I-10893, 27.
12 February 2008. Case C-2/06. Kempter. *European Court reports* 2008 Page I-00411, 58.
15 April 2008. Case C-268/06. Impact. *European Court reports* 2008 Page I-02483, 78.
8 May 2008. Case C-491/06. Danske. *European Court reports* 2008 Page I-03339, 83.
25 July 2008. Case C-237/0. Janecek. *European Court reports* 2008 Page I-06221, 20
16 December 2008. Case C-213/07. Michaniki. *European Court reports* 2008 Page I-09999, 84.
16 December 2008, Case C-210/06. Cartesio. *European Court reports* 2008 Page I-09641, 73.
16 July 2009. Case C-12/08. Mono Car Styling. *European Court reports* 2009 Page 00000, 23.
3 September 2009. Case C-2/08. Olimpiclub Srl. *European Court reports* 2009 Page 00000, 66.
6 October 2009. Case C-40/08. Asturcom. *European Court reports* 2009 Page 00000, 66.

ISBN 978-3642125461 -1

9 783642 125461

Printed in Japan
E0006633